Praise for

MYSTERIES OF THE MALL

"It is the attention [Rybczynski] pays space—an enthusiastic and highly infectious kind of attention, something close to an architectural evangelism—that both freshens our eyes and grants new perspectives on the intentionality of our environment . . . A deft and sensible guide, Rybczynski charms, challenges, and, finally, welcomes us into a world we may never have realized could be so enthralling . . . This [book] is required reading for anyone interested in the story of architecture—or the shape of the modern world."   —Dustin Illingworth, *The Brooklyn Rail*

"Throughout the collection, Rybczynski's writing is clearheaded and thoughtful, knowledgeable but unpretentious . . . The awe, appreciation and wonder that Rybczynski has for architecture can be infectious."   —Anna Wiener, *The New Republic*

"[Rybczynski's] writing is, like his architectural leanings, clear and civil, and full of cocktail-worthy trivia."
            —Mike Doherty, *Maclean's*

"A superb book for those interested in architectural history, written in an easygoing style by a man with encyclopedic knowledge and an obvious great love for building."
            —*Kirkus Reviews* (starred review)

"[Rybczynski is] an eloquent critic with a range of interests as broad as his voluminous published work . . . The prose sparkles . . . Over the course of his career, Rybczynski has proven a deft guide to the work of countless architects; here, he is just as sage a curator of his own criticism."   —Anthony Paletta, *Publishers Weekly*
            (boxed signature review)

Witold Rybczynski

MYSTERIES OF THE MALL

Witold Rybczynski has written about architecture for *The New Yorker*, *The Atlantic*, *The New York Times*, and *Slate*. Among his award-winning books are *Home*, *The Most Beautiful House in the World*, and *A Clearing in the Distance*, which won the J. Anthony Lukas Book Prize. Winner of the 2014 National Design Award and the Vincent Scully Prize, he lives with his wife in Philadelphia, where he is a professor emeritus of urbanism at the University of Pennsylvania. Learn more about Rybczynski at his website, www.witoldrybczynski.com.

ALSO BY WITOLD RYBCZYNSKI

MYSTERIES
OF THE MALL

MYSTERIES OF THE MALL

AND OTHER ESSAYS

Witold Rybczynski

FARRAR, STRAUS AND GIROUX

NEW YORK

Farrar, Straus and Giroux
175 Varick Street, New York 10014

Copyright © 2015 by Witold Rybczynski
All rights reserved
Printed in the United States of America
Published in 2015 by Farrar, Straus and Giroux
First paperback edition, 2018

A list of the publications in which these essays originally appeared, in slightly different form, can be found on pages 293–94.

The Library of Congress has cataloged the hardcover edition as follows:
Rybczynski, Witold.
      Mysteries of the mall : and other essays / Witold Rybczynski. — First edition.
         pages   cm
      Includes index.
      ISBN 978-0-374-26993-7 (hardcover) — ISBN 978-1-4299-5324-5 (e-book)
      1. Cities and towns—United States—History.   2. City planning—United
States.   3. Architecture and society—United States.   I. Title.
      NA9105 .R944 2015
      720—dc23

                                                                                2014046633

Paperback ISBN: 978-0-374-53809-5

Designed by Jonathan D. Lippincott

Our books may be purchased in bulk for promotional, educational, or business
use. Please contact your local bookseller or the Macmillan Corporate and
Premium Sales Department at 1-800-221-7945, extension 5442, or by e-mail at
MacmillanSpecialMarkets@macmillan.com.

www.fsgbooks.com
www.twitter.com/fsgbooks • www.facebook.com/fsgbooks

P1

To Shirley

Contents

PART ONE

The Way We Live Today

Mysteries of the Mall

Most of us don't attach much importance to the mundane architectural settings of our everyday lives. We go in and out of supermarkets, fast-food restaurants, and gas stations without a second thought, perhaps because we understand these places so well that they seem merely a part of our natural surroundings. It's necessary to think back to childhood to recall what it was like when such ordinary places were new and strange. I remember my first schoolroom, with its imposing hierarchy of many little desks and one big, important desk. Or the first time I was taken to a museum, with its succession of large, silent rooms filled with labeled glass cases. Or the first, truly strange experience of a movie theater: sitting alone—in a crowd—in the dark. As children, we unravel these unknown, exotic places like anthropologists in a new world, without the encumbrance of foreknowledge. We are obliged to decipher for ourselves the meanings of each new place, and to find our own place in it.

As adults, we feel more or less at home more or less everywhere. This is not just a question of habit. I don't mean that there aren't locales that appear exotic, but it's rare that we find ourselves in places that are truly incomprehensible. This is not just because buildings fall into recognizable types (a concert hall designed by Frank Gehry is still a concert hall; the relationship between performers and audience follows a well-understood convention) but also because television and movies have brought us in contact with so many places we would never ordinarily visit: prisons, morgues, missile silos. Last summer, I toured a World War II submarine moored alongside San Francisco's Fisherman's Wharf; it was the first time I had ever been aboard such a vessel, but thanks to Lloyd Bridges and *Sea Hunt* as well as many submarine movies, the confined mechanical interior of the USS *Pampanito* felt, if not exactly familiar, at least not unfamiliar. Similarly, when I was obliged to go to a hospital, a place I had not been in for thirty years but had seen innumerable times on television, the layout of the long corridors flanked by dreary wards, and the curious hospital atmosphere that combines boredom and urgency, personal attention and impersonal neglect, felt normal, and I think I would have been surprised had it been otherwise.

So, I didn't expect to come upon a new kind of place, that is, a place that demanded unknown rules of behavior, not twenty miles from my house, and certainly not in a shopping mall. This encounter happened in the 1970s. I was walking through the mall, which had recently opened, when I came upon a large, open area with many tables at which people sat eating. There were no waiters visible, and the food appeared to come from a series of take-out counters where young people served food that could be taken away on trays, cafeteria-style. The counters were located on the periphery of the open area, and to judge from the colorful overhead signs, there was a choice of different kinds of food: Chinese, Tex-Mex, pizza, southern fried chicken. I lined up at one of the counters, ordered my food, paid, and then, holding my loaded tray, I realized that I wasn't sure what to do next. I had been in fast-food restaurants before, of course, but this was different. Here, the tables all looked the same. I wasn't sure if I was expected to sit opposite the kiosk where I had just picked up my souvlaki and Coke, or anywhere at all.

I had stumbled on a "food court." (The name was then unfamiliar to me, which was one of the sources of my confusion; knowing the name of a space is a big part of learning to recognize and use it.) The food court is an unusual eating place. A conventional restaurant is a highly stylized environment; we are called customers, but as the hostess shows us to our table, we really feel like guests in someone else's house. The atmosphere of a cafeteria, on the other hand, is different: uniform, regimented like an industrial assembly line, reflecting its mess-hall and refectory roots. The experience of a food court is neither of these. It feels neither domestic nor institutional. Because it's not clearly set apart from the surrounding mall and the crowds of strolling shoppers, it has something of the feel of the sidewalk café, except that there are no waiters and no need to buy anything. In a sense, it's like picnicking on a park bench.

I must confess that few of my architect friends share my interest in food courts. If they notice them at all, they find them commercial, lowbrow, beneath contempt. (One exception is the Toronto architect Jack Diamond, who based the design of the dining space of the student center of York University on a food court.) Those of us who find food courts, drive-in banks, and shopping malls worth a second glance owe a debt to the writing and teaching of John Brinckerhoff Jackson, who, for the last half century, has been drawing our attention to such neglected places. "I have wanted people to become familiar with the contemporary American landscape and recognize its extraordinary complexity and beauty," he writes.

When Jackson uses the word "landscape," he is referring not only to the natural countryside but to the man-made landscape, and not only to parks and gardens but to the full range of man-made environments: highways and roads, towns and neighborhoods, public buildings and houses. Now, all these categories of place, taken separately, are the objects of study of different specialists: agriculturalists, landscape architects, highway engineers, urbanists, and architectural historians. What distinguishes a landscape historian like Jackson is that he considers man-made surroundings not as works of art or engineering or economic necessity but as social artifacts, that is, as evocative backgrounds for human activities.

Jackson taught the history of the American landscape at Harvard University and the University of California, Berkeley, for many years, and his writing appeared monthly in the magazine *Landscape*, which he founded and edited from 1951 to 1968. Several collections of his essays have appeared in print: *Landscapes*, *The Necessity for Ruins*, and *Discovering the Vernacular Landscape*. Retired from teaching for the last decade, the indefatigable octogenarian has continued to observe the contemporary landscape in its large and small manifestations: national parks and backyards, Pueblo villages and mobile-home parks, country roads and suburban driveways. And he writes bracingly about all of these, and more, in his latest book, *A Sense of Place, a Sense of Time*.

A Sense of Place, a Sense of Time is a collection of fourteen essays, arranged in three major sections, covering roughly the Southwest (Jackson lives in New Mexico), the natural landscape (parks and gardens), and the landscape created by the automobile. This arrangement sounds quirky, but it allows the author to explore both large subjects in detail and detailed subjects in a larger setting. He writes evocatively about the prehistoric dwellings of the Pueblo peoples, for example, reminding us how conceptions of space and time are determined by culture. Unlike European-American buildings, which are conceived as a single unit subdivided into multiple rooms, Pueblo architecture is made by clustering individual rooms, usually in a stepped-back fashion, to produce the characteristic rambling buildings that resemble piles of children's toy blocks and that can still be seen in towns like Taos, New Mexico. Curiously, in view of this approach to building, the Hopi language contains no word for "room." Jackson speculates that this is because the Hopi conception of space is different from our own:

A Pueblo room (or basic dwelling) is thus nothing more than a three-dimensional interior space in which objects are contained or events occur. The room itself imposes no identity on its temporary content, and in turn the contents do not permanently characterize the room . . . It is as if the occupants were saying that the single space, the single event is of no consequence: it is *repetition* which creates the periodic or rhythmic recurrence of spaces and events, the cosmic order.

Contrary to conventional wisdom, these structures are not marvels of building ingenuity. The walls were built of mud or stone, whatever material was close at hand. The timber beams were never planed or smoothed, and such relatively simple devices as the arch and the column were unknown. The prehistoric Pueblo builders demonstrated a cavalier disregard for natural forces: there were usually no foundations, for example, and walls that supported three or four stories were neither thickened nor properly buttressed. As a result, the buildings quickly showed the effects of erosion and decay. Citing Benjamin Lee Whorf's research, Jackson suggests that this was an indication not necessarily of technological backwardness but of a different conception of time, a conception that he calls "antihistorical." "They built as if the present order were going to last, untroubled by age and neglect and decay," he writes.

Jackson uses the discussion of prehistoric Pueblo architecture as a base from which to move on to an examination of twentieth-century houses in rural New Mexico. Here, he identifies a different conception of the dwelling. The houses he came across in the 1920s when he first visited the region were simple two- and three-room structures, more or less alike, more or less undistinguished, with walls of adobe brick and corrugated-tin roofs. To a middle-class sensibility, they appeared little more than shacks offering minimal shelter. And so, in a sense, they were, for the surrounding villages were much more important to the people who lived in them than their homes, whether for work, for recreation, or for seeing friends; even memorable family events such as anniversaries and reunions were held in church basements and school gyms rather than at people's houses. Jumping ahead sixty years, Jackson describes the mobile homes and prefabricated houses that now dot the New Mexico landscape and are home to many low-income people. The trailers are healthier and more comfortable than the old adobe shacks of the 1920s, but they are used in much the same way. Like the shacks, the trailers are more or less alike and considered useful rather than individually expressive objects.

In his discussion of mobile homes, Jackson does not deride their lack of architectural appeal, their standardized appearance, and their temporariness. He prefers to examine what it is that has made them for many the most accessible form of new housing in the nation. (According to the U.S. Bureau of the Census, the average price of a new mobile home in 1991 was $27,800, compared with an average sales price of a new home, including land, of $120,000.)

This tolerant attitude toward what many see as the aesthetic shortcomings of the American built landscape is typical of Jackson's writing, and it has exasperated some critics. In *The Geography of Nowhere*, a spirited condemnation of the American built landscape, James Howard Kunstler has written,

> What J. B. Jackson appeared to lack, it turned out, were critical faculties. So caught up was he in the empirical dazzle of his observations that he seemed unable to make judgments about what he was observing. He was not interested in consequences, only manifestations.

In fact, Jackson does make aesthetic judgments, but it is true that he prefers to be an observer rather than an advocate of conventional beautification. I think the reason he appears uncritical (or is it merely tolerant?) is that often he really admires the various signs of human initiative and creativity no matter how commonplace, and he delights in the ordinary interactions that take place between people and their surroundings, whether it is the way they decorate their backyards, run small businesses out of their garages, or organize their lives along a highway—Jackson has much to say about truck stops and about the industrial landscape of loading docks and warehouses.

It's also possible that Jackson simply does not share the taste of his critics. After all, there aren't many academics who would publicly admit, "I am very pro-automobile, pro-car and pro-truck, and I can't imagine what existence would be without them." Or who would concede, "Like millions of other Americans I have no great liking for wilderness and forest, but like the majority of Americans I am fond of trees." Elsewhere he adds, "I am one of those who believe that our current guilt-ridden worship of the environment is a sign of moral and cultural disarray." Jackson is critical of groups like the Sierra Club that wish to isolate nature from human use and is more sympathetic to what he calls the humanized landscape of state parks, beaches, and recreation areas.

Three chief themes can be found in *A Sense of Place, a Sense of Time*. The first is the uniqueness of the American man-made landscape and the need to understand it on its own terms. Jackson writes vividly of the new kind of historical relationship that settlers in the New World developed with trees. The American forest was a resource to be exploited (unlike in most of Europe, where it was set aside as aristocratic hunting preserves), and the early colonists quickly developed ways of using timber in house construction.

At the same time as trees were exploited, they were also being planted, and ever since colonial Williamsburg the tree-lined residential street has been a characteristic feature of American urbanism. So, in their day, were town squares, courthouse squares, and village greens, usually ringed by trees.

The traditional town square is a symbol of social unity and cohesion that no longer exists, however. Cities became collections of ethnic neighborhoods and eventually spread farther and wider than anyone expected. This was partly, but by no means entirely, owing to the automobile. For, as Jackson rudely reminds us, Americans have never been decided about how they ought to live:

> In theory, but only in theory, we want to duplicate the traditional compact European community where everyone takes part in a rich and diversified public life. But at the same time most of us are secretly pining for a secluded hideaway, a piece of land, or a small house in the country where we can lead an intensely private nonurban existence, staying close to home.

The compact nineteenth-century railroad suburb was in many ways a solution to this dilemma, providing private houses and gardens, leafy common streets, nearby shopping areas, and access to the city. But it was quickly usurped by the automobile, which did much to break the connection between the city and its suburbs.

The ambivalence that Jackson identifies will probably take Americans in a different direction from traditional city planning. The title of this collection refers to his intriguing thesis that Americans' sense of place, their actual sense of physical belonging, is mainly conditioned not by architecture and urban design but by shared daily, weekly, and seasonal rituals and events, that is, by a sense of time. This has something to do with the immensity of the land and the relative newness of American cities and towns; on the whole, Jackson argues, there has not been enough time to establish the individuality and variety that mark the older cultures of Europe. Spaces are identified not so much by their physical features as by the events that take—and took—place in them. For example, the grand public spaces of Washington, D.C., have a lesser place in the national memory than, say, the remembered image of three-year-old John Kennedy saluting his father's funeral cortege or of Marian Anderson singing in front of the Lincoln Memorial. One might say, following Jackson, that the homecoming game matters more than the stadium, the parade more than the street, the fair more than the fairground. This also explains the relatively rapid changes that occur in American cities. Places like railroad depots, main streets, and public squares acquire significance in one period and lose it in another.

Jackson's second theme is the notion of the vernacular in building. This term was popularized by architects and architectural historians with reference to popular, traditional, nonacademic techniques and forms of building. Thus, Saxon barns and Norman farmhouses are examples of vernacular buildings, and so are New England saltboxes and southern shotgun houses. Vernacular originally implied preindustrial, folkloric creations, and some critics such as Bernard Rudofsky, the author of *Architecture Without Architects*, have argued the moral superiority of such "timeless" buildings. This is a romantic view. It is now beginning to be understood that just as in formal architecture the history of vernacular buildings is marked by evolution, invention, and change. It is even likely that fashion plays a role in vernacular designs. A history of popular housing in nineteenth-century America, for example, would show the clear influence of changing Victorian tastes in the way that parlors were decorated or in the kinds of ornaments applied to porches. The distinction between vernacular building and architecture has never been absolute: architects have often incorporated vernacular elements in their designs (most popular building methods, like wood framing or bricklaying, have vernacular origins), and vernacular building is not immune to formal architectural influences.

According to Jackson, modern vernacular spaces have particular characteristics. Although it does not appear in Jackson's book, the food court can serve as an example. The court has an overall structure—the food counters are on the periphery, the tables in the center—but there is no strict separation between the different parts, as in a traditional restaurant. This lack of spatial hierarchy reflects the lack of formal ritual. It also reflects a curious attribute of modern vernacular spaces. The identity of the food court has very little to do with architecture but is derived almost entirely from its function. This was brought home to me recently as I ate in a food court in a newly built rest stop on an interstate highway near Albany. The food court was housed in a dramatic, skylit space that resembled a converted barn. Under other circumstances—if this had been a library or a museum, that is, a formal space—the handsome design would have been evocative. Here, it seemed out of place and, worse, disconnected from the unstructured busy activity it contained.

The food court is characterized by extreme personal freedom: we choose the cuisine we want and the food we want, and we sit where we want for as long as we want. This combination of choice, freedom, and informality has taken the food court out of the shopping mall (where it originated in the 1970s) and into all sorts of unexpected places: not only highway rest stops, but also amusement parks, airports, and universities. Food courts are among those ubiquitous but almost invisible settings for modern life, like parking garages or sidewalk banking machines, whose origin is relatively recent but to which we have, apparently effortlessly, adapted.

A characteristic of the food court that I have not mentioned is that it is likely to be patronized chiefly by a combination of mall shoppers, salespeople, and blue-collar workers, the broad middle class, sometimes called Middle America. That is, of course, what makes it vernacular because, by definition, vernacular spaces are used by the majority of the population. Jackson's third theme concerns class distinctions. This is a difficult subject, for, as he observes, "Americans are reluctant to discuss class distinctions in our culture, probably because we feel this would be undemocratic and adversarial."

This reluctance has produced euphemisms like "real people" and "ordinary folk" but no broad agreement on definitions of class. Only half jokingly, the late Herman Kahn once described America as a two-class society: those who hunted and those who didn't. In *Fear of Falling*, Barbara Ehrenreich identified a relatively high-paid "professional" middle class that included managers and academics and that she estimated made up about 20 percent of the population. But she was not always consistent in her description of Middle America, which she sometimes referred to as the middle class and sometimes as the working class. Jackson, too, can be inconsistent. He generally distinguishes between the broad middle class and the professional middle class, and in an essay on mobile homes in the Southwest he also refers to unskilled wage earners, "the man or woman without capital, without any marketable skill, and with only a limited formal education." But he also tends to use generalizations like "the average American" and "blue-collar," and one is not always sure when "middle class" means Middle American and when it refers to the academic and professional elite.

Nevertheless, some of the most stimulating essays in *A Sense of Place, a Sense of Time* concern the specific ways in which class is reflected in how spaces are used. In the past, bourgeois houses were divided into rooms for specialized functions—parlors, boudoirs, breakfast rooms; today, in the new houses built for the professional middle class, although eating spaces are sometimes combined with kitchens, there are also media rooms, exercise rooms, bedroom suites. By contrast, many rooms in Middle American homes were—and are—characterized by being unspecialized and are used flexibly for different activities at different times of day. People watch television in the kitchen, visiting relatives sleep in the living room, the garage is also a workshop, the driveway is a place to repair cars. This reflects not merely different economic resources—houses are smaller and households larger—but also a different and more pragmatic relationship to spaces. Jackson underlines this difference in an essay titled "Working at Home," in which he examines the way that garages in postwar American homes provided an opportunity for the home to become, as it once was, a workplace as well as a living place. In the Quebec village where I used to live, garages were converted into barbershops, beauty parlors, and repair shops; most urban neighborhoods contain extensive networks of semi-legal repair shops in garages and basements. Elsewhere, Jackson writes about the way that the proliferation of vans and pickup trucks has altered the city, bringing local services to far-flung neighborhoods.

In the 1960s, when he was writing *Esquire* articles about car customizers and surfers, Tom Wolfe once likened his role to that of the "renegade cowboy" in Western movies, the outsider who lived with the Indians and returned to town to regale the settlers with tales of what was going on "out there." Jackson is a serious scholar and is not interested in shocking or titillating the reader. Still, his writing is similarly a report from "out there."

> I made no great discoveries and wound up in plenty of blind alleys, but as my text indicates, I have come back convinced beyond a doubt that much of our contemporary American landscape can no longer be seen as a composition of well-defined individual spaces—farms, counties, states, territories, and ecological regions—but as the zones of influence and control of roads, streets, highways: arteries which

dominate and nourish and hold a landscape together and provide it with instant accessibility. This means, I think, that architecture no longer provides the important symbols. Architecture in its oldest and most formal sense has ceased, at least in our newest landscapes, to symbolize hierarchy and permanence and sacredness and collective identity; and so far the road or highway has not taken over those roles. The road generates its own patterns of movement and settlement and work without so far producing its own kind of landscape beauty or its own sense of place. That is why it can be said that a landscape tradition a thousand years old in our Western world is yielding to a fluid organization of space that we as yet do not entirely understand, nor know how to assimilate as a symbol of what is desirable and worth preserving.

This is Jackson at his best: lucid, provocative, iconoclastic, elegant. His work also contains, I think, an important message. Much as we would like to, we cannot go back. Not only our landscapes have changed, but so has our way of seeing and experiencing places. If we are to improve our countryside and our cities—and Jackson is never complacent about the shortcomings of the contemporary American vernacular landscape—we must understand them. We must put aside our prejudices and see it, and ourselves, clearly, as we really are, food courts and all.

J. B. Jackson made many of his field observations of the American landscape while riding his BMW motorcycle across the continent when he was teaching at Harvard and Berkeley. Shortly after this essay was published in The New York Review of Books *in July 1994, I received a touching note from the author. He said that throughout his long career this was the first time that his work had received attention in other than an academic publication. Jackson died two years later.*

Godfathers of Sprawl

Cities have existed in one form or another since Gilgamesh, but the shape of the American urban landscape is unprecedented: tangles of highways and interchanges punctuated by roadside restaurants and neon-winking attractions; boxy shopping centers and multiplexes sitting among vast parking lots; fleets of trailer trucks surrounding distribution warehouses and manufacturing plants; a crush of office buildings, warehouses, and hotels at the airport; suburban tract houses. We call it sprawl. The word means easeful repose, but sprawl makes many Americans anxious, not relaxed. Sprawl is sometimes described as if it were a natural calamity, like a flood or a forest fire. But it's hardly sudden: sprawl has been taking place for most of the twentieth century, and it might be useful to recall the recent history of some of sprawl's pioneers.

FRANCIS C. TURNER

Francis C. Turner (1908–99), a Dallas native, studied civil engineering at Texas A&M University and joined the Bureau of Roads, as the federal agency charged with highway construction was then called. Over the years, he oversaw the construction of the fifteen-hundred-mile Alaska Highway, rebuilt highways and bridges in the postwar Philippines, and worked on the Inter-American

Highway. In 1954, President Dwight D. Eisenhower tapped him as executive secretary of the President's Advisory Committee on a National Highway Program.

This committee had a monumental task: to lay the groundwork for what was to become the Interstate Highway System. As the only experienced road builder on the committee, Turner was its de facto point man. After Congress passed the Federal-Aid Highway Act, he assumed greater and greater authority over the $130 billion construction appropriation, the largest public works project ever undertaken in the United States. Acting as liaison between the Bureau of Roads and Congress, Turner negotiated with the states and oversaw the planning of the highways. It was a relentlessly deterministic process. The country was divided into grids, and residents were polled to determine "desire lines," which became the basis for individual routes. By the time Turner retired as head of the Federal Highway Administration in 1972, the forty-two-thousand-mile highway system was the wonder of the world.

Eisenhower had been impressed by the autobahns he had seen in Germany during World War II, and the strategic goal of the national highway program was to reduce dependence on the Panama Canal by providing an overland means of transporting military forces from coast to coast. That, at least, was the original intention. But big-city mayors, wanting to increase access to their downtowns—and yearning for a share of the highway budget—lobbied for urban connections to the interstate system. Eisenhower and Turner were reluctant, because urban land was expensive, as was the cost of elevated highways in congested downtowns. But they needed the support of urban politicians to convince Congress, and so the final act included more than six thousand miles of urban highways.

Federal highway money flowed to the cities, but with unintended consequences. Unlike German autobahns, interstates went not only "to" the cities but also "through" the cities. Construction

destroyed vast amounts of housing stock, mainly in poorer neighborhoods. Elevated superhighways and interchanges created physical barriers in the centers of cities. Because the banks of rivers and
lakes had been blighted by industrial uses, they offered convenient
sites for the new highways. Later, when waterfronts were seen as
potential amenities, these highways would become barriers to development. A few cities are now beginning the difficult task of repair-
ing the physical damage done by this intrusion into the urban fabric,
but in most cases the harm will never be undone.

The effect of the interstate system on the country as a whole
has been momentous. High-speed public roads—"freeways"—
have changed the way Americans live, work, and play. The highway
system provides links to distant weekend cottages and recreation
sites, including national and state parks. Because it is more convenient to ship goods long distances by truck instead of rail, factories
that had once been located in cities next to railroad spurs are now
beside highway interchanges. So are shopping malls and office
parks. Urban highways make it easier to get into the city, but they
also make it easier to get *out*. An hour's commute on the interstate
describes a fifty-mile radius around the city, turning thousands
of square miles of countryside into potential suburbs. The country
has changed its shape, thanks in great part to Frank Turner, the
unwitting godfather of sprawl.

STANLEY H. DURWOOD

By 1960, the interstate highway system was well on its way to creating a spread-out suburban nation, but that was not Stanley H.
Durwood's problem. He was worried about something else: television. Durwood (1920–99), born in Kansas City, had gone to
Harvard and served in the U.S. Army Air Forces during World

War II, before returning to work for his father, who owned a small
chain of movie houses and drive-in theaters. Business was not
good. Instead of going to the movies, families were staying in their
sparkling new suburban homes to eat TV dinners and watch *Gun-
smoke*. Hollywood, and the giant movie palaces of the 1930s that
the Durwood chain owned, seemed destined for oblivion. One
evening, in the six-hundred-seat Roxy Theater in downtown
Kansas City, attendance was so poor that Durwood, who was the
manager, had to close the balcony. "I thought, 'If we could just run
another so-so picture up in the balcony, we'd double our gross,'"
he later told *Variety*.

After Durwood took over the faltering family business, more
out of desperation than anything else—and remembering the
Roxy—he started subdividing his large theaters into smaller halls.
It was the beginning of an idea that came to fruition in 1963 when
he built a brand-new movie theater specifically designed to show
several movies at the same time. Thus, in a suburban shopping
center in south Kansas City, the multiplex was born.

Multiplexes proved enormously popular, and Durwood's company, which he later renamed American Multi-Cinema (today
AMC), has become a familiar part of the metropolitan landscape.
Suburban multiscreen movie theaters offer moviegoers an array of
choices in one location, something that had previously been possible only in the largest cities. They also provide a venue for the
kinds of movies earlier shown only in downtown art-house cinemas. Does the recent rise of the independents owe something to
Durwood's brainchild? Probably. Multiplexes also create a pleasant and comfortable atmosphere—Durwood is credited with in-
venting the armrest cup holder—that revived the custom of a
"night at the movies." In 1993, the Motion Picture Pioneers Foundation named Stanley Durwood Pioneer of the Year, an honor
previously accorded to Cecil B. DeMille and Darryl F. Zanuck.

JAY PRITZKER

Jay Pritzker (1922–99) was born in Chicago. After graduating from Northwestern University Law School in 1947 and serving as a naval aviator in World War II, he worked for the law firm founded by his grandfather. Then he struck out into the business world, acquiring and managing assorted small companies. In 1957, Pritzker was in the coffee shop of a hotel at Los Angeles International Airport. The coffee shop and the hotel were filled with business executives like himself. Pritzker had never thought of an airport as a location for a businessmen's hotel. "It was simply the first first-class hotel that I had ever seen at an airport," he later recalled. The hotel—named after its owner, Hyatt von Dehn—was for sale, and Pritzker, always on the lookout for new acquisitions, bought it on the spot for $2.2 million. Not long after, together with his brother, Robert, Pritzker built a brand-new hotel near San Francisco International Airport. Additional airport hotels followed in Seattle and Los Angeles. This was the beginning of the Hyatt Hotels Corporation, which today has 182 hotels and made the Pritzker brothers among the richest men in the world.

In 1979, Jay Pritzker endowed the Pritzker Architecture Prize, which is annually awarded to an outstanding architect. Yet his real architectural legacy—a place for businessmen to sleep and meet at the airport—is at once more mundane and more influential. The airport hotel, widely imitated and today an international phenomenon, is not simply a successful marketing gimmick. We take it for granted that airports are surrounded by a dense agglomeration of car rental agencies, meeting facilities, restaurants, offices, distribution centers, manufacturing plants, and hotels. Airports began as simple transportation terminals. But, as Pritzker realized, the airport could be more than simply a place to park your car. In the railroad age, hotels, nightclubs, and offices had clustered around the downtown train station. Airports couldn't be built downtown, of course, but parts of downtown could be brought to the airport.

In 1967, Pritzker bought an unfinished hotel in central Atlanta and built a giant atrium hotel, initiating an architectural trend that has lasted until the present day. Over the last two decades, his downtown hotels have been a part of urban renewal in Chicago, San Francisco, Dallas, Pittsburgh, Minneapolis, Miami, and Memphis. Stanley Durwood's company, too, returned to the city. The multiplex was born in the suburbs, and the sprawling one-story buildings were built in suburban malls, often near one of Frank Turner's highway interchanges. This year, a thirteen-screen Loews Cineplex opened on Forty-Second Street in Manhattan. Early next year, AMC will open a twenty-five-screen movie theater across the street, incorporating part of the old Empire Theater into its design, neatly closing a forty-year-old circle.

There is a common theme in the visions of Turner, Durwood, and Pritzker; each filled a new market need. They made plans, to be sure, but these were often altered by chance—and by the vagaries of the marketplace. Their stories are a reminder that cities today are not the result of grand political visions but the expression of millions of individuals' choices. Those who anticipate and respond successfully to these choices, as Turner, Durwood, and Pritzker did, are the real planners of the American city.

This essay was commissioned in 1999 by The New York Times Magazine *for its end-of-year "The Lives They Lived" issue. I thought it an interesting subject, but perhaps the* Times *expected a more tongue-in-cheek treatment, for it spiked my piece. I published it in the* Wharton Real Estate Review *instead.*

Big-City Amenities. Trees.
High-Tech Jobs. Cappuccino.
Retirement Paradise. Nose Rings

Places Rated Almanac bills itself as a "guide to finding the best places to live." It compares and ranks all 343 metropolitan areas in the United States and Canada, taking into account cost of living, job opportunities, transportation, housing, recreation, climate, and so on. The metropolitan areas surrounding large, vibrant cities like Seattle, San Francisco, and Toronto are highly ranked: after all, these places tend to boast a variety of employment, entertainment, and recreational opportunities; they also offer a wide choice of health-care facilities and are usually important transportation hubs. It's a surprise, then, to discover that the fifth-rated place to live in the United States is Raleigh-Durham in North Carolina. This is a metropolitan area whose largest city, Raleigh, has only about 230,000 people; Durham is even smaller, with fewer than 150,000. Yet little Raleigh-Durham is hot: in 1992, *Inc.* magazine rated it as one of "the best places in the country to own a business," and last year *Money* magazine gave it the coveted No. 1 spot in its "best places to live in America" issue.

The runners-up to Raleigh-Durham as *Money*'s best places to live were Rochester, Minnesota, and Provo-Orem, Utah. Likewise small-to-midsize regional centers that share several characteristics other than their size. They score high in that ephemeral but crucial category, "quality of life." They are near recreational amenities like lakes and mountains. They have strong local economies and have lower unemployment, poverty, and crime rates than the national average. But Raleigh-Durham, Rochester, and Provo-Orem are not merely examples of successful small cities. They are also examples of a new urban trend: the rise of what might be called the college city.

The college town is an American institution. Throughout the nineteenth century, it was common practice to locate private colleges in small towns like Amherst in Massachusetts, Middlebury in Vermont, and Claremont in California. The idea was that bucolic surroundings would provide the appropriate atmosphere for the pursuit of learning and (not incidentally) remove students from the distractions and temptations of the big city. The influence of the small college on its town was minimal, however, beyond providing a few local residents with service jobs.

The college city is different. At its heart is a large research university. In the case of Raleigh-Durham, there are actually three: Duke in Durham, North Carolina State in Raleigh, and the University of North Carolina at Chapel Hill, just down the road. Provo has Brigham Young University, and Rochester has the Mayo Clinic, which also runs a graduate school. Not only are modern research universities vast undertakings—the three North Carolina universities have about sixty thousand students among them—but they also act as magnets for private enterprise, attracting industries that provide well-paying jobs in the high-tech and medical fields. For example, the sixty-eight-hundred-acre Research Triangle Park outside Raleigh is now home to more than eighty research enterprises that employ about thirty-five thousand people.

It's not just jobs that lure people to these places. Simply put, life in most smaller cities is cheaper. A family moving from the metropolitan area of a large city like Philadelphia, say, to Raleigh-Durham would need considerably less income—about 30 percent less—to maintain the same standard of living. The savings come chiefly in the form of lower housing prices and property taxes as well as lower state and local taxes.

In the past, a lower cost of living usually translated into a lower *standard* of living. Life in small cities, with or without colleges, might have been cheaper, but it was also restricted in terms of entertainment, shopping, and recreation. Today, DVDs, sports channels, cineplexes, clothing and housewares catalogs, national distribution chains, and the Internet have changed that. You don't have to travel to Manhattan anymore to shop at Bloomingdale's; all you need to do is go down to the mall or call an 800 number. This is more than merely a matter of convenience. It means that small cities can offer many, if not all, of the everyday services and amenities that used to be the exclusive province of the metropolis.

Where people live has always been influenced by technology. Once, the seaport, the railroad, and the huge factory complex encouraged concentration in large cities. Truck transport and the automobile have had the opposite effect; so has the deregulation of airplane travel and telecommunications. Generally speaking, recent technological developments like cellular telephones, cable television, personal computers, and fax machines have all supported dispersal. Indeed, it is difficult to think of a single invention in the past fifty years that has not been inspired by the desire to make modern life more decentralized.

The forces of decentralization account for much of the appeal of the college city. For example, the largest American cities—New York, Philadelphia, Chicago, Boston—have traditionally had the most sophisticated hospitals. The decentralization of medical skills now means that a regional medical center, like the Duke University Medical Center or the Mayo Clinic, can provide world-class health care. Another appeal of a college city is the access to continuing education, not only for people in mid-career, but also for retirees. Mild climates and golf courses used to be the main attractions in retirement communities, but college cities, with their high-quality athletic programs, their university drama and music departments, and their art galleries and museums, offer a variety of diversions not available in most cities of comparable size. Life in a college city, whether it is Raleigh-Durham, Santa Cruz, California, or Charlottesville, Virginia, can be as cosmopolitan as it is in larger cities. The list of such college cities is long and growing longer: Madison, Wisconsin; Ann Arbor, Michigan; San Luis Obispo, California; Eugene, Oregon; Austin, Texas; Bloomington, Indiana; Boulder, Colorado; Iowa City, Iowa; and Lawrence, Kansas, are some examples.

The college city I know best is Burlington, Vermont. This little city is in the foothills of the Green Mountains and on the shore of Lake Champlain. (Burlington itself has a population of about 40,000, while the metropolitan area has about 214,000 people.) The setting is as idyllic as it sounds. Undoubtedly, it was the unspoiled surroundings and the recreational opportunities that drew many newcomers here during the 1960s and 1970s. Burlington became a destination for those who wanted to escape big cities but were not quite ready for a dropout's life on a farm or in a commune. (The rest of Vermont offered those alternatives.) Burlington also attracted young professionals and entrepreneurs who were looking for a low-key urban life. The city's most famous success story of that era is Ben & Jerry's, whose first ice cream parlor was located in an abandoned service station downtown. High-tech corporations also found Burlington congenial, and IBM and Digital Equipment Corporation established plants in the area. While not quite in the same league as booming Raleigh-Durham, Burlington exhibits many of the characteristics of the larger college city: a busy regional airport and university medical center, growing white-collar employment, and a beautiful environment.

I used to live close to Burlington, just over the Canadian border. My wife and I would frequently make the ninety-minute drive, sometimes to shop, sometimes to visit the nearby Shelburne Museum—an extraordinary collection of historic buildings and

artifacts—and sometimes to go sailing with friends on Lake
Champlain. But most often we would go with no particular aim in
mind, just to stroll the streets.

We would usually end up on Church Street, where a legacy of
that urban design fad of the 1970s still exists: the main street converted into a pedestrian mall. The malls of that period were usually
a last-ditch effort to resuscitate declining downtowns; today, with
their crumbling planters and unpainted benches, most downtown
malls are deserted. Church Street is an exception: it's a busy and
thriving thoroughfare crowded with adults, children, and dogs.
There are sidewalk vendors, several good bookstores, an art supply
store, the inevitable Banana Republic, and a number of restaurants,
bistros, and cafés—a veritable Green Mountain Saint-Germain-
des-Prés.

I exaggerate, but there is at least one real similarity to Paris's Left
Bank: the place is teeming with students. (There are about twelve
thousand of them in Burlington, enrolled at the University of Vermont and two other colleges.) The presence of so many young
people may be one of the secrets to the success of college cities like
Burlington. College students are generally bright, healthy, social,
and usually unencumbered by serious financial worries. They typically don't have large, comfortable homes to retreat to—or families to take care of—and so they tend to inhabit the public realm.
At night, students are out and about; downtown Burlington has
two independently owned cinemas as well as a renovated theater.
Although some might complain that students, by their nature, can
be bothersome, they contribute a vital ingredient to urban life.
Unlike their career-focused elders, college students really do have
the time to sit in a café or dawdle on the village green, which is why
many college cities have retained the vibrant kind of public street
life that was once characteristic of larger cities. Who would have
thought that the ivory tower would nurture that precious but rapidly
disappearing commodity: city life.

Designs for Escape

Last summer, I was in Montreal on a brief visit from Philadelphia, where I now live. I had some small business to conduct there, but the visit was mainly an opportunity to look up old friends. I called Danièle, whom I hadn't seen in a couple of years, and we arranged to have dinner together that evening. She promised to take me to a new bistro, and I looked forward to it; Montreal is no longer the premier city of Canada—that role now belongs to Toronto—and it was a little shabbier than I remembered, but it still has more than its share of exceptional restaurants.

"Shall we meet there?" I asked.

"No," she said, "you must come by the apartment first." She told me excitedly that she wanted to show me the plans of a weekend house that she and Luc were going to build. Danièle is not an architectural neophyte: she had been married to an architect for twenty years. True, the marriage had ended in divorce—Luc, her current beau, is in public relations—and I didn't remember her having expressed strong ideas about architecture in the past. But I knew her ex well; he had been a student of mine. You can't live with someone for twenty years and not be influenced by what that person does. At least, that's what my wife tells me. So I was curious to see what sort of house Danièle had come up with.

She and Luc and I sat around the kitchen table, and they showed me snapshots of the site, which was in the Laurentian Mountains,

a popular recreation area north of Montreal. The Laurentians are
an old volcanic range, and the worn, rounded hills recall the Catskills
or the Berkshires, but they're wilder, with fewer signs of human
habitation. Though I prefer pastoral landscapes—rolling fields
and gentle slopes—to mountains, I could see that Danièle and
Luc's land was beautiful: a wooded hilltop with long views in several directions.

I sensed that Danièle was a bit nervous about showing me the
drawings of the house. That was understandable. She knew that I
teach architecture and write about domestic design. She and her
husband had helped my wife and me when we built our own house
in the country. Now it was her turn. Building a house for yourself
is exciting because of the feeling of possibility that a new house
carries and because creating shelter is a basic human urge, whether
or not you are an architect. It's the same urge that makes children
erect playhouses out of blankets and cardboard boxes and build
sand castles at the beach. But building a house—a real house—is
also scary, and not just because of the money involved or the fear
of making mistakes. A new house is revealing. It tells you—and
everyone else—"This is how I live. This is what's important to me.
This is what I dream about." I think that's why home magazines—
from *Ladies' Home Journal* to *Architectural Digest*—have always
been popular. It's not just a matter of looking for decorating hints.
Rather, houses intrigue us because they tell us so much about their
owners.

Danièle spread out the sketches, which had been prepared by a
local architect. Siting is always a crucial consideration for a country
house. I could see that the house would stand at the top of the hill,
and so would be approached from below, as, ideally, houses should
be; walking *down* to a house is always unpleasant. The hilltop had
obviously been chosen for the views it offered, but it also meant
that the house would be some distance from the road and would
require a short walk through the trees to arrive at the front door.

The floor layout of the house was simple enough. Because of the sloping site, the lower level, containing two bedrooms and a bathroom, was dug partly into the ground. The floor above, which could be entered directly from the upper part of the slope, would contain the living areas, and there would be a sleeping loft in a sort of tower. Danièle explained that they wanted to be able to rent rooms to skiers during the winter season, which was why the lower level would have its own front door and could be cut off from the rest of the house. The exterior was mainly wood, with several sloping roofs. It was hard to put your finger on the architectural style of the house. It didn't have the curved eaves and dormer windows of the traditional Breton style, which continues to be popular with many Quebecois. Although the functional-looking window frames and rather spare exterior couldn't be called old-fashioned, neither did they seem aggressively modern. I suppose most people would describe the style as contemporary.

The three of us got into a long discussion about how best to rearrange one of the bathrooms. I pointed out that if they moved the door to the other side and changed the location of the toilet, they could gain space and improve the circulation in the kitchen area as well. Not very inspirational stuff. I could see that Danièle and Luc expected something more. I had unconsciously fallen into a bad habit of architecture teachers: if you really don't know what to say about a project, focus on some practical improvement, no matter how small. How often had I sat on design juries at the university, taking part in interminable discussions about fire exits and corridor widths, when the real problem was something else entirely.

It wasn't that Danièle and Luc's house looked boring—quite the opposite. "The architect told us that she worked hard to make each side of the house different," Danièle explained. Differences there certainly were, and, I thought, that was part of the problem. The little house was trying too hard to be unusual and interesting.

The perimeter was animated by indentations and protrusions—
architectural bumps and grinds. Instead of a single sheltering
gable, the roof was broken up into several slopes. This is a favorite
device of commercial home builders and is obviously a crowd-
pleaser, although the roof has always seemed to me an odd thing to
spend your money on. The complexity of the roof was mirrored by
the intricacy of the windows: there were half a dozen different
shapes and sizes. The modest house was hardly in a league with
Frank Gehry or Peter Eisenman, but it *was* busy.

I realized that I had to say something more substantive, but I
wasn't sure where to start. I believe that small, inexpensive houses
like Danièle and Luc's should be as simple as possible. This is
partly a question of economics; complexity costs money, after all,
and I would rather see a restricted budget devoted to better-quality
materials than to architectural bravura. But it is also an aesthetic
issue. I like plain farmhouses and straightforward country buildings. They usually look good in the landscape, and they have a
kind of directness and honesty that appeals to me. True, they are
often really just boxes, but boxes can be given charm through relatively inexpensive details of construction, such as bay windows,
trellises, and shutters.

The simplest way to dress up a house is to add a porch. Porches,
with their columns, balustrades, and ornamental fretwork, are
pleasant to look at, and they are also pleasant places to sit. They
are like rooms without walls, and they encourage the sort of lazy
inactivity that has always seemed to me the essence of leisure. I
noticed that Danièle's house didn't have any covered outdoor area,
and I suggested that they consider adding a screened porch. This
would also be a useful feature because the Laurentian summers are
hot and are also notorious for their mosquitoes and blackflies.

"No," Luc said. "A porch wouldn't do at all. Porches and balconies are something for a city house. We want our house to look
rustic."

That was interesting. I had always associated porches and verandas with country houses. Evidently, for Danièle and Luc they
were an urban feature. (Indeed, Montreal row houses traditionally
do have verandas.) A little later, they asked me what sort of material I thought should be used to finish the inside walls. I said that I
liked plaster wallboard: it was inexpensive, you could paint it whatever color you wanted, and, furthermore, it was fire-resistant—an
important consideration when you're building miles from a fire-
house. They looked skeptical and said that they had been thinking,
rather, of wood. "We want this to be a different sort of place, where
we can get away from our city life," Luc said.

A lot of architecture has to do with images—and imaginings.
The image may be the result of a remembered family photograph,
or a painting, or the experience of a real porch somewhere. For one
person, getting away means a shady porch with a rocking chair
and a slowly turning ceiling fan. That particular image has haunted
me for years—I think I first saw it in a magazine ad for whiskey.
And for me one of the pleasures of watching the film *Out of Africa*
is the beautiful porch of Karen Blixen's house in Kenya, with
Mozart's Clarinet Concerto playing on a windup gramophone.
Alas, for Luc a porch was just a utilitarian appendage. Moreover,
the image it conjured up for him was not rural but urban. I also had
the impression that he considered porches to be old-fashioned—or
maybe just places for old people.

I have always liked farmhouse kitchens—large comfortable
rooms where you can cook and eat and socialize around the kitchen
table. (That's probably a remembered image too, although I have
never actually lived in a farmhouse.) The plans of Danièle and
Luc's house, on the other hand, showed a small efficiency kitchen,
with a separate dining area. It was an arrangement that reminded
me—but, obviously, not them—of an urban studio apartment. I
realized that their idea of getting away from it all was more dynamic than mine: not a cabin in the woods but a striking ski chalet

on a hilltop, with different views from each room, beamed ceilings, knotty-pine walls, and a dramatic fireplace. I was starting to understand why the house looked the way it did. It was not a question of money—theirs was hardly an extravagant house. It reflected a different idea of rusticity.

Getting away from it all has a long history; almost as soon as people started living in towns, they felt the need to build country retreats. In ancient times, it was the common practice of wealthy Romans to decamp periodically to country estates. "You should take the first opportunity yourself to leave the din, the futile bustle, and the useless occupations of the city," Pliny the Younger wrote in a letter to a friend. Pliny owned two country retreats, one a large agricultural estate in present-day Umbria, the other his famous seaside villa in Latium, of which he wrote, "There I do most of my writing, and, instead of the land I work to cultivate myself." The sentiment—re-creation—is recognizably modern. Modern-sounding, too, is the Renaissance architect Leon Battista Alberti's advice that "if the villa is not distant, but close by a gate of the city, it will make it easier and more convenient to flit, with wife and children, between town and villa, whenever desirable."

In nineteenth-century America, such flitting usually meant taking a steamboat or a train. Summer houses sprang up along the Hudson River, in New York, and the Schuylkill, in Philadelphia, or in places like Newport, Rhode Island. Newport has many early examples of the so-called Shingle Style, one of the high accomplishments of American architecture. The William Watts Sherman House, designed by the great architect H. H. Richardson in 1874, is irregular in composition, and the granite, the half timbering, and the wooden shingles on the exterior give it the picturesque appearance that is a trademark of the Shingle Style. Still, it is provided with a drawing room, a dining room, and a library, and

so is not really a radical departure from a typical middle-class suburban or urban house of the period.

Although wealthy New Yorkers commuted to their villas in
Newport, these were summer houses, not weekend houses. Indeed, the full weekend—a two-day holiday at the end of the
workweek—didn't appear until the twentieth century. It arrived
first in Britain, as a one-and-a-half-day holiday, and by the early
twentieth century more and more Americans were also working
"short Saturdays." Eventually, the five-day workweek became
commonplace, and the combination of a two-day holiday with the
automobile produced the proliferation of weekend retreats that we
know today.

The weekend cottage continues the time-tested tradition of
the summer getaway house, but with a crucial difference. Instead
of being used for an entire season, it is chiefly a two-day retreat.
Hence it is a place less of long and lazy summers than of sometimes
frantic spurts of recreation. Perhaps that's why the architecture is
often intentionally unusual, with dramatic fireplaces, cantilevered
decks, and tall spaces. That was what Luc meant when he said he
wanted "a different sort of place." It was probably the late architect
Charles Moore who started the trend toward spatial excitement. In
the mid-1960s, he designed a series of weekend houses, chiefly in
Northern California, with deceptively simple exteriors and interiors that were a cross between barns and jungle gyms. Although
designed with considerable sophistication, these houses could also
be described as the architectural equivalent of the then-popular
leisure suit. That is, they were intended to put people instanta-
neously in a different mood and also to tell the world that here the
owner was off duty. Moore's approach was influential, and versions of his houses sprang up in vacation spots from Vail to Stowe.

Like many people, I spend my weekends in a worn pair of shorts
and an old polo shirt. Perhaps that's why my ideal of a weekend
house is more like a farmhouse—commodious rather than exciting,

a place to kick your shoes off and relax, a place that can get scuffed up and still feel comfortable. Now, I don't want to give the impression that I think weekend houses should be Thoreau-style shacks, without conveniences or even without luxuries. I would have no objection to a Miele range and a Sub-Zero refrigerator in my country kitchen. After all, that has always been the paradoxical thing about second homes: we want to feel that we're roughing it, but we want our comforts, too. When Richardson designed the Watts Sherman House in Newport, he made it look rustic, but he also incorporated a novel amenity: central heating. Even Thoreau, whose cabin at Walden Pond didn't have a kitchen (in warm weather, he cooked outside over an open fire), regularly walked to nearby Concord to have dinner at friends' houses.

I remember once visiting an Adirondack camp on Lower Saranac Lake. It was one of many in the area that had been built by wealthy New Yorkers during the Gilded Age. The house itself was typical—a charming, rough-hewn log building with a massive granite fireplace, columns made of peeled and polished tree trunks, and spartan Arts and Crafts–style furniture. Here was rusticity laid on with a trowel. When this particular camp, Knollwood, was built in 1899, it consisted of six cottages, a so-called casino (a social gathering place, not a gambling hall), and a boathouse, all designed by William Coulter, the architect of some of the buildings at Sagamore, the Vanderbilts' famous camp. Although the ample cottages at Knollwood contained several bedrooms, there were originally only small service kitchens. That was because the six families and their guests had their meals prepared and served to them in the casino, which had a large kitchen. You went boating on the lake and hiking in the forest, but that was no reason you couldn't have a proper dinner, prepared by your New York cook. The Knollwood boathouse contains canoes and handmade Adirondack guide boats but also, on the upper floor, a huge billiard table. I don't think I would require a billiard table in my ideal weekend house, but on the other hand I couldn't do without a compact-disc player. Getting away from it all has always involved compromise as well as a certain degree of make-believe.

It's hard to comment on—let alone judge—other people's fantasies. If Danièle and Luc wanted a house in the country, well, they would have to make their own compromises. I don't think I was really much help to my friends; our ideas of weekend houses were just too different. Anyway, we all went out to dinner, the atmosphere in the bistro was convivial, the food was excellent, and everyone had a good time. A week later, when I got home to Philadelphia, I couldn't resist making some sketches of my own, trying to accommodate all their requirements. I drew a little cottage, twenty feet by thirty feet, clapboard above and with a stone base— for the two bedrooms—below. The house was sheltered by a broad gable roof (to accommodate the sleeping loft). The loft looked down on the main living space, a large family room with a kitchen at one end and a sitting area at the other. In the center of the room, a Franklin stove served for warming cold toes and cold plates. A pair of glazed doors opened onto a large screened porch. It was only a sketch, just to keep my hand in, I told myself. But if I shut my eyes, I could almost hear the strains of the Clarinet Concerto in the woods.

I sent my sketch to Danièle and Luc, although I hardly expected them to follow it. Nor did they. A few years later, I visited their Laurentian cottage, which had turned out pretty much like the drawings they had shown me. No porch.

Tomorrowland

Famous firsts are recorded by sports statisticians, academic journals, and *The Guinness Book of Records*. Everyday firsts are not. There is no statue to the person who held the first garage sale, or used the first cash machine, or to the pioneering consumer who sprinted through the first shopping mall. I have these thoughts standing in front of 931 Jasmine Street. It is unlikely that there will ever be a commemorative plaque here, but there should be. The building itself, while attractive, is unremarkable. It is a one-story house of a type that is not uncommon in the South: a hipped roof extends over a deep veranda across the entire front, the walls are clapboard, the double-hung windows have shutters. There's a U-Haul trailer in the driveway. I'm standing on the sidewalk, watching Larry Haber moving into his new home. He's a good sport and pauses so that I can take a photograph. Larry, his wife, Terri, and their two young children are the first residents of an unusual town, a town that is being built by an organization whose chief business is storytelling and make-believe: the Walt Disney Company.

It was Walt himself who had the idea. Thirty years ago, he announced that he was going to create a showcase for advanced technology, a kind of urban laboratory. It would be called EPCOT—Experimental Prototype Community of Tomorrow—and it would be an actual residential community. But Disney died before realizing his vision of a city of the future. When EPCOT finally opened in 1982, it did feature futuristic technology, but there were no residents—it was a theme park.

EPCOT is located in Walt Disney World, on the enormous tract of land that the Disney Company owns outside Orlando, in central Florida. There are two other theme parks—the Magic Kingdom and Disney-MGM Studios—and a fourth, Disney's Animal Kingdom, is slated to open in 1998. That still leaves about a third of the twenty-eight thousand acres unused. The idea of building a residential community had lingered on in the Disney Company's corporate memory, and when a master plan was being prepared under the new CEO—Michael Eisner—it was determined that it was finally time to implement Walt's original vision. "At that point, we could have gone in any direction," says Disney Imagineering's Tom Lewis, who was responsible for the first five years of the project. "It could have been a second-home community, a resort, or a retirement village. Instead, we decided that it would be a place where families would have their primary residences. We wanted it to be a real town."

The town is called Celebration. It will have a school, a health campus, and an office park. Recreational facilities will include a golf course, a lake, and miles of walking trails and bike paths. The town center will have restaurants, shops, offices, a supermarket, a bank, a small inn, and a cinema. When it's complete, which will take about ten years, Celebration will have twenty thousand inhabitants. It's the first comprehensively planned new town of this size since Columbia, Maryland, and Reston, Virginia, were founded thirty years ago.

The project was made public in mid-August last year. Although there was nothing actually built, not even a model home, twenty thousand prospective home buyers showed up in the first two months. The demand was so great that it was decided that the only fair way to sell lots was to draw names out of a hat. (Disney employees were not given preference.) Twelve hundred prospective residents put down deposits for the chance to become one of the 351 home buyers or 120 apartment renters in Celebration's first phase. "Things have moved very quickly, more quickly than we expected," says Don Killoren, general manager of the Celebration Company. "But I'm not really surprised. We did a lot of research. We knew the type of houses that people wanted."

Killoren is being slightly disingenuous. One reason people wanted the houses was undoubtedly because they were *Disney* houses. A 1990 international study identified the five brands that were most recognized and most highly esteemed around the world. They were Coca-Cola, Sony, Mercedes-Benz, Kodak—and Disney. Does the Disney name assure success no matter what? Perhaps (although Disney has stumbled from time to time), but you don't become one of the five most powerful brands in the world by being second-rate. The house that the Habers are moving into was built by David Weekley Homes, one of two production home builders picked by Disney through an exhaustive selection process. Half a dozen leading home builders were approached and asked to provide a complete customer list going back five years, up to ten thousand names in some cases. Disney interviewed a random sample of several hundred names from each list regarding satisfaction with customer service, construction quality, warranty, attention to detail, and so on. Among the survey questions was, would you use this builder again or refer him to a close family member? "That was the answer we were really interested in," says Lewis. The two top-ranked builders were Weekley of Houston and Town & Country Homes of Oak Brook, Illinois. Production house prices range from about $130,000 for a row house to over $300,000 for the largest detached house. A similar process was used to select ten local builders who are building the more expensive one-of-a-kind houses that constitute a quarter of the total. The custom houses start at $425,000.

You would look in vain for manifestations of any of the current

vogues in high-fashion architecture. There is no free-form deconstructivism here, no corrugated-metal high tech, no tongue-in-
cheek postmodernism, no glass-and-steel modernism. Instead, there
are gable roofs with dormers, bay windows and porches, balustrades and columns. Like all houses built commercially in the
United States today, the Celebration homes reflect distinctly traditional taste. The Habers' house on Jasmine Street is in a style Disney calls Coastal, a loose interpretation of the types of houses that
were built in the South Carolina Low Country. It is a style characterized by deep one- and two-story porches, high ceilings, full-
length windows, and first floors raised above the ground. Coastal
is one of six—and only six—permissible architectural styles; the
others are Classical, Victorian, Colonial Revival, Mediterranean,
and French. "At one point we actually identified as many as twenty-
seven different residential styles," Joe Barnes, a young architect
working for Disney, told me, "so this is really a distillation." The
six styles are described in a pattern book that ensures the builders
achieve a degree of architectural clarity that is missing in most
builder homes. Unusual, too, is the approach to parking. Alleys run
behind the houses and give access to garages in the rear. Many of
these garages have rooms above them. Larry Haber has a suite for
his mother-in-law above his garage. The only problem, he says,
is that he can't mount the basketball hoop in the usual place—it
would be too noisy.

Leaving the Habers' house, I drive down Campus Street, which
is lined with town houses, directly across from the site of the future
school. The town houses are still under construction, but ahead of
me is a large group of completed buildings: the town center. There
are about twenty buildings, most of them three stories high, fronting narrow streets with sidewalks; not a pedestrian mall in sight.
The buildings look vaguely familiar, the sort of small-town architecture that is found across America. Or used to be, for this
looks like a nineteenth-century downtown. The buildings line

up to the sidewalk, and I can't see any parking lots (the lots are behind the buildings, shoehorned into the center of the blocks). It doesn't really feel historical, however, for there is no consistency to the architecture. There is a plain office block that might be of the late nineteenth century, a two-screen cinema—the only building not quite finished—that looks as if it might turn out to be Art Deco, and a bank whose colored horizontal streamlining stripes are straight out of the 1920s. In addition, there are buildings that look quite modern, such as the town hall, the post office, and a visitor center.

Michael Eisner is an architecture buff, and in the past he has commissioned world-famous architects to design buildings for Disney: Arata Isozaki, Michael Graves, Frank Gehry, Aldo Rossi. Celebration, too, has a cast of celebrated architects. Graves designed the post office, Philip Johnson the town hall, Robert Venturi and Denise Scott Brown the bank, Cesar Pelli the cinema, and Charles Moore the visitor center. I dislike the town hall; like so much of Johnson's work, it tries to be monumental and manages to be merely bombastic. Most of the other signature buildings appear to me to be lackluster rather than inspired, although Graves's little post office is delightful, Venturi and Scott Brown's bank manages to look both old and new, and Pelli's cinema will be appropriately theatrical. But it is the rest of the buildings that I find most impressive. They are what architects call "background buildings"—the ordinary buildings that give character to a town. Here, they are both unpretentious and charming, which is more difficult to do than it sounds. They are the work of either Robert A. M. Stern or Jaquelin T. Robertson, of Cooper, Robertson & Partners.

Stern and Robertson are also the planners of the town, although the credits for the design of Celebration resemble a Hollywood screenplay. First, Disney held a design competition. It invited Andrés Duany and Elizabeth Plater-Zyberk, whose concept of traditional neighborhood development is a major influence on

Celebration, Charles Gwathmey of Gwathmey Siegel, and Stern. Then, instead of choosing a winner, Disney asked the architects to work together to develop a consensus design. An enlarged program and a new expressway required a revised plan, which was prepared collaboratively by Skidmore, Owings & Merrill and Cooper, Robertson & Partners. Finally, Stern and Robertson were commissioned to prepare the master plan and also to design the health campus (Stern), the golf clubhouse (Robertson), and all the secondary downtown buildings.

The downtown buildings are owned by Disney, which leases them to retail tenants. But there is no Banana Republic here. Instead of major national chains, Disney has chosen only local and regional shops and restaurants. The intention is to attract the public by creating an experience that is different from that found in a typical shopping mall, Killoren told me. With its single landlord, Celebration's downtown functions like a mall, albeit one that is decentralized and outdoors. But there is one crucial difference. This is a commercial area where people will also live. All the 120 apartments are located in the downtown area, many of them above shops and restaurants. As I walk around, construction workers are adding finishing touches to the apartment buildings; the tenants are due to start moving in next week. When Celebration opens to the public, which will be in August (the formal opening is scheduled for November), the mixture of tourists, shoppers, residents, and office workers—there are also two small office blocks—will provide precisely the sort of round-the-clock activity that is the hallmark of a successful downtown.

A lively downtown, apartments above shops, front porches, houses close to the street, and out-of-sight garages all add up to an old-fashioned sort of place, more like a small town of the 1920s than a master-planned community of the 1990s. But there is more to

Celebration than nostalgia and tradition. What families like the Habers really want—what most Americans really want—has less to do with architecture and urban design than with good schools, health care, safe neighborhoods, and a sense of community. "We understand that community is not something that we can engineer," emphasizes Todd Mansfield, an executive vice president with Disney Imagineering, "but we think that it's something we can foster." Despite Disney's reputation for obsessively leaving nothing to chance, fostering has not meant controlling. The Celebration school (kindergarten through grade twelve) will be owned and operated not by Disney but by the Osceola County School Board. The school will serve about fourteen hundred students from the surrounding county as well as the town. It will open next year; this fall, students will start classes in the so-called Teaching Academy, a teacher-training facility owned by Disney but run by Stetson University and housed in a handsome building designed by William Rawn, who is also the architect for the school. What will be unusual about the school, apart from pedagogical innovations, will be its central location in the town. Many of the children will be able to walk and bike to class.

The health campus, now under construction, is a large facility belonging to Florida Hospital and includes outpatient surgery, advanced diagnostics, primary-care physicians, and a fitness center. A fiber-optic network will link both the school and the health facility to individual homes. This is just the sort of technological innovation that Walt Disney imagined would be the cornerstone of life in the future. But Michael Eisner's Celebration is actually the exact opposite of Walt Disney's urban vision. Walt Disney imagined a world where all problems would be solved by science and technology. Celebration puts technology in the background and concentrates on putting in place the less tangible *civic* infrastructure that is a prerequisite for real community. Home buyers agree to be governed by a homeowners' association and a set of restrictive deed covenants, whose purpose is to strike a balance between individual freedom and communal responsibility. You can park in front of your house, for example, but only two cars. You can sublet your house—or your garage apartment—but you can't lease individual rooms. You can hold a garage sale—but only once a year. Writers or artists can work out of their homes, but not dentists— unless they live in the "home business neighborhood," where professional offices are allowed. A real sense of community cannot develop in a vacuum, however. Disney seems to have gone out of its way to ensure that Celebration will not become a hermetic place. It is neither walled nor gated, unlike many recent master-planned communities. The streets are not private property. Policing is by the county sheriff's office, not by hired security guards. The golf course, designed by the Robert Trent Joneses—father and son—is a public daily-fee facility, not a private club.

Nevertheless, despite these efforts, much of the public assumes— or at least hopes—that a Disney town will be a perfect town. "It's one of my fears," says Todd Mansfield, who is himself building a house in Celebration. "We have people who have purchased houses who think they're moving to Utopia. We keep having to remind them that we can't provide safeguards for all the ills of society. We will have everything that happens in any community." He's right. I'm confident that despite the advanced Honeywell security systems, there will be break-ins. Despite the fiber-optic networks, there will be children with learning problems. Despite the state-of-the-art medical technology, there will be sickness. And despite the sociable appearance of the front porches, there will be neighborly disputes. If there weren't, Celebration would not be the real place that Disney wants it to become.

Charles E. Fraser has thought a great deal about creating real places. As a developer, he pioneered many of the concepts such as deed covenants, architectural review boards, and neighborhood planning that are today standard practice in master-planned communities. Fraser is the creator of Sea Pines Plantation on Hilton Head Island, South Carolina, where, between 1956 and 1975, he built about thirty-four hundred homes. I asked him how a sense of community had been created at Sea Pines. "My wife and I gave a party every Saturday night for the first ten years. We invited all the new residents and second-home owners who were on vacation. I was only twenty-seven and not very knowledgeable, but I knew it was important to introduce people to each other." Fraser was right; by the time that there were two thousand residents, Sea Pines had as many as two hundred clubs and social groups. Modern mobility means that the process of neighborhood creation, which previously took decades, must be "jump-started." "I've come to the conclusion that relatively small groups—two or three hundred families—that share a common responsibility such as a swimming pool or a park are the answer," he says. At Celebration, where he has been a consultant for seven years, innovative covenants have been written to permit the creation of precisely such small subneighborhoods.

Fraser points out that the population of the United States is increasing at the rate of about twenty-five million people every decade. Most of this growth is now occurring randomly in metropolitan areas, which are too large to have a single focus like the old center city downtown. What is needed, he suggests, are smaller planned communities that can offer people a sense of belonging. "Celebration is a model of such a smaller-size town," he says. "It can offer the range of neighborhood services and amenities—schools, churches, shops—that used to be the benefits of small-town living."

After leaving Celebration, I drive to Winter Park, which is just the sort of small town that Fraser had in mind. Winter Park, which has a population of twenty-five thousand, is part of greater Orlando. It started life as a master-planned community in the 1880s. The main commercial street, Park Avenue, was laid out beside a

six-acre strip of green, named—what else?—Central Park. The
focus of the park was a railroad depot, once the chief place of arrival for winter visitors from the North. The surrounding residential neighborhoods have curved, comfortably shaded streets and
a variety of houses. Park Avenue is lined with low buildings containing shops and restaurants with offices and apartments on the
second floor. I'm sitting in a bar, open to the sidewalk. It's five
o'clock, and people are stopping in for a drink before going home.
It is noisy, bustling, and convivial. People appear to know each
other. It is not hard to imagine that this is what Celebration may
become. More than thirty years ago, the developer James Rouse
(who would go on to build Columbia) called the Disneyland theme
park "the outstanding piece of urban design in the United States."
Just as Disneyland radically transformed the amusement park, Celebration, with its curious mixture of old-fashioned values and new-
fangled organization, will change the way we think about planning
new communities. Which is probably what Walt had in mind in the
first place.

Tina Brown, editor of The New Yorker, *must have liked the first piece
I wrote for the magazine ("Designs for Escape"), for she invited me to
lunch at her famous table at the Royalton. I was unprepared when she
asked me what I would like to write about next. I mentioned that I had
just visited the new town that Disney was building in Florida, and she
said, "That sounds interesting. Go ahead."*

Thoughts on *Home*

The way that we arrange and use our homes is governed by fashion, by custom, and by culture. Fashions change relatively quickly. Chintz was fashionable in the seventeenth century, distinctly unfashionable in the nineteenth ("chintzy" came to mean cheap or vulgar), and fashionable again in the early twentieth century. The picture window arrived in the American bungalow in the 1950s but within thirty years was considered passé. Beanbag chairs were even more fleeting. I remember having one in the 1970s; it was red and Italian, whatever happened to it?

On the other hand, social customs—the way that we use our homes—are more durable. At the end of the nineteenth century, the living room supplanted the parlor as the main public gathering space in the house. Today, a hundred years later, the family room is on the ascendancy, but the living room has hardly disappeared, and I expect it to endure for some time. Who knows, it may even make a comeback.

The most enduring influences on our homes, however, are deeply embedded cultural ideas such as privacy, domesticity, and comfort. These took hundreds of years to emerge and, being deeply rooted, are resistant to change. The modernist movement tried to eliminate bourgeois comfort from the domestic interior but was brought up short. Modernism has survived, but it has had to

come to terms with the idea of comfort—think of Eero Saarinen's
cozy womb chair.

I wrote *Home* more than twenty-five years ago. In the interim,
a number of fashions have come and gone. Traditional furniture,
such as wing chairs, Windsor chairs, and sofas, is still popular, but
there has been a rediscovery of mid-twentieth-century modern
furniture. This is not simply a retro fashion; the period 1940–60
represents one of the high points of furniture design, equivalent
to the British eighteenth century. Another revived modernist idea
is the open plan. Open-plan family homes were never popular—
too noisy, not enough privacy—but the concept has become popular in the unexpected form of the urban loft. The most powerful
domestic fashion trend is the importance given the kitchen, which
is the result of our fascination with cuisine, cooking, and food in
general. Grand nineteenth-century houses had kitchens that resembled commercial kitchens because they prepared food for so
many people, but who would have thought that restaurant kitchen
equipment would become the height of chic?

Has behavior in the home changed? Only slightly. Everything
points in the direction of greater informality, hence the popularity
of the family room, where people can eat, relax, and watch television, both as a family and with friends. In some ways, the family
room is a version of the medieval hall, which did not discrimi-
nate between family and public behavior. But what is more striking is how many customs have not changed: sitting around a
fireplace, sharing special celebratory meals, decorating the home
for holidays.

What has also not changed is our idea of domesticity. The
home is still a refuge from the outside world, especially as that world
becomes more commercialized, more vulgar, and in some places
more violent. The home as a private world has gained in importance, reflecting the atomization of taste and behavior. As there is

no consensus about how we should behave, dress, and act in public, the public realm has become increasingly undisciplined. On the other hand, each of us can be whatever we want to be in the privacy of our own homes.

When Marco Velardi, the editor of Apartamento, *a self-styled "everyday life interiors magazine" based in Milan and Barcelona, invited me to contribute something "to celebrate the fact we were inspired by your words five years ago when we started doing our magazine," I couldn't resist.*

PART TWO

Our Urban Condition

Tocqueville, Urban Critic

Alexis de Tocqueville is celebrated for *Democracy in America*, his classic study of American civilization at the beginning of the nineteenth century. The author was only twenty-five when he visited the United States, but he had a wide-ranging intellect, a keen sense of observation, and a journalist's knack for eliciting the opinion of others. Consequently, one can pick almost any subject—slavery, religion, education—and find that he had something interesting to say about it. It's hardly surprising, then, to discover that Tocqueville, the political scientist and the comparative sociologist, was also a penetrating urban critic.

Tocqueville and his friend and traveling companion, Gustave de Beaumont, disembarked on May 9, 1831, in Newport, Rhode Island. Tocqueville found the harbor town "very attractive" (it still is) and wrote to his mother that Newport was "distinguished by a cleanness that is a pleasure to see and that we have no conception of in France." (Today, it's Paris that surprises Americans by its tidiness.) It is Tocqueville's letters and the fourteen notebooks that he kept during his travels, more than his famous book, that are the best source for his opinions about American cities and towns. In general, he was impressed by small towns. While traveling through Massachusetts, he recorded, "Almost all the houses are charming (especially in the villages), and there prevails a height of cleanliness which is something astonishing." It was not only the architecture

that impressed him. Tocqueville considered the New England town
an exemplary democratic institution because it involved a large
number of citizens in managing their own affairs; he called the
town "the ultimate *individual* in the American system." He was
also astute enough to observe that the political independence of
these small communities lay in what he called their municipal spirit.
"Americans love their towns," he wrote, "for much the same reasons that highlanders love their mountains. In both cases the native
land has emphatic and peculiar features; it has more pronounced
physiognomy than is found elsewhere." Here, more than a century
before Capra's *It's a Wonderful Life*, is clear evidence of the widely
held American affection for the small town.

Most New England towns remained small; they rarely had
more than 2,000 residents, which undoubtedly facilitated their self-
government. But such small settlements were no longer typical of
the United States. A very different sort of town was coming into
being in the American interior—the boomtown. Tocqueville
passed through a number of such places: Rochester, whose population had increased from 150 to 15,000 in only a decade; Memphis, only four years old but already a busy cotton port; and
Louisville, where a local merchant proudly told him that the town
had grown from 3,000 to 13,000 inhabitants in only seven years.
But the fastest-growing inland river port was Cincinnati, where
Tocqueville and Beaumont spent three days in December 1831.

When Tocqueville arrived, Cincinnati was only forty-three
years old, but thanks to the opening up of the Ohio to steamboat
traffic in 1816, it was a busy city of about thirty thousand people.
"Cincinnati presents an odd spectacle," he recorded in his note-
book. "A town which seems to want to get built too quickly to
have things done in order. Large buildings, huts, streets blocked
by rubble, houses under construction; no names to the streets, no
numbers on the houses, no external luxury, but a picture of industry and work that strikes one at every step." Tocqueville's

reservations are understandable; the town had little in the way of
civic refinement. A regular grid of intersecting streets divided the
land into square blocks and demonstrated no regard for topography or for the great river. It is not surprising that the founders of
the city wasted no effort on niceties of urban design; they were
property developers, and like most nineteenth-century American
towns Cincinnati was founded strictly as a real estate venture.

Tocqueville and Beaumont spent slightly less than nine months
in North America (they also went to Canada), and they visited all
the major Eastern Seaboard cities—New York, Philadelphia, Boston, Baltimore, Montreal—although they missed those two attractive southern colonial towns, Charleston and Savannah. Montreal
reminded Tocqueville of an ugly French provincial town, but he
liked Boston—"a pretty town in a picturesque site on several hills
in the middle of the waters." Boston, unlike Cincinnati, had created
a civic waterfront (the rare American city to do so), which happened shortly before Tocqueville's visit—Quincy Market opened
in 1825. The Massachusetts city was the cultural center of the
United States—it was, for example, the heart of the Greek Revival
that was sweeping the nation—and the young French aristocrat
(Tocqueville was technically a baron, although he refused to use
the title) appreciated Boston society, which he compared favor-
ably to the upper classes in Europe. "One feels one has escaped
from those commercial habits and that money-conscious spirit
which makes New York society so vulgar," he wrote in a letter.

Tocqueville spent a total of two months in New York, because
it was the base from which he and Beaumont set out on their several trips, but he never warmed to the city. In a letter to his friend
Ernest de Chabrol, he described the island site of New York as
"admirable" but complained about the lack of noteworthy public
monuments and added that "it does not resemble in the least our
principal cities in Europe." "To a Frenchman the aspect of the city
is bizarre and not very agreeable," he wrote to his mother. "One

sees neither dome, nor bell tower, nor great edifice, with the result
that one has the constant impression of being in a suburb. In its
center the city is built of brick, which gives it a most monotonous
appearance. The houses have neither cornices, nor balustrades,
nor *portes-cochères*." The only good thing he found to say about
New York was that although the streets were badly paved, there
were sidewalks in all of them.

Was it really that dismal? Probably. Large sections of New
York had been destroyed by two disastrous fires during the British occupation, the population shrank to as low as ten thousand
people immediately after the War of Independence, and the economy did not revive until about 1790. So what Tocqueville saw was
a newly growing, newly built city; that, and the lack of an architectural heritage, would have given it a makeshift air. The monotony that he comments on was also the result of the Commissioners'
Plan of 1811, which divided almost the entire island of Manhattan
north of Washington Square into a regular grid consisting of east–
west streets at two-hundred-foot intervals, crossed by a dozen
north-south avenues, more than seven miles long. The blocks were
divided into twenty-five-by-one-hundred-foot plots. It was a real
estate agent's dream, but it was not much more than that.

In 1811, when the population of New York was fewer than 50,000
people, laying out such a vast grid must have appeared hopelessly
optimistic, and even twenty years later when Tocqueville stayed
there, although the city had mushroomed to over 200,000, less
than a third of the grid was filled in. Two hundred thousand
doesn't sound like a major city today—it's smaller than Anchor-
age, Alaska—but in the beginning of the nineteenth century it
signified an important city the size of Amsterdam, say, or Vienna,
or Berlin.

But one should not imagine New York as a smaller, more livable version of today's metropolitan behemoth. This was a pre-
modern city that lacked most of the urban technologies that we

take for granted. There were no underground sewers to carry off household wastewater, for example. The fecal matter of 200,000 people was either collected by night-soil scavengers and dumped in the river, carted to the countryside to be used as fertilizer, or deposited into pits and cesspools; kitchen slops were thrown into the street. Because there was no municipal water supply, backyard wells easily became contaminated: it's little wonder that the first cholera epidemic in the United States broke out in New York, in 1832. As Tocqueville noted, most streets were unpaved. The mud was mixed with horse manure, and domestic refuse was scattered everywhere, for there was no garbage collection—which is why modern Manhattan streets are typically five to fifteen feet higher than their original levels.

Urban life was uncomfortable and unhealthy—and dangerous. What seems to have struck Tocqueville most about the largest cities like New York and Philadelphia was the presence of a turbulent urban lower class, which he described as consisting of freed black slaves ("condemned by law and opinion to a hereditary state of degradation and wretchedness") and poor immigrants, whom he considered to be motivated by self-interest rather than citizenship. The urban rabble was a common feature of European cities and would hardly have surprised Tocqueville, but in a democracy he foresaw (more or less correctly) that the large size of American cities and the volatile nature of the urban underclass (although he did not call it that) would eventually threaten republican institutions. He also predicted that the government would be obliged to create an armed force to suppress the excesses of the mob, which had already instigated serious riots in both New York and Philadelphia. He was right about that, too: in 1833, Philadelphia formed its first regular, daytime police force, and eleven years later New York followed suit.

It is understandable that a native Parisian was not impressed by unruly, mercenary New York. There was another American city, however, that might have elicited a more favorable opinion—Washington. After all, it was planned by Tocqueville's countryman Pierre Charles L'Enfant, and it was intended to be a leading example of civic beauty. L'Enfant was trained as an artist, and his plan incorporated such Baroque-inspired devices as broad diagonal avenues, civic squares, and monumental vistas. It was a visionary scheme that dwarfed anything being built in Europe, including even Peter the Great's St. Petersburg, then taking shape on the Neva.

When Tocqueville and Beaumont visited Washington—they spent about two weeks meeting public officials and consulting government archives—the city was forty years old, but lacking a good port and commerce, it was growing slowly and held only about twenty thousand people. Because there was no indication in L'Enfant's plan of how the city might expand in phases, construction was taking place in a scattershot fashion, with groups of houses here and there; it gave the impression, according to Tocqueville, of a town composed of five or six villages. Compared with the carefully drafted plans made first by L'Enfant and later by the surveyor Andrew Ellicott, the reality was almost comical. The mile-long mall was used as a cow pasture; the *rond-points* scattered throughout the city, which were to commemorate the states of the Union, were planted with vegetables. The monumental avenues (130 to 160 feet wide) that L'Enfant had created to link important sites were there all right, but they were flanked not by buildings but by virgin forest or raw earth; the White House and the Capitol stood in forlorn splendor. There is disbelief in Tocqueville's voice when he notes that "they have already rooted up trees for ten miles around, lest they should get in the way of the future citizens of this imagined capital." Eventually, the imagined capital would be splendidly realized (thanks to the 1901 McMillan Commission), and the future citizens of Washington would spread out far beyond ten miles around, but that was in a future that even the prescient Frenchman could not foresee.

We're All Venetians Now

It is common enough, when asking people if they've recently been somewhere interesting, to be told Paris, London, or New York. We find this normal—to visit a big city for pleasure. But in the past, people were more likely to go to the seaside or the mountains for a holiday; the city was for work. The fact that many people now perceive cities as primarily tourist destinations is something new.

Forty years ago, Marshall McLuhan became famous for making pithy if somewhat obscure pronouncements. In hindsight, many of his theories seem dated. Does anyone really remember the difference between hot and cool media, for example, or believe that in an era of 24/7 newscasts and reality television the medium really is the message? Yet I am reminded of him every time I see an ad for an expensive chronometer watch. McLuhan once observed that obsolete technologies often resurface as objects of aesthetic veneration. Sailing ships, for example, once a mundane—and rather dangerous—mode of transportation, become romantic "tall ships." Steam locomotives, which at least in industrialized countries have long disappeared from everyday use, take pleasure seekers on special outings, the smoke, smell, and noise suddenly quaint and charming rather than annoying. It is as if by shedding their function, utilitarian devices acquire the aura of cultural icons or works of art.

What could be called McLuhan's Law of Technological Second

Lives serves to explain what has happened to cities in the last fifty years. A little bit of history. The evolution of cities is the story of changing functions: military outposts becoming peaceful trading centers, trading centers becoming transportation hubs, transportation hubs becoming manufacturing centers. As functions changed, obsolete buildings were generally replaced by new ones. Medieval fortifications, for example, were razed and turned into parks and avenues, craftsmen's cottages and guild halls gave way to textile mills, industrial tenements were replaced by high-rise office buildings. During the last great transformation, when cities ceased to be manufacturing centers, something unusual happened: instead of demolition, preservation.

One of the first American examples of urban preservation was Ghirardelli Square in San Francisco's Fisherman's Wharf district. This retail and commercial complex was contained in a disused chocolate factory whose tall ceilings and brick-and-timber construction made for a unique setting. Down the coast in Monterey, a row of fish canneries made famous by John Steinbeck was turned into a stylish promenade of boutiques, art galleries, and restaurants. That was in the 1960s. Today, what architects call adaptive reuse is commonplace. In Philadelphia, an old steel-and-glass railroad terminal is turned into the gala space of the new convention center; in Baltimore's Inner Harbor, a shopping mall is shoehorned into a disused brewery. Perhaps the most ambitious example of industrial reuse is the mill town of North Adams, Massachusetts, where a museum of contemporary art has been installed in a group of mammoth industrial sheds that once housed a textile factory.

These relics of the Industrial Revolution are not being saved because of sentimentality; after all, many of these buildings were debilitating sweatshops where workers toiled under inhuman conditions. Rather, as McLuhan observed, having lost their original functions, they are now worthy of aesthetic admiration. Factory lofts, with their vast spaces and rough-and-ready building materials and their patina of age, contrast sharply with the increasingly sterile environments of contemporary commerce. The truth is that a nineteenth-century warehouse exhibits greater craft in its construction than all but the most expensive modern buildings. The beautiful cast-iron structure of the cattle market at La Villette in Paris, which now contains science exhibits and a conference center, is a reminder of a period when even four-footed users were granted a measure of architectural grace. The overwhelmingly favorable reception accorded to the Tate Modern in London is due less to the rather heavy-handed modern interventions than to the splendid spaces of the original 1940s power station.

The most prominent example of an entire city becoming obsolete and then remaking itself is Venice. After the collapse of the Venetian Republic at the end of the eighteenth century, the city fell on hard times; by 1820, it is estimated that as much as one-quarter of the population survived by begging. There were attempts to revive manufacturing and shipbuilding, but the most successful stimulus to economic activity turned out to be tourism. Today, the outskirts of Venice bristle with factories, refineries, processing plants, and residential suburbs. La Serenissima itself has only about seventy thousand inhabitants, less than half its sixteenth-century population, but it entertains ten million visitors a year. Once considered an urban anomaly, Venice turned out to be an early prototype. Elsewhere, as manufacturing and industry have moved to the suburbs— and to the developing world—and as economic activity has become increasingly decentralized, large cities have also turned to tourism.

This trend has been fueled by globalization and lower airfares. Nineteenth-century industrial centers such as Glasgow, Bilbao, the Ruhr valley, and Pittsburgh are remaking themselves into cultural attractions. People—tourists and visitors—come not to trade or work, as they once did, but to be entertained, educated, and informed. Hence the proliferation of urban festivals devoted to music, theater, film, comedy, art, historical reenactments, food—you name it.

Equally important, people come to cities simply to experience urbanity. The urban experience has become cities' new product. The experience is a blend of the old and the new, of old streets and old architecture, of museums and opera houses (some old and some new), and also of new restaurants, entertainment malls, festival marketplaces, hotels, and waterside promenades.

The corollary to McLuhan's law is that the attraction of an urban place is in inverse proportion to its actual economic productivity. No one is interested in guided tours of Silicon Valley or Boston's Route 128; such places may be economic powerhouses, but they are too spread out, too new, too, well, ugly. Paradoxically, many of the very qualities that have contributed to cities' shaky position in the new economy—their density, their out-of-date buildings, their aging infrastructure, their reliance on mass transit rather than automobiles—heighten their appeal to tourists and short-term visitors. Cities have many resources that complement their new identity: nineteenth-century railroad stations and markets that can be turned into museums and shopping malls; cultural institutions such as symphony orchestras and theater, opera, and ballet companies; magnificent parks; venerable luxury hotels; and historic cultural sites. Indeed, the historic places that large cities inherited from the past—the cathedrals, the palaces and grand houses, the squares and monumental avenues—are unlikely ever to be replicated and are an important part of our heritage.

Nor is urban tourism restricted to aging industrial cities. Even cities that are dynamic centers of international finance, media, and fashion depend on leisure visitors. New York City had almost thirty million domestic visitors in 2001, of whom about three-quarters were tourists; Paris, a much smaller city, welcomed thirty-six million visitors, 60 percent of them foreign.

•

Tourism is sometimes referred to as the hospitality industry, but it is an odd sort of industry. On the one hand, like traditional industries, it contributes to the urban economy by providing employment. It is estimated that in New York City, for example, tourism supports more than 280,000 jobs, which is only slightly fewer than the important finance, insurance, and real estate sectors. In London, about 200,000 are employed in the tourism sector. It is true that these service jobs are not as highly paid as those in the financial sector, but the low level of skill they demand makes them useful entry-level positions for immigrants and other new urban arrivals.

Unlike traditional industry, the hospitality industry doesn't make anything. But if it doesn't export goods, it does import people—lots of them. And just as the smokestack industries of the past belched soot into the atmosphere and altered their urban surroundings, present-day hospitality industries also change the city—and not always for the better. The story of the neighborhood restaurant that was ruined by tourists is universal. Short-term visitors have particular needs and demands, usually different from those of local inhabitants. They place a higher premium on entertainment and cultural facilities, for example. They are more likely to patronize luxury— as opposed to everyday—shops. Tourists are less resistant than residents to paying more for a gift or souvenir—or for a theater ticket. Thus, tourists drive up living costs, for they will be in the city a relatively short time, and in any case they are on holiday.

Tourists expect a city to be interesting, enjoyable, and memorable. They don't particularly care about the quality of the schools or the efficiency of mass transportation to the suburbs. Probably the chief concerns that tourists share with the locals are a demand for good policing and clean streets; an unsafe or a dirty city soon loses its appeal. A city that wants to attract visitors—whether tourists, conventioneers, or after-hours suburbanites—has to reorder its priorities. It will invest in parking garages, downtown stadiums and other sports facilities, and ever-larger convention centers. It will organize business improvement districts that augment municipal services. It will subsidize the construction of shopping malls and entertainment centers. This investment will be almost exclusively in the downtown. After all, when people say that such and such a city is "lively" or "exciting" or "interesting," they are really talking about its center, not its residential districts.

Architecture plays an important role. Cities have always built monumental buildings—city halls, opera houses, concert halls—but out of civic pride and for local consumption. Now cities erect buildings whose chief aim is to attract visitors. Following the remarkable success of the Guggenheim Museum in Bilbao, which since it opened in 1997 has brought almost five million visitors to that aging industrial port city, the formula for success is clear. Eye-popping architecture + cultural attractions = more tourists. This unprecedented wave of high-profile construction projects has been good for architects; it is less clear how good it is for cities. How often can the Bilbao effect be replicated before it wears thin? Not only are signature buildings extremely expensive, but they tend to cancel one another out, producing a sort of architectural fatigue. There is some indication that the museum construction bubble, at least, has burst: recently, several high-profile museum projects in New York, Los Angeles, and San Francisco were either canceled or put on indefinite hold.

In their heyday, manufacturing cities specialized: Philadelphia was a textile center, Detroit made cars, Milwaukee brewed beer. Today's recreational cities offer essentially the same product; hence they compete fiercely for the same shrinking tourist dollars and euros. In addition, manufacturing fun has turned out to be more complicated than manufacturing carpets. Consumers have always been fickle, but global tourists are also highly mobile. They want to be constantly entertained, diverted, and enthralled, and they are easily beguiled by the next new fad. If one city begins to look faded and shopworn, there are plenty of others that beckon. Casino owners in Las Vegas have always understood this, which is why their properties are in a constant state of renewal. In that regard, conventional cities may have to become more like Las Vegas, as has already happened in Times Square and on Forty-Second Street in New York.

The advent of tourism in big cities is generally welcomed by municipal governments, which regard the hospitality industries as fortuitous substitutes for lost manufacturing and industrial jobs and a useful new source of revenue for depleted municipal coffers. But reconciling the opposing interests of tourists and residents is not easy. How to allocate scarce city resources—build affordable housing or more museums? How to solve serious social problems while also providing occasions for fun? How to balance the needs of downtown with those of the outer neighborhoods? There are many contradictions in cities' new roles as tourist attractions. Of course, cities have always incorporated contradictions: medieval walled cities were safer, but their densities also made them susceptible to fire and disease. Today's fun cities will have to learn to balance new demands; their inhabitants will have to adapt to their new roles. In any case, they have no choice—we're all Venetians now.

The recreational role of cities is demonstrated in what one might call tourist urbanism, of which New York City's High Line is the most prominent example. Like Vienna's early Ringstrasse and Paris's more recent Promenade Plantée—old urban infrastructure transformed— the High Line is an example of McLuhan's Law of Technological Second Lives.

Downtown

"The almighty downtown of the past is gone—and gone for good," writes Robert Fogelson in *Downtown*, his stimulating new history of a long-neglected subject. "And it has been gone much longer than most Americans realize," he continues. The provocative second part of this statement encapsulates his thesis: that long before the failures of urban renewal, the intrusions of urban interstate highways, and the competition of suburban shopping malls and office parks, the primacy of downtown was on the wane.

Most recent books that deal with downtowns have done so in the context of urban advocacy, describing them as a precious part of our heritage that needs to be saved, revitalized, restored. They tend to cast a rosy and nostalgic light on the past. Fogelson, who is a professor of urban studies and history at the Massachusetts Institute of Technology, writes dispassionately and meticulously about the subject and in the process punctures a few myths.

First of all, he reminds us how unusual, indeed unique, is the concept of an extremely dense, nonresidential district in the center of the city. Although the popular media regularly refer to "downtown Madrid" or even "downtown Kabul," these cities do not have downtowns in the American sense. Work, entertainment, shopping, and living are combined across the entire city.

On the other hand, the concentration of the American downtown, particularly in its heyday (in the second and third decades of the twentieth century), was extraordinary. Typically covering less than a square mile, the downtown district included all the city's business offices, all its government offices, most of its professional offices, all its department stores, all its large hotels and restaurants, and a host of other services. Conspicuously absent were residences. You didn't live downtown, but if you wanted to see a lawyer, or go to a nightclub or a movie, or shop, or have dinner, this is where you came. On a typical day in 1920, more than three-quarters of a million people poured into downtown Chicago or Philadelphia. "It is safe to say that most people who lived in big cities—as many as one-half to two-thirds, according to one transit engineer—went downtown every day in the mid and late 1920s," writes Fogelson.

They went on foot or riding streetcars and street railways, another American phenomenon. In 1890, Philadelphia, an average American city in regard to street railways, had more than three times as many miles of track per capita as Berlin, five times as many as Paris, and eight times as many as London. However, as American downtowns became denser and streets more congested, the effectiveness of surface transport decreased. Something had to be done. Chicago and New York City built elevated railways. Because the El darkened the street as well as adjacent properties— and was noisy—this "solution" produced much opposition and was not copied by other cities. Underground railways, pioneered in London, were an alternative. But going underground was extremely expensive, and many believed that it would only increase, not cure, downtown congestion.

One of Fogelson's themes is that even as they built it and used it, Americans were deeply ambivalent about downtown. For example, he details the intense debates that took place concerning the advisability of providing mass transit to downtown. Whereas today's support or opposition to mass transit often marks the divide between liberals and conservatives, this was not the case in the past. Opponents to downtown mass transit included such progressive groups as the Regional Plan Association of New York and the American Institute of Architects. Supporters included downtown property owners and city administrations, for whom downtown property taxes were a major source of revenue. However, few American cities were dense enough to justify the cost of rapid transit, and when the new subways of Boston and New York experienced financial difficulties in the 1930s, that effectively discouraged further experiments. By the late 1920s, Fogelson writes, in the entire country there were only about 350 miles of rapid transit lines (of which a little more than a third ran underground, mostly in New York City and Boston), compared with 41,000 miles of street railways.

One reason that Americans, unlike Europeans, did not live downtown was that downtown was crowded, noisy, and insalubrious—and also dark, the streets and low buildings being shaded by their taller neighbors. All European cities had height limits: in the late nineteenth century, the height limit in Paris was 65 feet; in Berlin, 78 feet; and in Brussels, 72 feet. But as American downtowns expanded between 1880 and 1930, they tended to get taller. This is a crucial part of the story, for vertical growth not only created the requisite density but also tended to raise property values, discouraging all but commercial and retail uses.

Skyscrapers are a popular symbol of downtown, yet Americans were not universally enthusiastic about tall buildings. Between 1880 and 1910, a remarkable number of cities adopted height limits (though these limits were considerably higher than in European cities, ten stories rather than six or seven). Boston had a 125-foot height limit; Chicago, though it is considered the cradle of skyscraper architecture, long had a height limit of 130 feet, though this was often broached in practice. Other cities that established height limits were Baltimore, St. Louis, Cleveland, Buffalo, Milwaukee, New Orleans, Los Angeles, San Diego, Indianapolis,

Denver, and Washington, D.C. The holdouts were New York City, where the majority of early American skyscrapers were built, as well as Detroit, Pittsburgh, and Minneapolis.

In the end, whether downtowns allowed tall buildings or not didn't really matter. Downtown Philadelphia, which had many tall buildings, and downtown Boston, which had only two buildings higher than twenty floors, declined equally in importance. The cause for downtown's decline lay elsewhere. In 1941, John A. Miller, a transportation consultant, observed, "The basic question is whether we can retain the city as a central market place, and at the same time decentralize residences to the extent that everyone lives out in the suburbs or country." It was a rhetorical question, because for more than a decade the answer had been apparent: once people lived far from downtown, and especially once they traveled by automobiles rather than street railways (which were crowded and unreliable), it was no longer logical to have a single center for the entire metropolitan area. Downtown merchants and bankers, seeing the writing on the wall, built suburban branches; downtown hotels gave way to suburban motels. Although the advocates of downtown claimed that it was the indispensable "heart" of the city, many healthy cities had "weak" hearts. The second-largest city in the country, Los Angeles, became an economic powerhouse without ever having an important downtown, and Houston, Dallas, and Atlanta repeated this pattern.

Fogelson describes various attempts in the 1930s and 1940s to stem the tide and attract citizens back to downtown. These included not only expanded mass transit but also road improvements and solutions to automobile parking. Immediately after World War II, there was also slum clearance—the antecedent to the urban renewal projects of the 1960s. If the blighted areas adjacent to downtown could be improved, the reasoning went, the middle class would return, and downtown would thrive once more.

By then, it was too late. The chief reason that Americans

stopped going downtown, according to Fogelson, is that they no longer wanted—or needed—to. "For the average person it might have been a thrill to go downtown in the late nineteenth and early twentieth centuries," he writes. "It might even have been a thrill in the 1920s, when the downtown hotels, department stores, office buildings, and movie theaters dazzled the senses—and, with their doormen, bellhops, elevator operators, shoeshine boys, salesgirls, floorwalkers, and ushers, offered a level of service that all but disappeared in the second half of the twentieth century. But by the mid twentieth century the thrill was largely gone."

Fogelson breaks off his account in 1950, so he doesn't deal with the ballyhooed downtown revivals of the 1980s and 1990s. But his balanced, sobering history leaves little doubt that whatever the future holds for downtown, its glory days are past. It is now but one of several metropolitan centers, and in many cities not even the most important.

Downtown contains an evocative photograph of the Chicago Loop—the corner of State and Madison Streets—taken around 1910. The scene is enormously crowded. Lines of streetcars are backed up on the street, which is flooded with people who have spilled over from the broad sidewalks. It's a serious crowd, the men in suits and hats, the women in long, dark dresses. The atmosphere is one of busyness and purposeful activity—the proverbial beehive. What a contrast to downtowns today, which are never this crowded and whose chief occupants are either the poor or idling tourists. Truly, the almighty downtown that didn't just dominate the metropolitan region but came to stand for the American city itself is gone.

Bauhaus Blunders

Cabrini-Green is a large, inner-city public housing project on Chicago's Near North Side. It attracted national attention in October 1992, when a seven-year-old boy walking to school was fatally shot (for no apparent reason) by an unknown sniper from an abandoned apartment in one of the project's high-rise buildings. The tragic shooting was widely reported, and journalists drew predictable, if far-fetched, parallels with violence-ridden Sarajevo. What struck me was how much the background behind the television reporters really did resemble Sarajevo; that is, it looked European rather than American. It was not only the bleak expanses of grassed public spaces rather than streets, and the lack of private gardens, but also the sight of tall, institutional-looking apartment blocks rather than of neighborhood streets lined with single-family houses.

What I saw on television was a reminder, as the housing critic Catherine Bauer wrote more than thirty-five years ago, that "life in the usual public housing project just is not the way most American families want to live." That this was not always so is evidenced in Cabrini-Green itself, which is a veritable Olduvai Gorge of American public housing policy evolution.

The oldest housing on the site dates from 1941, not long after the Housing Act of 1937 that signaled the first involvement of the federal government in funding housing for what were then called the deserving poor. Frances Cabrini Row Houses was named after a soon-to-be-canonized Chicago nun, famous for her charitable work, and it was built on the site of a notorious Italian-American slum known as Little Hell. The new housing consisted of almost six hundred dwellings in two- and three-story brick buildings; the total area of the project was relatively small: sixteen acres. The unassuming architecture of these row houses—every dwelling had its own front door on the street—was not substantially different from the popular urban housing then being built by the private sector in the surrounding city. The brick facades even incorporated some decorative elements. The overall design, like that of most prewar public housing projects, was modest but unremarkable; it was taken for granted that poor people would prefer to live like everyone else.

During World War II, construction of publicly subsidized housing virtually ceased, and in 1949 the Truman administration passed a new housing act intended to reactivate the government's commitment to providing rental housing for those who could not afford the private market. The ambitious new act provided funds for more than 800,000 new public housing units across the country. In Chicago, the 1940s and 1950s coincided with a large immigration, much of it black: by 1960, the number of the city's black residents had grown from 278,000 (in 1940) to more than 800,000. Some of these were from the rural South, some were from other northern cities, but most were poor, and many needed social assistance, at least for a time.

The Chicago Housing Authority responded to a big problem with big solutions. In 1955, work started on a huge extension to Frances Cabrini called William Green Homes, after a Chicago labor leader. This was the era of urban renewal, and more than fifty acres of the surrounding neighborhood were cleared. This time there were more than nineteen hundred apartments in fifteen freestanding buildings, ten and nineteen stories high; in 1962, eight additional fifteen- and sixteen-story apartment slabs were added. While the residents of Frances Cabrini Row Houses had been

almost entirely white families, the ten thousand people who occupied what was now called Cabrini-Green were almost all black.

Although Cabrini-Green occupies almost as much land as the
Loop itself, it is not the biggest public housing project in Chicago;
that dubious honor belongs to Robert Taylor Homes, said to be the
largest public housing project in the world. Cabrini-Green was the
first of the big projects, and it became a model for how municipal
authorities would rehabilitate deteriorated inner-city real estate and
provide large amounts of public housing. The solution—bulldoze
existing houses and replace them with tall apartment slabs spaced
far apart in open parkland (created by closing off existing streets
to make immense "superblocks")—reflected the prevalent social
and architectural thinking of the time. As Bauer pointed out, this
was not how the majority of Americans really lived—or would
choose to live—but the idealistic housing reformers felt that they
knew best.

The French architect Le Corbusier, who proposed that cities
consist of freestanding high-rise buildings in a parklike landscape,
is often given the credit—or the blame—for this new urban vision. But the model for the public housing projects of the 1950s
was closer to home. The urban design of Cabrini-Green closely
followed the ideas of Ludwig Hilberseimer, a German planner
who had lectured at the Bauhaus, immigrated to the United States,
and taught at Chicago's Illinois Institute of Technology (IIT).
The man who had brought Hilberseimer to IIT was Ludwig Mies
van der Rohe, another German expatriate and fellow Bauhausler
living in Chicago. His influence was evident in the utilitarian appearance of the Cabrini-Green apartment slabs (designed by Epstein
and Sons and Pace Associates), which resembled high-rise factories with exposed concrete frames filled in with glass and brick.
Mies had built exactly such an apartment tower in Chicago in
1949, and in 1955 he and Hilberseimer designed a large commercial housing project in Detroit.

Architects and planners maintained that high-rise buildings were better because they occupied less land and provided their occupants with sunlight and unobstructed views, but the Chicago Housing Authority was probably attracted to modern architecture for the same reason that many commercial developers were partial to the designs of Mies van der Rohe—their low cost. Standardized, stripped-down, and undecorated tall buildings can be erected quickly and inexpensively. It is also likely that the plain architecture suited the puritan view of many Americans—and certainly of the housing reformers—who felt that social housing should not be fancy. Soon, utilitarian high-rise apartment towers were accepted as the best solution for public housing.

However, it was one thing to design apartment towers for the upper-middle class, as Mies did, and quite another to adopt them as solutions for housing the poor. The well-off have doormen, janitors, repairmen, and babysitters; the poor have none of these things. Without restricted access, the lobbies and corridors were vandalized; without proper maintenance, elevators broke down, staircases became garbage dumps, roofs leaked, and broken windows remained unreplaced; without babysitters, single mothers were stranded in their apartments, and children roamed unsupervised sixteen floors below. In Cabrini-Green, there were problems with the design of the buildings: to save money, no private balconies or terraces were provided, access galleries and elevator lobbies were left open to the elements (in frigid Chicago!), and despite the lack of air-conditioning, the unshaded apartment windows of the tall buildings faced east and west.

Equally unsuccessful was the overall layout, which dispensed with the familiar street and supplanted it with parkland, although what little landscaping there was quickly disappeared and was replaced by beaten dirt and asphalt parking lots. In any case, the open pedestrian spaces were problematic: windy, unappealing, and more crime prone than conventional streets and sidewalks overlooked by individual homes. In the name of housing the poor, the well-meaning social reformers of the 1950s invented a new type of urbanism, quite foreign to any previous American ideal of city planning. It is hardly surprising that the projects acquired a social stigma. This, as well as the crime, drugs, and poor management, explains why today one-third of the apartments at Cabrini-Green remain unoccupied.

One drastic solution to dealing with what had become, in effect, high-rise slums was simply to abandon them. This is what happened to the infamous 2,740-unit Pruitt-Igoe public housing project in St. Louis, which was built in 1956 but which was so vandalized that it was completely vacated in 1974 and was torn down two years later. But what to put in their place? Nothing, some would say—the Reagan administration effectively stopped providing federal funds for the construction of new public housing: provide employment, and housing will take care of itself. In this hands-off approach, for those without work or in strained circumstances there would be some form of housing vouchers. (A housing allowance program was initiated on an experimental scale by the Nixon administration in the 1970s and is currently practiced by several cities, including New York and Washington, D.C.) Housing vouchers are an attractive solution inasmuch as they get municipal governments out of the housing business, but there are drawbacks: the poor are not as mobile as the middle class and cannot seek out the best housing opportunities (in that sense, housing vouchers are different from food stamps), nor are commercial builders eager to provide new rental housing at rock-bottom rates, at least not while they are subject to rent control.

Others have proposed that the government assist poor people in purchasing houses or in forming housing cooperatives. While this might help some families, the added burden of homeownership is a questionable benefit for those already battered by the multiple difficulties of poverty. (There is also a political obstacle: in

America, homeownership has always been considered an economic reward, not a right.) Those who would continue a government role in constructing housing for the poor suggest that public
housing be dispersed throughout the community: a house here, a
house there. This strategy, tantamount to disguising soup kitchens
as Burger Kings, would at least get rid of the stigma of the projects,
although it would also create an administrative system of daunting
complexity. Still, even if some enlightened and pragmatic combination of housing vouchers, assisted homeownership, and dispersed
housing were to replace large public construction of housing in the
future, the problem of the projects, where some 3.5 million Americans currently live, would remain.

What to do about existing public housing projects was the focus
of an international architectural competition announced by the
Chicago Tribune in February 1993. The site of the competition was
Cabrini-Green, and entrants were asked to show how the project
could be reconfigured "to provide a model for decent and humane
public housing." The entrants were free to demolish or retain existing buildings and dispense with existing zoning and building
regulations. Although there was no cost limitation, it was pointed
out that "the Chicago Housing Authority is a cash-strapped public
agency," and the emphasis was clearly on practicality rather than
utopianism.

The results were exhibited at the Chicago Athenaeum last
summer. Altogether, there were about three hundred entries from
ten countries, including several by prominent architects: Lucien
Kroll of Brussels, Thomas Beeby and Stanley Tigerman of Chicago,
Morphosis of Los Angeles. The solutions were a mixed bag, ranging
from the touching entry of two young girls who live in Cabrini-
Green to the sort of conceptual posturing that characterizes so
much of contemporary architecture. One entry mysteriously

linked Cabrini-Green to the tidal cycles of Lake Michigan, another incorporated an amusement park into the public housing project, yet another nastily suggested "circling the wagons for safety" by creating fortresslike housing structures surrounded by masts with batteries of high-intensity spotlights. One designer, apparently a devotee of Buckminster Fuller, produced a solution to low-income housing based on prefabricated concrete spheres: the houses resembled lightbulbs.

The winning project was the work of two assistant professors of architecture at North Dakota State University in Fargo and a newly graduated student. Jim Nelson, Don Faulkner, and Larry Carcoana's proposal brims with midwestern good sense. Rebuild the old street grid, the designers suggest, and fill in the open spaces with traditional row houses oriented to the streets. Save as many of the existing apartment blocks as possible and mix in commercial buildings (public housing traditionally had no commercial or industrial functions), and introduce small parks and squares as well as civic buildings like police and fire stations, churches, and day-care centers. Create avenues linking two large neighborhood squares. Replace the two large schools with several smaller elementary schools.

The carefully crafted project of the winning team is representative of a current approach to urban design that has been termed neo-traditional but whose adherents prefer to call it New Urbanism. New Urbanism represents a turning away from the principles that have characterized American urban design since the 1950s and a rediscovery of the virtues of traditional, gridded streets scaled to the pedestrian and of cities that integrate a diversity of urban uses—commercial and industrial as well as residential—rather than being zoned according to single functions. So far, the accomplishments of architects and planners like Peter Calthorpe, Daniel Solomon, and Andrés Duany and Elizabeth Plater-Zyberk have been predominantly suburban and aimed at an upper-middle-class clientele, but the commercial successes of New Urbanism are evidence of its broad appeal to consumers and developers alike. It seems appropriate that such a mainstream, pragmatic approach should be applied to the remedial design of public housing.

An appealing feature of New Urbanism is architectural design whose flavor is regional rather than international. In Nelson, Faulkner, and Carcoana's proposal, moreover, the traditional design approach means that public and private housing are indistinguishable. "One must avoid the danger of building for the poor under regulations or in a style very different from that to which the middle class is accustomed," wrote Nathan Glazer in the pages of *The Public Interest* in 1967. Just so. Despite the argument of one of the Cabrini-Green competition entrants that "architecture is not the solution, architecture is not the problem," it's obvious that large islands of high-rise apartment blocks that contribute to social isolation *are* a problem.

But more than architectural alterations are required to make the projects part of the city again. The most radical change that Nelson, Faulkner, and Carcoana suggest is that the Chicago Housing Authority sell off a good part of the land that it owns to private developers who would build residential, commercial, and retail functions. According to the designers, of the eight thousand dwellings in the final scheme, which also takes in land next to Cabrini-Green, adjacent to the Chicago River, almost two-thirds will be privately owned. In such surroundings, the public housing would finally have a chance to be socially and economically—as well as architecturally—integrated into the surrounding city.

Instead of the monumental plan of the 1950s, whose proud proclamation of public largesse ultimately created a vast island of poverty, the new Cabrini-Green would be woven back into the surrounding fabric of Chicago. Could it work? Maybe. It can hardly be expected to solve all the problems that plague public housing: the senseless shootings, the crime, the gangs and drugs, the chronic dependency on welfare. Still, a more supportive physical environment in conjunction with the sorts of managerial changes that the Chicago Housing Authority has slowly begun to implement at Cabrini-Green—security checks, supervision of apartment lobbies, better maintenance, better responsiveness to tenants, better policing, more thorough screening of prospective tenants—would help. It will also be necessary to persuade the private sector to invest in housing and commercial developments in physical proximity to public housing, and this will undoubtedly be the most difficult aspect of the proposals to realize.

Vincent Lane, the chairman of the Chicago Housing Authority, was a member of the jury that unanimously picked the winning project. (The jury also included architects, a housing historian, a journalist, and the president of the Cabrini-Green residents' advisory council.) Lane has been careful to point out that the prize-winning proposal will not be carried out in its present form, although he feels that many of the ideas can be implemented.

One of the *Chicago Tribune* competition entries, prepared with the collaboration of a group of Cabrini-Green residents, angrily describes the current architecture of the housing project as a "trap." This was surely the last thing on the minds of the liberal framers of the first public housing legislation, who called for "decent, safe, and sanitary dwellings for families of low income," more than fifty years ago. Their failure is a reminder that whatever is done—and clearly something *must* be done about public housing—should be done with great caution.

This article was written in 1993. The last of the Cabrini-Green slabs was demolished in 2011, and the area has since been rebuilt with a combination of low- and high-rise housing that mixes residents of different income levels.

Downsizing Cities

Urban America is changing, and as has so often happened, the change is largely unplanned. Fields turn into housing developments; housing developments turn into suburban towns; suburban towns grow into cities; commercial strips and malls grow into full-fledged urban centers. Moreno Valley and Santa Clarita, both in California, not even incorporated in 1980, are today among the fastest-growing cities in the country. Forty years ago, Mesa, Arizona, was a town outside Phoenix; today, with 325,000 inhabitants, Mesa is bigger than Louisville or Tampa. As for Phoenix, it is now the eighth-largest city in the United States, with more than 1 million people, and makes up only part of a metropolitan area that covers more than four hundred square miles.

A metro area—or a metropolitan statistical area, as the Census Bureau calls it—is defined as a central city of at least 50,000 inhabitants together with adjacent communities with which it has a high degree of social and economic integration. A metro area without a central city must contain at least 100,000 people in all (or, in New England, 75,000, as the term is defined there); major metro areas of more than 1 million, which in practice always contain central cities, may be designated consolidated metropolitan statistical areas. Although the concept of a metro area was introduced in 1949 as a demographic convenience, the city proper remains a distinct legal entity.

In *Cities Without Suburbs*, David Rusk, a former mayor of Albu-
querque, convincingly demonstrates that those central cities that
have expanded their limits to annex suburbs, or that have enough
vacant land to accommodate suburban growth, do better than static
cities in a number of significant ways. A comparison of two Ohio
metropolitan areas, Columbus and Cleveland, serves as an example. Since 1950, the city of Columbus has been aggressively expanding and now covers about two hundred square miles, while
Cleveland's area—seventy-seven square miles—is almost un-
changed. Although metro Cleveland is comparable in income level
and racial composition to metro Columbus, and both metro areas
have grown significantly in population in the past four decades, the
present situation of the two cities is very different. Cleveland has
fallen behind Columbus in economic growth and job creation, it is
more racially segregated, and it has a significantly lower per capita
income, more poverty, and a lower municipal-bond rating. The city
of Cleveland, despite being the center of a consolidated metropolitan
statistical area, is anything but integrated with its surrounding
communities. By every measure (income, education, employment,
poverty), the city is less well-off than its suburbs. The same pattern is repeated across the country in cities like Detroit, St. Louis,
and Chicago, which are increasingly isolated—economically and
racially—within their metro areas.

Can old manufacturing cities and their suburbs be unified?
Rusk concedes that true metropolitan government is unlikely (the
only American metro area with a directly elected regional government is Portland, Oregon) and suggests revenue sharing between
rich and poor jurisdictions, metro-wide housing assistance programs, and economic development plans. But helping ailing center
cities by transferring funds from the suburbs is unlikely to garner
much political support.

What is more likely is a new federal program, such as the recently created empowerment zones, aimed at revitalizing inner-city

slums. This is another version of what used to be called urban renewal, or enterprise zones, and it is as unlikely to succeed as its predecessors. Nicholas Lemann made this point forcefully last year in a *New York Times Magazine* article titled "The Myth of Community Development." "Nearly every attempt to revitalize the ghettos has been billed as a dramatic departure from the wrongheaded Government programs of the past," he wrote, "even though many of the wrongheaded programs of the past tried to do exactly the same thing."

Even if it were possible to expand the tax base of isolated central cities to capture at least some of the wealth of surrounding suburbs, doing so would not solve another problem. A city like Cleveland is not just poorer, less dynamic, and less racially heterogeneous than it used to be; it's also considerably smaller. Since 1970, the city of Cleveland's population has decreased by 33 percent—one of the most precipitous declines of any large city. (During the same period, the city of Columbus grew by 17 percent.)

Cleveland is an example of an increasingly common urban phenomenon: the shrinking city. From 1970 to 1990, the total population of the two hundred U.S. cities with more than 100,000 inhabitants apiece increased from 59 million to 64 million—a 9 percent growth rate. (The nation's population grew by 22 percent in the same period.) But growth was not experienced equally by all cities. In fact, cities fell into two distinct categories: about two-thirds grew vigorously, while the rest actually lost population. Over the two decades, the average population decline was 12 percent, and the average growth was an astonishing 81 percent. The cities that lost population tend to be the older manufacturing cities; the gainers are newer suburban-style cities, chiefly in the West and the Southwest. The trend has continued; nine of the twenty largest cities in the country now have smaller populations than they did in 1950, and some cities, such as Boston and Buffalo, are smaller today than they were in 1900.

These and many smaller cities now have what is referred to in the real estate business as a low occupancy rate. In a shopping mall with a low occupancy rate, the owner can refurbish the mall or offer special leases. If these strategies don't work, in the short run the owner will absorb the loss; in the long run, either rents must be raised or the owner will go bankrupt. But if rents are raised too high, more tenants will leave, and bankruptcy will only be accelerated.

Like a mall owner, the administration of a city with a low occupancy rate can try to increase its tax base by refurbishing the downtown area to make it more attractive to business. It can organize riverboat gambling and build aquariums and world trade centers. It can stimulate employment by enlarging the public sector. (It cannot, however, create the sorts of manufacturing jobs that were the basis for the earlier prosperity and growth of great cities like New York, Chicago, and Philadelphia.) It can also try to balance its budget by raising revenues through higher property taxes, business taxes, and income taxes and by curtailing services— although these tactics, like raising rent, will eventually only hasten population decline.

The mall owner who has tried everything and finds that there is simply no demand for space has a final option. Make the mall smaller: consolidate the successful stores, close up an empty wing, pull down some of the vacant space, and run a smaller but still lucrative operation. Many cities, such as New York, Detroit, and Philadelphia, don't stand a chance of annexing surrounding counties. Downsizing has affected private institutions, public agencies, and the military, as well as businesses. Why not cities?

Two things happen when a city loses population. The reason for the first is that although a city is often said to be shrinking, its physical area remains the same. The same number of streets must be policed and repaired, sewers and water lines maintained, and transit systems operated. With fewer taxpayers, revenues are lower, often leading to higher taxes per capita, an overall deterioration of services, or both. More people depart, and the downward spiral continues. The reason for the second is that urban vitality has always depended on an adequate concentration of people. In 1950, the average density in cities like Detroit, Cleveland, and Pittsburgh was more than twelve thousand people per square mile; by 1990, it was around six thousand—a dramatic decline. The reality is even worse than it sounds, because the decline is not distributed equally across the city, and certain areas experience much more dramatic reductions.

Without sufficient concentrations of people, not only is the provision of normal municipal services extremely expensive, but urban life itself begins to break down. There are not enough customers to support neighborhood stores and services or even to provide a sense of community. Empty streets become unsafe, and abandoned buildings become haunts for drug dealers and other criminals. A national study of housing abandonment found that the "tipping point" in a neighborhood occurred when just 3 to 6 percent of the structures were abandoned. Vacant lots and empty buildings are more than just symptoms of blight; they are also causes of it. Central cities of metro areas that have aggressively expanded their borders face these problems too, even if the cities have a broader and richer tax base.

The first need of a city whose population has declined radically is to consolidate those neighborhoods that are viable. Rather than mounting an ineffectual rearguard action and trying to preserve all neighborhoods, as is done now, city planners should encourage the de facto abandonment that is already in progress. Housing alternatives should be offered in other parts of the city, partly occupied public housing vacated and demolished, and private landowners offered land swaps. Finally, zoning for depopulated neighborhoods should be changed to a new category—zero occupancy—and all municipal services cut off. Efforts should be made to concentrate in selected areas resources such as housing assistance and social programs.

Inevitably, consolidation would involve the movement of individuals and families from one part of the city to another. It is true that private freedoms would be sacrificed for the common good in the process, just as they are when land is expropriated to build a highway or a transit system. Does this sound heartless? Surely it is less so than the current Pollyanna-ish pretense of providing services to many poor and depopulated neighborhoods, which are occasionally half revived with community development projects and then left on their own to decay even further.

The comprehensive downsizing of cities faces formidable obstacles—not only the lack of legal and bureaucratic tools (town planning has traditionally dealt with growth, not decline), but also political opposition. Historic preservationists will likely oppose the demolition of many old buildings. Local politicians whose electoral base would be eroded can also be expected to resist attempts at consolidation.

In 1976, Roger Starr, a past administrator of New York City's Housing and Development Administration, published an article suggesting "planned shrinkage," a reduction in New York's municipal services. "I profoundly wish I'd never coined that phrase," he says today. "It was a most unfortunate term that was misinterpreted by many people as a plan to drive poor blacks out of New York, and I still receive calls that accuse me of being a racist." It is important to underline that the act of consolidating neighborhoods would not move people out of the city, and no loss of benefits and services would ensue. Nevertheless, because the most depopulated parts of the city tend to be the poorest, and because the poorest city inhabitants are predominantly black and Hispanic, relocation would undoubtedly affect members of these groups more than others. Much would depend on the ability of minority leaders to see that given the lack of real alternatives, abandoning half-empty neighborhoods is not necessarily a political defeat.

Much of the housing in older industrial cities is as dense as it is because of high land costs, a history of property speculation, and the greed of the original tenement builders. Consolidating neighborhoods would provide an opportunity to relieve congestion and encourage variety in kinds of housing. Two-story attached and semidetached houses can be built at net densities of sixteen to twenty-four houses per acre, instead of the higher densities that characterize nineteenth-century neighborhoods of three- to five-story buildings. There may even be an opportunity, in some cases, for cities to compete directly with the suburbs by providing detached single-family housing. In cities such as New York and Philadelphia, detached single-family housing, built with a mixture of public and private support, is appearing in previously high-density areas.

Oscar Newman wrote in *Community of Interest* that "architects and architectural historians have been damning the suburban tract development since the 1930s, but social scientists and Realtors will tell you that tract houses continue to be the most sought after and the most successful form of moderate- and middle-income housing ever built." The success of the tract house is one reason that cities have been losing people to suburbs. If cities are to attract—or at least keep—moderate- and middle-income citizens, they will have to provide the sort of housing those citizens want. If cities cannot annex suburbs, they can do the next best thing: rezone areas to permit the construction of suburban-style housing.

The consolidation of residential neighborhoods would produce stretches of empty blocks where buildings would have to be knocked down, services stopped, streets closed, and bus lines rerouted. It would be comforting to think that such vacant land would find new use as recreational parks and wilderness areas. On a small scale, empty lots could be converted into allotment gardens or playing fields. But there is little likelihood of large new urban parks on the scale of Frederick Law Olmsted's nineteenth-century creations. The costs associated with the removal of basements and old foundations, soil amelioration, drainage, and planting would be out of the reach of cities already in financial difficulties. Vacated urban land would more likely be left empty, streets and buried infrastructure in place, available for use at some future date.

The objection may be raised that zero-occupancy zoning would create large tracts of empty land whose presence would disrupt the proper functioning of a city. In fact, many cities have grown up around cemeteries or have enveloped earlier industrial areas such as quarries and railroad yards, and most cities already have large areas of land such as tank farms and container depots that are cut off from everyday use. The only difference between these areas and zero-occupancy zones would be that the latter would be unused and would not create noise or air pollution.

Cities have another option: divestiture. Contiguous parcels of, say, at least fifty acres could be put up for sale, with one of the conditions of sale being that the land would cease to be part of the city. According to Peter Linneman, the director of the Wharton School's Real Estate Center, large tracts in proximity to cities but without the burden of city taxes and bureaucracy would very likely attract developers who would otherwise shun them. The new developments, whether residential or commercial, would be responsible for their own municipal services, as new developments already are in suburban locations. Assuming that questions of ownership of rights-of-way and underground infrastructure could be worked out, the prospect is attractive. Cities would increase their income (although they would not gain taxpayers), and they would divest themselves of unproductive land. At the same time, people and economic activities would be attracted back into the urban vicinity.

The idea of downsizing goes against the progressive, optimistic American grain. Surely, conventional wisdom says, one should attack the root of the urban problem, not merely its symptoms. The solution to urban decline has always been assumed to be a combination of economic development (leading to renewed growth, more jobs, a larger population, and a larger tax base) and financial aid from federal and state governments. The problem is that population loss has gone on for too long: generally, cities that have stopped growing and are losing population have been doing so for more than forty years. If metro-wide tax sharing were to be implemented, and if a more equitable allocation of financial resources finally gave cities a chance to deal more effectively with problems of poverty and immigration, the rate of population decline might be reduced, or at best the population might be stabilized. Great manufacturing cities like St. Louis, Detroit, Philadelphia, and Cleveland would not return to their earlier predominance or their earlier size. Downsizing alone would not solve the problems of unemployment and urban poverty, but it would permit shrinking cities to marshal their resources more effectively as they make their way to a stable—albeit smaller—future.

Almost twenty years after The Atlantic Monthly *published this article, still only very few cities are coming to terms with the need to manage urban shrinkage. In Detroit, Mayor Dave Bing reduced municipal services in certain neighborhoods, but too late; in 2013, the city was forced to declare bankruptcy. Consolidation has also been tried in neighboring Flint, Michigan. In 2005, Youngstown, Ohio, which has lost 60 percent of its population in the last forty years, adopted a master plan that aimed at stabilizing the population at current levels, although implementation has proved difficult. As* The New York Times *reported, "Despite the city's efforts to entice residents in far-flung areas of the city to move closer to the center, no one has agreed, and the city's footprint remains unmanageably large."*

The Fifth City

Specific cities currently serve as backdrops for most television dramas. New York dominates; San Francisco, Boston, and Chicago are runners-up; Indianapolis, Cincinnati, and Baltimore have all made at least one appearance. Dallas lent its name to a long-running show; so did Miami. Seattle is the setting for the award-winning *Frasier*; Washington, D.C., for *Murphy Brown*. Yet there is one conspicuous absence. Not since *Thirtysomething*, which was actually set in a suburb outside Philadelphia, has the City of Brotherly Love figured in a prominent television series.

It is a striking omission. Philadelphia is the fifth-largest city in the country. It is in one of the most populous—and prosperous—metropolitan areas in the United States. It has the Liberty Bell as well as Independence Hall, the greatest concentration of museum art after New York, a legendary orchestra, and an Ivy League university. Despite these attributes, Philadelphia occupies a curious position in the national consciousness. It is not merely neglected; it is almost invisible.

Philadelphia was never an American favorite. *Bartlett's Familiar Quotations* lists four entries for the city; three are distinctly uncomplimentary. "On the whole I'd rather be in Philadelphia," famously quipped that ungrateful native son, W. C. Fields—he meant it as his epitaph. "Philadelphia is the most pecksniffian of American cities," observed H. L. Mencken, "and thus probably leads the world." Mark Twain weighed in: "In Boston they ask, How much does he know? In New York, How much is he worth? In Philadelphia, Who were his parents?"

Twain wrote that in 1899. He was right about upper-class Philadelphians' obsession with heredity (it continues to be a preoccupation). But if turn-of-the-century Philadelphians did not ask, "How much is he worth?" there was another reason: they were rich. In 1900, Philadelphia was one of the greatest and most diversified manufacturing cities in the world. Its textile industry was unrivaled. The city was the headquarters of the mighty Pennsylvania Railroad and the home of the Baldwin Locomotive Works. It was also the site of one of the largest shipbuilding yards in the country. Philadelphia led all other American cities in industrial production in the following: petroleum refining; knit and lace goods; upholstery; carpets and rugs; cardboard and paper making; cigar and cigarette manufacturing; clay products; and plumbers' supplies. It was a powerhouse.

Here, then, is one explanation for the city's long-standing lack of national prominence. This was a blue-collar, smokestack town. It was slow and steady. It did not have the sizzle of New York, the gentility of Boston, the down-at-heel charm of New Orleans, or the sunny glamour of Los Angeles. It was not "Hog Butcher for the World" like Chicago or a city of blast furnaces like Pittsburgh; it made carpets and cardboard boxes. Not that these were less useful, but they did not stir the national soul. There was no Whitman or Sandburg to celebrate the makers of plumbing supplies.

In 1900, Philadelphia was one of the ten most populous cities in the world and, at about 130 square miles, one of the most expansive. Philadelphians generally did not live in crowded tenements like New Yorkers or cramped triple-deckers like Bostonians. They owned houses. In fact, more people owned their own houses in Philadelphia in 1900 than in any other city in the United States— or anywhere else, for that matter. Philadelphia was the site of another urban innovation: the suburb. In that regard, Philadelphia resembled New York and Boston, but with a difference. Unlike Brooklyn and Brookline, Philadelphia suburbs were not middle class; they were wealthy. Rich New Yorkers lived in the city and had country houses on Long Island or up the Hudson; rich Philadelphians had small second homes in town and lived on imposing suburban estates on what came to be known as the Main Line.

This combination of almost universal homeownership, with its emphasis on home life and privacy, and the retreat of the urban elite from the center of the city to exurban splendor produced a determined introspection. "Philadelphia, in 1900, was provincial and patrician," wrote John Lukacs in *Philadelphia: Patricians and Philistines*. "Provincial, because, unlike the older Boston or the newer Chicago, incurious about what was happening in New York. Patrician, because of the close relationship of families composing its principal social and financial institutions; indifferent, rather than hostile, to the rising new rich, even when the latter were ready to make their public contributions to the benefit of the city." The provincialism that Lukacs described did have its benefits, among them a healthy conservatism that kept extremely tall skyscrapers out of the downtown until the 1980s. Philadelphia, despite the occasional grand gesture—Fairmount Park, the enormous city hall, a parkway modeled on a Parisian boulevard—retained an old-fashioned, cozy atmosphere of blue-collar and bourgeois domesticity. This comfortable and self-sufficient city did not much care what was going on in the rest of the country; understandably, the rest of the country reciprocated.

Between 1900 and 1950, Philadelphia grew larger, richer, and more productive. Its future seemed assured. The ambitious 1960 master plan for the city predicted an increase in jobs and population. Like so much that passes for city planning, this was mostly civic boosterism. The reality was that for Philadelphia—as for most older American cities—the postwar period would be marked not by growth but by decline. This should have been apparent as early as the 1930s, when the expansion of automobile ownership and truck transportation signaled the end of the concentrated railroad city. World War II, with its government-supported wartime industries, gave Philadelphia only a brief respite.

Philadelphia was far from being a single-industry town like Pittsburgh or Cleveland. It had the manufacturing diversity that Jane Jacobs maintains is the pillar of urban economies. Nevertheless, Philadelphia's complacent entrepreneurs did not capitalize on this variety. Like the infrastructure and the entrenched municipal bureaucracy, management proved too atrophied and too resistant to change. The loss of manufacturing jobs was nothing less than catastrophic. In 1960, there were about 300,000 manufacturing jobs in the city; thirty years later, there were only 85,000.

As jobs departed, so did people. By 1990, instead of gaining 225,000 residents, as the optimistic master plan had predicted, the city lost 400,000, almost a quarter of its population. Six percent of Philadelphia's housing stock now consisted of abandoned buildings, not counting vacant lots. The city spent more than $5 million a year demolishing dilapidated buildings. The poverty rate surpassed 20 percent; 14 percent of households were on public assistance, twice the national average. The education system deteriorated, and 40 percent of those enrolled dropped out before finishing high school.

The departure of the middle class meant the loss of tax revenues precisely at a time when the demand for social services was rising. It was an untenable combination. The city raised wage taxes; employers responded by relocating to the suburbs. When the city cut services, those taxpayers who could likewise moved away. Deficits began to accumulate. In June 1990, Moody's Investors Service rated Philadelphia bonds below investment grade. In

1992, *City and State* magazine ranked the fiscal soundness of the
nation's fifty largest cities. Philadelphia was at the very bottom of
the list.

It is at this point that Buzz Bissinger's *Prayer for the City* begins.
It is January 1992. Edward G. Rendell has just been inaugurated
Philadelphia's mayor. David Cohen, Rendell's chief of staff, and
John White, a financial consultant, are running a computer model
of the city budget. It is based on projected expenditures, salaries
and benefits, state and federal aid, and projected tax revenues. The
computer calculates and produces a number. It makes no sense—
they must have made a typing error. After all, it is 2:30 in the morning. So they repeat the procedure.

> The computer again paused momentarily, then returned the
> Number once again.
> John White looked at it, and so of course did Cohen,
> and they quickly noticed the same thing. It was exactly the
> same as when White had punched in the data the first time.
> There had been no clerical error. There had been no mistake.
> $1.246 BILLION
> That was the Number glaring at them from the com-
> puter screen. That would be the budget gap over the next
> five years if nothing was done; *one billion two hundred forty-
> six million dollars*—a budget deficit bigger than the entire
> budget of Boston or Houston or Baltimore.
> John White looked at David Cohen. David Cohen looked
> at John White.
> "Holy shit," said White. "This is bad."

Much has been written about the sorry state of American cities.
Many authors describe generic urban problems—poor education
systems, drugs, crime, unemployment, public housing. They imply
that these difficulties constitute a sort of disease. Administer the

correct antibiotic, the argument goes—for example, charter schools, community policing, methadone clinics, empowerment zones, housing vouchers—and the disease can be put into remission. Other books, such as J. Anthony Lukas's *Common Ground*, describe the same conditions but are based on a different assumption: there are no such things as urban problems; rather, there are problems that beset individual cities. These books, often written by journalists, describe the problems in terms of a city's peculiar history, its character, its citizens, and its politicians. The particular serves to illuminate the general.

A Prayer for the City belongs firmly to the second category. Bissinger is a journalist who has worked for *The Philadelphia Inquirer*, where he won a Pulitzer Prize for investigative reporting. In May 1991, while living in the Midwest, he learned that Rendell was running for mayor. He contacted Cohen, who was managing the campaign, with a request. If Rendell was to win, would he give Bissinger access to the administration for four years—a full term— to write a book? Rendell's answer was yes. After the election, Bissinger moved in, literally. "David Cohen and I basically shared an office for four years," he writes. The result is an extraordinary book, an insider's account of the daily workings of a big-city administration, warts and all.

"Spending four years on the couch of a mayor is a bizarre way to make a living," writes Bissinger, "but if you're going to do it, there is no better person to do it with than Ed Rendell." Well, yes. Bissinger made a very lucky—or a very smart—guess. When Rendell was elected, Philadelphia was bankrupt in all but name. Yet in only two years, Rendell's administration eliminated a structural deficit of almost $200 million without raising taxes, negotiated a cost-cutting contract with the city employees' unions, and privatized many municipal services. Rendell avoided the billion-dollar sinkhole and worked what many would call a miracle.

Rendell's previous political record was hardly promising. He

was a native New Yorker who went to college at the University of
Pennsylvania, graduated from Villanova University Law School,
and stayed in Philadelphia to work in the district attorney's office.
In 1976, he ran on the Democratic ticket for district attorney and
won. He was popular and gained an easy reelection. In 1986, after
finishing his second term, he decided to run for governor of the
state. He was defeated in the primary. A year later, he entered the
Philadelphia mayoral primary, opposing the incumbent, W. Wilson
Goode. Goode, the city's first black mayor, appeared beatable;
he had authorized the infamous bombing of a radical group's
headquarters that resulted in the destruction of sixty-one West
Philadelphia row houses. Instead, Rendell ignominiously lost that
primary, too. He was beginning to look like a perpetual loser.

In 1990, despite not having won an election in nine years, the
forty-six-year-old Rendell decided to run once more for mayor
of Philadelphia. This time he was lucky. Philadelphia has a two-
term limit, and Goode had to step down. Two black candidates
split the large black Democratic vote (by 1990, Philadelphia was
40 percent black). Rendell won the primary. He was opposed by a
popular Republican veteran, Frank L. Rizzo, former mayor and
police chief, who unexpectedly died the summer before the election. Rendell won the election in a landslide.

Rendell was also fortunate to obtain the services of David
Cohen. Cohen had been his press secretary during the failed mayoral campaign of 1987. Then thirty-one, he was a successful corporate lawyer in a prominent Philadelphia firm. As Bissinger
describes him, he is a prodigious worker with a steel-trap intelligence, a stickler for detail, and a patient negotiator. Rendell, by
contrast, comes across as undisciplined, expansive, intuitive. The
cool technocrat and the charismatic politician were a good match,
something that both men seem to have understood almost immediately. It was an intense relationship. "We are best friends," Cohen told Bissinger, "but we are also like brothers. He's my father.

I'm his father." Cohen was one of the few who stuck with Rendell after his loss to Goode. When Rendell was finally elected mayor, he asked Cohen to join his administration as chief of staff, a position created specially for him.

Rendell and Cohen found a city in financial ruin. It was not just the growing deficit; according to Bissinger, there was only enough money in the treasury to last roughly a week and a half. Drastic action was required. Rendell and Cohen offered the city employees' unions a stark alternative: accept a wage freeze and across-the-board cutbacks in benefits, or as much as a sixth of the workforce— four thousand employees—would be laid off as their contracts expired. The offer was not taken seriously by the unions, one of which demanded a wage increase of 18 percent. The city responded by leaking some of the most outrageous work requirements. For example, how many employees did it take to change a fluorescent tube at the Philadelphia International Airport? Answer: three. One to remove the fixture cover, one to replace the tube, a third to sweep up. Cohen proved a skilled tactician. He played off factions against each other. At one point, he threatened to privatize garbage collection (a bluff, but the union didn't know that). The recalcitrant unions prepared to strike. Bissinger vividly describes the crisis atmosphere as the strike date approached. The city's contingency plan included changing locks, backing up computer data in case of sabotage, preparing secret contracts for the removal of sewage sludge, providing security to fire departments, even stockpiling toilet paper.

In the end, Rendell and Cohen won. Wages were frozen for two years, and later increases kept to a minimum. Benefits were reduced. The city gained representation on the boards that administered the unions' health and pension benefits. Moreover, the city gained the right to set workforce rules, monitor performance, contract out certain services, and even lay off workers in certain instances. "By any measure, it was a remarkable contract," writes

Bissinger, "a nationwide model for what a city government could do under the right conditions of crisis." This is an overstatement. It is true that wages were frozen, but they were frozen at already unrealistically high levels. If this is a model, it is hardly a sustainable one.

The conditions of crisis continued. There were defeats and victories: the educational bureaucracy proved more resistant to reform than the municipal unions; a new downtown convention center was built; Philadelphia-Camden was awarded one of the federal government's urban empowerment zones. In 1992, the federal government took control of the Philadelphia Housing Authority, considered by many to be the most incompetent and corrupt in the country. It was the largest takeover of its kind. Then, in an unprecedented arrangement between the city and the federal government, Rendell became chairman of the housing authority board, and the Department of Housing and Urban Development allocated funds to improve the ailing public housing stock, a quarter of which was actually vacant. The story of the Navy Yard is the climax of Bissinger's book. The yard was about to close after 194 years of service, putting thousands out of work. A German shipbuilding corporation that was interested in establishing an American operation to build cruise ships was approached by the city. There was a promise of six thousand jobs, in exchange for tax benefits as high as $30 million. As a result of complex negotiations, the cost of modernizing the facilities was to be shared between the Germans, the states of Pennsylvania and New Jersey, the regional port authority, and the city. Then the Republican governor, Tom Ridge, withdrew his support. Cohen devised a plan to float a bond issue to make up the shortfall. At the last minute, Ridge, in an apparent fit of pique, publicly (and inaccurately) attacked the German shipbuilder for not making a larger investment. The chagrined Germans withdrew; the deal fell through.

Bissinger also chronicles the small, daily vicissitudes that befall a big-city mayor: the threat of the closure of a local factory, the shooting of a policeman, the flare-up of neighborhood racism. Indeed, most of the time Rendell seems more like a municipal father figure than an administrator—commiserating, cajoling, backslapping, pacifying, scolding. Some of the most lively scenes in the book concern these ordinary occurrences, where Rendell's simple but affecting humanity shines through. The mayor is also a kind of referee. Philadelphia, more than most American cities, consists of neighborhoods that enjoy great autonomy. An experienced community activist once described Philadelphia ward politics to me in this way: "Something for everybody; not too much for anybody." It is an extreme form of localism that frequently stymied even as able a politician as Rendell. "The racial politics that had been displayed during the first term made easy decisions difficult and fractious," writes Bissinger, putting his finger on a truly structural urban problem. "The extortionate threats of every self-interest group imaginable, vowing to heap embarrassment and woe on the mayor if he didn't do exactly what they wanted, had a similar impact, to the point where the public interest often seemed irrelevant."

A Prayer for the City is a journalist's chronicle of urban political life. It has some of the qualities of a dramatized diary, although Bissinger also includes useful digressions on Philadelphia's recent history. The focus is on Rendell and Cohen, but the book also provides a moving account of how politics touches individuals. The author interweaves the stories of four persons living in the city: a hardboiled prosecutor; a seasoned Navy Yard welder who loses his job; a white-collar worker who anguishes about living in—or leaving—the city she loves; and a grandmother who struggles to prevail against the multiple adversities of inner-city life. These stories are predictable, but no less affecting for that. They are also a useful reminder that urban policies can succeed or founder because of the individual decisions of citizens. Those decisions are not always rational; that is, while motivated by self-interest, they are also influenced by personal experiences and perceptions, by emotional attachments and a sense of identity. For example, as the prosecutor says of his decision to remain in Philadelphia despite its wage tax and deteriorating services, "I like being a Philadelphian. Once you leave Philadelphia, you lose your standing to care and complain about it." Such emotional attachments notwithstanding, while Rendell and Cohen successfully attacked Philadelphia's budget deficit, people continued to move out of the city. During the period that Bissinger describes, about forty thousand jobs left the city, and the population further declined by sixty-one thousand. The poverty rate went from 20 to 30 percent.

Shortly after I moved to Philadelphia, in 1993, I heard Rendell deliver the Wriston Lecture at the Manhattan Institute in New York City. It was a lively talk, during which the Democratic mayor both charmed and chided his conservative audience. The mayor closed with a metaphor. He likened the first two years of his administration to an emergency room operation. The patient had been brought in with a shotgun wound to the stomach. They had stopped the bleeding, sewn up the injury, and stabilized the situation. Now—and here Rendell paused for dramatic effect—they had to get around to treating the cancer.

The cancer has been growing a very long time. It is not that the plight of American cities has been ignored, but so many of the well-intentioned interventions—public housing, for example, or urban renewal, or busing—have only worsened the condition. The fragmented polity that allows metropolitan regions to develop without metropolitan responsibility also has hurt cities. If large cities are the home of the nation's poor, as is now the case, should not the nation shoulder at least part of the burden? This is not a message that most Americans want to hear.

A Prayer for the City ends on a sober note, as it must. The recent

news of falling crime rates and downtown revival, of popular new
baseball stadiums and waterfront entertainment centers, suggests a
turning point in the fortunes of cities. Nothing could be further
from the truth, as Bissinger eloquently concludes:

> The idea that cities had come close to reversing themselves
> was dangerously misleading, ignorant of poverty rates; ig-
> norant of the timeline of decline that occurred not just for
> five years but for nearly fifty; ignorant of social and racial
> stratification; ignorant of the types of jobs that the audience
> economy threw off; ignorant of what would happen in the
> next recession when the disposable dollars of tourists and
> suburbanites were no longer disposable. There was also the
> danger that what lay behind the fancy wrap of the down-
> town, the gray areas of abandoned factories and worn-out
> neighborhoods, had been rendered invisible, the Bermuda
> Triangle of American life.

Bissinger's pessimistic conclusion proved all too prescient. Further ef-
forts to revive the Navy Yard foundered after a Swedish shipbuilder,
which was enticed with generous public subsidies, went bankrupt; the area
is currently being transformed into an office park. Downtown Philadel-
phia has prospered, experiencing a growth in population during the
condo boom, but outlying urban neighborhoods continue to lose jobs and
population. In the middle of the first decade of the twenty-first century,
the fifth city briefly became the sixth city, surpassed by Phoenix. The
latest bleak statistic: of the nation's ten largest cities, Philadelphia now
has the largest portion of its population living in poverty.

Bollard Burg

It used to be that Washington, D.C., architecture consisted of graceful Georgetown mansions, neoclassical federal buildings—and, of course, the monuments. When the U.S. Commission of Fine Arts was founded in 1910 to guide Washington's architectural development, it reviewed designs such as the Lincoln Memorial and the Federal Triangle. However, during the seven years I've served on the commission, an increasing amount of time is spent discussing security improvement projects: screening facilities, hardened gatehouses, Delta barriers, perimeter fences, and seemingly endless rows of bollards. We used to mock an earlier generation that peppered the nation's capital with Civil War generals on horseback; now I wonder what future generations will make of our architectural legacy of crash-resistant walls and blast-proof glass.

How did we become so insecure about our buildings? Although the September 11, 2001, attacks loom large in the public's imagination, the event that changed the way federal buildings in America are designed and used—perhaps forever—was a presidential directive issued six years earlier. Historically, U.S. presidents have shown little interest in architecture. You can count the exceptions on one hand: Franklin D. Roosevelt, who designed his own presidential library; Theodore Roosevelt, who had many architect friends and added the West Wing to the White House; and of course America's two great architect-presidents, Thomas Jefferson and

George Washington. Mostly, however, presidents have preferred
to leave design to designers, whether of public buildings, war
memorials, or double eagles. President Bill Clinton, whose most
prominent addition to the White House was a hot tub, was not
known as an architecture buff. But by issuing Executive Order
12977 in October 1995, he set in motion a process that thrust politics squarely into the center of design.

The executive order was the result of the Oklahoma City bombing. The day after the destruction of the Murrah Federal Building,
which claimed 168 lives and injured more than 680 people, Clinton
directed the Department of Justice to assess the vulnerability of all
federal facilities to acts of violence. The resulting report, prepared
by a large team headed by the U.S. Marshals Service, is generally
known as the Marshals Report. To implement the report's recom-
mendations, Executive Order 12977 established an interagency security committee charged with developing standards for all federal
facilities as well as "long-term construction standards for those
locations with threat levels or missions that require blast-resistant
structures."

The Marshals Report classified all federal buildings according
to rising levels of threat. The Murrah Building, which had 550
employees and housed ATF and DEA offices, would have been
Level IV, a high-risk category that includes federal courthouses and
all large federal office buildings, as well as ATF, DEA, and FBI
offices. Level V is reserved for the highest-risk agencies such as
the Department of Defense, the CIA, and Homeland Security.

Because the authors of the Marshals Report were security experts, they focused on the immediate security problem—that is,
safeguarding the occupants of federal buildings against explosives
and other domestic threats. It is hard to question the good intention of protecting federal employees. However, as bombings in
Madrid and Oslo later showed, terrorism does not confine itself to
official targets; hardening government buildings simply moves the

threat elsewhere. It is like deciding to protect only the flight crew rather than safeguarding the plane and all its passengers.

The Marshals Report proposed no fewer than fifty-two specific criteria, which resulted in the deployment of a host of building security devices. Some, such as reinforced structure, blast-resistant glass, and hardened curtain walls, have a small impact on a building's appearance. That is not the case with perimeter security.

"Depending on the facility type," the report cautions, "the perimeter may include sidewalks, parking lots, the outside walls of the building, a hallway, or simply an office door." Because truck bombs are the simplest and cheapest way of creating large detonations, and given what happened in Oklahoma City, the focus has been on keeping vehicles far away from their target by creating a so-called standoff distance. The optimal standoff is large—at least a hundred feet—and new buildings, such as the ATF headquarters in Washington, D.C., achieve this setback by creating a sort of landscaped demilitarized zone between the building and the street. The Marshals Report came out at a time when the federal agency with the greatest experience of terrorism was the State Department, which had developed its expertise hardening diplomatic buildings abroad in the wake of several embassy bombings. This may explain why federal buildings are protected as if they were divorced from their surroundings and why so many federal buildings today, surrounded by barricades and layers of security, resemble foreign outposts.

Existing urban buildings are generally near the street. The only alternative to closing a street completely—as with Pennsylvania Avenue in front of the White House—is to keep the potential truck bomber from driving right up to the building. This is achieved by a device that could serve as a symbol for our insecurity: the bollard.

Bollards are hardly new—Baroque Rome was full of them. But the attractive marble bollards that Bernini placed in St. Peter's

Square or those that prevented carriages from driving into his fountain in the Piazza Navona are a far cry from the security bollards of today. Old bollards were typically low enough to make a convenient seat and were spaced far apart, sometimes linked by chains. Cast-iron bollards were installed by nineteenth-century Dutch townspeople in front of their houses, but those decorative so-called *Amsterdammertjes* (little Amsterdammers) were not intended to stop a speeding truck, only to discourage driving on the sidewalk.

Modern post–Oklahoma City bollards are not delicate. Designed to halt a fifteen-thousand-pound vehicle going fifty miles per hour, they are big: eight to ten inches in diameter, typically three feet high, and spaced no more than four feet apart, according to current standards. A large, block-size building might be encircled by several *hundred* of these oversize fireplugs. To reduce the monotony, architects have tried mixing in hardened fences, low walls, planters, and reinforced benches and light poles. However, when a security line occurs at the curb, as is usually the case, solid barriers are impractical because people need to be able to exit cars, so bollards remain the chief perimeter protection. Whether they are clad in stainless steel or granite, they are a visual intrusion on the streetscape; they also pose a nuisance for pedestrians and bicyclists.

Some agencies don't seem to mind this intrusion, as it's an external marker of their buildings' strategic importance. In Washington, we've come to see the bizarre phenomenon that one federal official characterized to me as "bollard envy," where the degree of protection becomes a symbol of bureaucratic status, like a choice parking spot or a corner office.

Government officials regularly speak of integrating perimeter security "unobtrusively" into the design of a building. A rare case where this has been achieved is the landscape improvement to the Washington Monument. Designed by the Olin landscape architecture firm, the perimeter security is disguised as a set of curving stone retaining walls, which are invisible from the monument itself and are designed to be sat upon. A similar retaining wall provides security for the Lincoln Memorial, although here the topography requires additional intrusive bollards as well.

The security plan being designed for the Jefferson Memorial will depend on walls as well as scores of bollards. Where to put the perimeter security is a Hobson's choice: put it farther away and you need more bollards; nearer and you need fewer, but they are more visually intrusive. In either case, the experience of John Russell Pope's handsome building will not be enhanced. The directive to secure the Jefferson Memorial is intended to protect a precious national icon. It may end up having the opposite effect.

The Marshals Report did not mention the potential architectural impact of new security standards, but simply assumed that the criteria would be met—somehow. That "somehow," after sixteen years of the war on terrorism, has generally come at the expense of aesthetics. Standards, whether they govern the precise height of bollards or the minimum dimension of standoffs, tend to be inviolable and leave little discretion to the designer. And because everyone (at least everyone inside the same risk-class building) must have the same level of protection, there can be no exceptions. Most building design decisions are trade-offs—between cost and benefit, maintenance and durability, and appearance and performance. Security—"Are you ready to risk a life?"—brooks no compromises.

And yet if that question were answered by citizens instead of by security consultants, the response might be different. Most of the decisions regarding building security have been the result of executive-branch directives, either from the president or from department heads, rather than from Congress. These decisions are not the result of public debate. The possibility of an open discussion about security—for example, when is too much, too much?—is further constrained by the necessary veil of secrecy that surrounds the subject. After all, security measures are intended to foil terrorists—whether foreign or domestic—and revealing too many details defeats the purpose.

Herein lies the problem. The design of public buildings today is usually subject to review by design boards, municipal arts councils, neighborhood associations, and various community groups. But security concerns, which can greatly affect building design, are "off the table." Instead of reasoned discussion by citizens and their representatives, debate is stifled by the unarguable pronouncements of security experts.

Last year, the Supreme Court decided that the public would no longer be able to ascend Cass Gilbert's iconic marble steps to enter the Supreme Court Building. Instead, visitors would be redirected to a side door leading to a screening facility. Justices Stephen Breyer and Ruth Bader Ginsburg called the change unfortunate and unjustified, and Breyer pointed out that no other high court in the world has closed its front entrance over security concerns. He said that the main entrance and the front steps of the 1935 building "are not only a means to, but also a metaphor for, access to the court itself."

But Breyer and Ginsburg were in the minority. Justice Anthony Kennedy, who supported the closure, told the House Appropriations Subcommittee that from a security perspective entering from the side is "mandatory." According to ABC News, Kennedy said that the court spent millions of dollars on an updated security facility "but decided, after talking to experts, that visitors no longer should be able to enter through the main front entrance." Once more, the experts carried the day.

•

Users of airports know that security can vary: one year liquids are for-bidden, another year not; sometimes belts and shoes must be removed, sometimes not. The trouble with our misguided hardening of federal buildings is that it is not as easily reversed: the intrusive bollards and screening centers will remain for a long time, becoming our generation's architectural legacy.

New York's Rumpus Room

I can't imagine Manhattan without Central Park. Without the park, meadows and lakes would be miles away, instead of just behind the Metropolitan Museum. Without the park, taxis couldn't take those east–west shortcuts that are like sudden excursions into the country. Columbus Circle would be simply a circle, like Piccadilly Circus, instead of an arc opening onto a generous green wood. I would never see the top of the Dakota sticking up out of the trees like a spooky Transylvanian castle. Without the intervening park, the Upper East Side would blend into the Upper West Side—unthinkable. Without its enchanted setting, Tavern on the Green would be just another tourist eatery, and the Bethesda Fountain would be simply an ordinary plaza. New York City without Central Park would be like Chicago without the lake, San Francisco without hills, or Los Angeles without sunshine.

Most urban parks reflect the style of their cities. Parisian parks and gardens exhibit a Gallic sense of good order and neat urbanity; London parks are casual and elegant, like London buildings and streets. Central Park is different. The uniform Manhattan grid was laid out for the convenience of real estate subdivision and traffic flow, just building lots and streets, no frills. Pragmatic, standardized, commercial, artless—and largely treeless—the grid represents an urbanism that only a surveyor could love. The creators of Central Park turned their backs on this mercantile diagram.

They made the park all loopy curves; even the streets crossing the park lose their straightness. Despite its matter-of-fact name, Central Park is romantic, non-standardized, uncommercial, artful—and full of trees. It is *all* frills.

It was Edmund Burke who coined the famous description of parks as "the lungs of the city," but Central Park is also New York's heart. Without Central Park, New York would risk becoming as callow and mercenary as many of its critics maintain. The park is part of New York's better nature. That is why crimes in the park—the attack on the Central Park jogger, the preppy murder, the wilding after the Puerto Rican Day Parade—have special resonance with the public. Central Park is one place where the city that never sleeps lets down its guard. Urban crime has always been a part of city life; a crime in a park is a particularly shocking affront, not only to civility, but also to our image of ourselves.

Whenever I walk down Fifth Avenue next to the park and I am not in a hurry, I get drawn in. I can't resist. Maybe it's all those shady trees, or the glimpse of sparkling water, or the sinuously curved path that disappears behind a clump of bushes. Before I know it, I am in another world. It's easy to forget what a distinctly odd world it is. Generally, urban parks are conceived as large public gardens with gravel paths, flower beds, and manicured lawns. Central Park is a swath of Adirondack landscape—woodland, rocky outcroppings, lakes, and all. City and park meet at a simple, rugged stone wall. On one side of the wall, a sidewalk, women in frocks, traffic, and the bustle of the city; on the other, a dark, silent primeval forest. Jay Gatsby meets Natty Bumppo. The abruptness of the change—from man-made to natural, from natural to man-made—is so absolute it takes my breath away. Even though I know that the park is as much an artifact as the surrounding city, as with any work of art, it's what it makes you feel that's important.

Above all, Central Park is horizontal—in the most vertical city in the world. The contrast is underlined by the looming cliff of skyscrapers that encloses the park like an architectural frame. The experience of any urban park is always the experience of temporary escape, but in Central Park the distant view of tall buildings is a constant reminder of the city. Paradoxically, this heightens the experience of retreat and lends a particular zest to everyday, ordinary occurrences. That's why so many memorable movie scenes have been filmed in the park: romantic carriage rides, park-bench conversations, harrowing chases, echoing steps in a shadowy underpass. Always that delicious and slightly unsettling sense of dislocation, of being in the city—and not. A walk in Central Park always makes me feel that I'm playing hooky.

This remarkable place came into being 150 years ago, when, after three years of cantankerous public debate, the New York State legislature passed a bill that authorized the construction of a large public park on Manhattan Island. In fact, it was not a straightforward decision—this was New York City, after all—because there were two competing sites. The affair was settled in the courts, and the "central" site prevailed.

The southern portion of Central Park opened to the public in the winter of 1859, about two years after the competition for the design of the park was held. Can one imagine such speed today? Surely not. New Yorkers immediately took to skating on the frozen lake. In the summers, they went boating in rented skiffs, cruised silently in electric launches, or lounged in one of several Venetian gondolas, listening to the singing boatmen. The park had an elaborate system of bridle paths and carriage drives, an elm-lined mall for promenading, a ball ground for games, and a parade ground (today, Sheep Meadow) for military exercises. There were rustic arbors and the Belvedere viewing platform, but the only building was a genteel watering hole, the Ladies' Refreshment Salon. In all, Central Park was a mannerly place, mirroring the high-minded ideals of William Cullen Bryant, an early advocate, who hoped that a park in New York would promote "good morals and good order."

Frederick Law Olmsted and Calvert Vaux are often praised for the farsighted vision of their design, but they did not anticipate how popular Central Park would become. By 1865, before the park was complete, there were already more than seven million visits a year, at a time when the city's population was about half a million (today, there are more than twenty million visits annually). From its opening—and ever since—Central Park played catch-up, trying to adapt itself to the various demands of its voracious clientele. Vaux added a boathouse at the head of the lake, a dairy that served milk to children, and a spa pavilion that served mineral water to adults. The 1880s saw a welter of new outdoor activities in the park: roller-skating, bicycling, baseball. There was a craze for tennis, and more than a hundred grass courts were set up in the South Meadow.

Olmsted introduced free concerts to the park as early as 1859, and these proved so popular that an ornate bandstand was built beside the Mall. Nineteenth-century concerts were decorous affairs: people were not allowed to sit on the grass. For many years, park commissioners, notably Robert Moses, who ruled from 1934 until 1960, had a strict notion of which recreational activities were appropriate, and that did not include large public gatherings. Ironically, it was Moses who was responsible for creating the ninety-acre Great Lawn on the site of the filled-in Lower Reservoir. The flat open area turned out to be the perfect place for outdoor concerts. In the summer of 1966, 75,000 people gathered on the Great Lawn to hear the New York Philharmonic led by Leonard Bernstein, and the following year an unprecedented 135,000 people listened to Barbra Streisand. It took sanitation workers three days to clean up the trash, raising the question—not for the last time—of whether the park should be open to mammoth crowds.

Nevertheless, more concerts followed, culminating in the historic reunion of Simon and Garfunkel, who played to a crowd of almost half a million.

Musical concerts have a long tradition in Central Park, so it is easy to forget that the park has also served as a place for mass demonstrations. This is a relatively recent development, for during the nineteenth century political meetings were not allowed in the park. That changed on Suffrage Day in 1914, when a group of suffragists marched down the Central Park Mall. "The crowd was as large as that drawn by a municipal band concert," marveled *The New York Times*. In the early 1930s, during the Depression, a group of unemployed homeless men built a so-called Hooverville on the site of the future Great Lawn to protest federal policies; the two hundred temporary shacks remained in place for two years. What is still the largest recorded public gathering in Central Park's history took place in Sheep Meadow on October 27—Navy Day—in 1945. An audience estimated at one million people listened to President Harry Truman give a foreign policy address. Photographs show an attentive crowd, seated on orderly rows of wooden folding chairs. Most of the men are wearing hats.

The 1960s saw a variety of distinctly less orderly public events—love-ins, be-ins, kite-ins. The park continued to be a magnet for a large variety of political causes: rallies for and against the Vietnam War, protests against nuclear weapons and apartheid, celebrations of Gay Pride and Earth Day. Such events would have surprised Olmsted and Vaux, who imagined the park as a contemplative retreat, not a public forum. But each generation of New Yorkers has redefined the meaning of Central Park to suit itself: a place to promenade, a place to listen to Sousa, a place to demonstrate, a place to in-line skate dance. Whatever.

Central Park was conceived with a very specific function, but it has not been static. It is a historical place, but it is also a place with a history—a changing history. It took a long time before the park was open at night, for example. A hundred years ago, letting automobiles use the carriage drives must have seemed like a good idea; today, it feels—and sounds—like an imposition. One day, no doubt, we will further restrict the use of cars, and not only on weekends. But that does not mean that there is a "right" way to use the park. Uses come and go, users jostle each other, sometimes the odd elbow is thrown. Central Park is often described as a democratic space, but it is really a democratic arena where there is no fixed consensus, just a constant conversation whose tenor rises and falls with the times.

I've always liked Napoleon's description of the Piazza San Marco in Venice as "the finest drawing room in Europe," a somewhat ingratiating remark because he had just conquered the city. A decorous Parisian park could be described as a sort of salon, with nothing more strenuous going on than a game of *pétanque*; a London park is more like a comfortable living room, with people dozing in scattered deck chairs. Central Park is like neither; it's too informal to be a drawing room and too sweaty and boisterous to be a living room. On any given day, you can see dog walkers and birdwatchers, bicyclists and joggers, horseback riders and folk dancers, soccer and baseball teams, and yes, *pétanque* players. Central Park is the city's outdoor rumpus room.

Olmsted had foreseen that the time would come when Manhattan Island would be covered by "rows of monotonous straight streets, and piles of erect, angular buildings" and there would be "no suggestion left of its present varied surface, with the single exception of the Park." But I'm not sure if even he could imagine just how precious its 843 acres would be to a city grown unimaginably large and dense. Mayor Bloomberg, in a rare burst of eloquence, recently described the park as "our picnic spot, our playground, our nature preserve, our band shell, our field of dreams." Not only dreams, *memories*. There's something about parks that makes people want to fill them with commemorative statues. It must be the tranquil surroundings—I always think that if he were able, William Tecumseh Sherman would leap his horse over the yellow cabs that circle Grand Army Plaza and find himself a quiet spot overlooking the pond. He would have plenty of company. There are now more than fifty fountains, monuments, and sculptures in the park, though there is no memorial to Calvert Vaux, who deserves one; Olmsted, who disliked flowers, is honored by, of all things, a flower bed. The monuments are a decidedly odd mix. The men on plinths reflect the city's various ethnic groups— Simón Bolívar, Christopher Columbus, the Polish king Jagiello— and celebrate famous artists (Beethoven), notable New Yorkers (Alexander Hamilton), obscure New Yorkers (the newspaperman Arthur Brisbane), and adopted New Yorkers (John Lennon). There are hallowed authors such as Shakespeare and Sir Walter Scott and literary characters such as Mother Goose. My favorite statue is Balto, the heroic Alaskan sled dog, whose bronze surface is rubbed bright by the stroking of innumerable tiny hands.

New York is a city relentlessly driven by change, with one eye always cocked on the future, the latest fashion, the next new thing. Yet Central Park looks obstinately backward. It is a repository of the past, other people's pasts (Cleopatra's Needle) as well as our own. Perhaps that's why the park, picnic spot and playground that it is, is also—at times—a sort of shrine. It is where New Yorkers go to remember, to commemorate, and to grieve. When George Harrison died, bouquets piled up in Strawberry Fields, which also serves as the site of an annual memorial for John Lennon. On the day after 9/11, people gathered spontaneously on the Great Lawn, simply to feel the warmth of each other's companionship on that mournful day. On the first anniversary of 9/11, flickering candles marked an evening vigil.

No one is buried in Central Park, but those little brass plaques on the park benches that memorialize loved ones—privately famous people, as opposed to the public variety—have always seemed to me as moving as gravestones. Here they once sat, the plaques testify, doing not much of anything, taking a break, listening to the birds, reading a book, eating a sandwich, watching the children play, hearing the hum of traffic far away, daydreaming, convivially alone. In the park.

Why We Need Olmsted Again

Sprawl is shaping up to be an issue in the 2000 Bush-Gore presidential elections. It is easy to see why. The public is concerned about gridlock and the relentless urbanization of the countryside. Existing communities erect barriers to growth, pushing development yet farther out; rural towns feel threatened. There is a general feeling that things are out of control. Yet there is no consensus about how growth should be accommodated. On the whole, the public is undecided: we are alarmed at the consequences of sprawl but suspicious of the chief means of reining it in—centralized planning.

The public's confidence in planning was soured by the debacles of the 1960s. High-minded urban renewal left thousands homeless, crosstown freeways fractured neighborhoods, and public housing superblocks, conceived by the best minds in the field, created high-crime zones. Faced with another round of planning "solutions," the public is right to be skeptical. Yet the suspicion of planning runs further back in time than these relatively recent events. Americans have always been uncomfortable with centralized planning. We admire European cities, but we have resisted vesting as much power in an individual as, say, Rome did in Pope Sixtus V or Paris in Napoleon III. Instead of the grand gesture, we have preferred the generic grid, plain old Main Street, and its modern counterpart, the ubiquitous highway strip. This is not simply laziness. These modest planning solutions have generally provided a level playing field for "life, liberty, and the pursuit of happiness." In the grid, or on the strip, everyone is treated equally. The house stands beside the church, which is next to the drive-in restaurant. Each has equal prominence; none assumes precedence over the other.

The history of planning the American city has been chiefly a story of private accomplishments and private monuments: palatial department stores, railroad terminals, skyscrapers, baseball stadiums. There is one exception, and it is a big one. During the second half of the nineteenth century, almost every large city—New York, Philadelphia, Boston, Chicago, San Francisco—planned and built a public park. European cities already had parks, but London's Hyde Park and Paris's Tuileries Garden were relatively small. The American parks were huge: 843 acres in the case of New York's Central Park, more than 1,000 acres in San Francisco, more than 3,000 in Philadelphia. This was planning on a heroic scale.

Many of these great public works were laid out by Frederick Law Olmsted, the remarkable planner and landscape architect who, with Calvert Vaux, built Central Park and Brooklyn's Prospect Park as well as parks in Buffalo and Chicago. Later, working alone, Olmsted planned parks in Boston, Detroit, Louisville, Rochester, and Montreal. What was it that made Olmsted's brand of city planning so successful?

Olmsted lived at a time of spectacular urban expansion. "We have reason to believe, then, that towns which of late have been increasing rapidly on account of their commercial advantages, are likely to be still more attractive to population in the future," he wrote in a paper delivered in 1870 to the American Social Science Association, of which he was a founder. "That there will in consequence soon be larger towns than any the world has yet known, and that the further progress of civilization is to depend mainly upon the influences by which men's minds and characters will be affected while living in large towns."

Although Olmsted loved the countryside, like most of his contemporaries he never suggested that urbanization could—or should—be curtailed. Nor was he nostalgic about the past. He understood the attractions of city life, cultural as well as commercial, social as well as economic. As a young man, enthusiastic about "scientific farming," he had farmed for a living and knew about rural isolation and hardship. He had traveled across the South and the Texas frontier writing regular reports for the *New-York Daily Times* before the Civil War and had no romantic illusions about life in small, backward rural communities. Although he had grown up in a small New England town—Hartford, Connecticut—he had been apprenticed to a trading company in New York and understood that the future lay with the burgeoning metropolis.

Olmsted had spent many years writing—though never finishing—an ambitious book on American civilization. He was always concerned with the big picture. Huge cities were inevitable, of that he was sure. The questions were how to make them livable and how to influence "men's minds and characters" so that civilization would prosper. He was far from sanguine about the future of the latter. After spending two years during his early forties managing a gold mine in California's untamed Sierra Nevada, he had firsthand experience of the crudeness and roughness of frontier life. He was afraid that the booming industrial city would likewise brutalize its inhabitants.

His solution was the public park. It provided city dwellers with easy access to nature. That is something that distinguishes the American city park of that period: it is not an urban garden, nor a manicured parterre, nor a fantasy landscape. It is pastoral countryside, sometimes resembling wilderness. This rural quality is already present in Central Park's Ramble with its rocky

outcroppings, but it becomes more evident in later works such as
Prospect Park's ravines and waterfalls and the twisting mountain
road of Montreal's Mount Royal Park.

Olmsted was influenced by two landscapes: the picturesque
grounds surrounding English estates, particularly those laid out
by Lancelot "Capability" Brown, whose work Olmsted first saw as
a young man; and Yosemite Valley. He visited the valley during his
California sojourn, and as head of a commission to chart its future
as a national park, he studied it closely. Yosemite was an eye-opener.
Not only because of its grand scale—its American scale—but also
because of the poignant contrast between the rugged cliffs and
mountains and the tame, domestic atmosphere of the gentle valley
floor. This contrast became a theme of many Olmsted landscapes.

Olmsted was not an aesthete, and the public park was not only
a place to commune with nature. "Men must come together, *and
must be seen coming together* [emphasis added], in carriages, on
horseback and on foot, and the concourse of animated life which
will thus be formed, must in itself be made, if possible, an attractive and diverting spectacle." The public park was to be the great
outdoor living room of the city, where its citizens would mingle
and meet. In a sense, it was a large version of the New England
town green that Olmsted knew so well. However, in a vast city
even a thousand-acre park had a limited impact. In response, Olmsted and Vaux devised the parkway—an American version of the
Parisian boulevard (and no relative of the later automobile rural
highway). The original parkway was an urban pleasure drive,
with traffic lanes in the center for carriages, two broad green treed
strips for pedestrians and bridle paths, and additional lanes for
local traffic. The 260-foot-wide swaths were linear parks that gave
breathing room to the congested industrial city, brought green
spaces into neighborhoods, and created fashionable settings for
large residences. The latter point was important, for parkway construction was financed by the income from new property taxes.

The first parkways were in Brooklyn, stretching miles from Prospect Park to the edges of the city. In Buffalo, Olmsted went further and created an entire park system, three separate parks joined to one another and to the downtown by avenues and parkways (sadly, long since converted into expressways). It turned Buffalo, which became known as the City of Elms, into the best-planned city in the country. In Boston, where Olmsted moved in 1881 after he became frustrated by political bickering over Central Park, he laid out his masterwork of urban design, the so-called Emerald Necklace. Nine continuous parks forming a seven-mile-long system, stretched from the Common to Franklin Park.

Of course, it was a different time. Decisions were taken by a relatively small, educated urban elite of city fathers and patricians, without public hearings and the oversight of countless private interest groups. There were no environmental impact studies, no experts, no consultants. When Olmsted was invited to Buffalo in 1868 to give advice on the park system, for example, he spent two days visiting sites, personally digging test holes to evaluate the soil conditions. The following day, he addressed a public meeting for an hour and presented the rough outlines of a plan. It was immediately accepted, and he was hired to prepare a preliminary report to be submitted six weeks hence. In the meantime, the park backers petitioned Albany to form a park commission that would issue public bonds. The legislature approved the project the following year, and work began. With enthusiastic civic leaders, supportive state politicians (the federal government played no role in financing urban parks), and a public that expected results, these large public works were undertaken with astonishing rapidity. In the case of Central Park, the competition for the design was held in 1858, and by the following summer work was sufficiently advanced that a program of free concerts was inaugurated and daily attendance in the park reached as high as 100,000. The following winter, the frozen lake was ready to receive skaters.

New Yorkers still skate in Central Park in the winter and boat on the lake in the summer. What is striking about Olmsted's parks is their endurance. Generally, American cities have proved impervious to planning. The City Beautiful movement lasted three decades after its birth in 1900, but except in Washington its grand plans remained largely incomplete. Today, only forty years after urban renewal we are demolishing public housing projects, and some cities have even dismantled urban freeways. The fad for pedestrian malls closed to traffic was likewise fleeting. Yet in the 140 years since Central Park was built, no one has ever suggested that it was a mistake. True, the park experienced periods of neglect, especially during the post–World War II decades. There were unforeseen encroachments such as the zoo and the skating rink. Joggers and Rollerbladers have replaced promenading ladies and gentlemen. There is probably too much automobile traffic for what were originally conceived as pleasure drives for horse-drawn carriages. Yet while the activities that take place in the park have changed, its fundamental role as a place of retreat and renewal remains. Today, Central Park is as much used—and cherished—as ever.

Olmsted was not merely a park builder; he was a visionary city planner. He planned a new town for the western railhead of the Northern Pacific, devised a street layout for the Bronx when it was annexed by the City of New York, and oversaw a comprehensive regional plan for all of Staten Island. Yet there is no record that he ever designed an "ideal city." He was no utopian. That, too, explains his success. Unlike later planners, Olmsted did not try to impose a predetermined template on the city. When Leland Stanford approached him to plan a new college in California, the railroad magnate wanted a New England–style campus; Olmsted reasonably pointed out that the arid climate demanded a different solution. Likewise, when the city of San Francisco commissioned a park expecting a version of Central Park, Olmsted proposed a different solution tailored to that city's particular climate and geography.

Olmsted could be dictatorial. Once, when he was working on South Park in Chicago, one of the commissioners asked him, "I don't see, Mr. Olmsted, that the plans indicate any flower beds in the park. Now where would you recommend that these be placed?" Olmsted's curt answer: "Anywhere outside the park." He immersed himself in details, not only creating a Central Park police, but designing their uniforms. Yet as a planner, he purposely avoided trying to control everything. He understood that the city was too volatile, too changeable, to be easily tamed. The parks and parkways were big enough to hold their own; in between, he left the ebb and flow of city life largely to its own devices. Similarly, in his suburban plans, while he laid down certain broad rules governing public areas, he left individual homeowners room for personal expression and liberty. His was a peculiarly American approach to planning: open-ended, pragmatic, tolerant.

He approached cities with the long view of a gardener. "I have all my life been considering distant effects and always sacrificing immediate success and applause to that of the future," he once observed to his son Rick. "In laying out Central Park we determined to think of no result to be realized in less than forty years." This proved to be a good principle for city planning. His ability to see into the future was uncanny. In the Bronx, he proposed acquiring railroad rights-of-way well in advance of development, ensuring cheaper land costs and more efficient routes. In Staten Island, he advised laying out residential subdivisions in advance of the demand for suburban homes that he felt sure would come. When he was advising on Yosemite, he correctly foretold that the annual number of visitors, which was then two or three thousand, would in a century surpass a million.

Olmsted's landscaping contracts always included a clause requiring follow-up visits for several years. The plan was not an end in itself but the beginning of a process. He assumed that over time adjustments and improvements would be required. Mistakes would be made. Some trees would thrive; others would have to be replaced. Unpredictable natural effects would have to be taken into account. This pragmatic quality served him well as a city planner and is another reason, I think, for his marked success in a field where so many have failed. He not only took the long view; he was prepared to adjust his plans as circumstances demanded.

Olmsted's thinking about cities was not confined to the center. Although he and his family lived for a number of years in a Manhattan brownstone on West Forty-Sixth Street, he spent the bulk of his adult years in suburban towns: Clifton on Staten Island and Brookline outside Boston. He liked suburban life and wrote that suburbs combined the "ruralistic beauty of a loosely built New England village with a certain degree of the material and social advantages of a town." This was the way that cities would expand. "The construction of good roads and walks, the laying of sewer, water, and gas pipes, and the supplying of sufficiently cheap, rapid, and comfortable conveyances to town centers, is all that is necessary to give any farming land in a healthy and attractive situation the value of town lots," he wrote.

Olmsted, the godfather of sprawl? He did build the country's first large planned suburban residential community outside Chicago, and he was responsible for several master-planned communities, not least, beautiful Druid Hills in Atlanta. He assumed—correctly, it turned out—that future urban growth in the United States would take place at a relatively low density. Yet in his suburban plans, he always emphasized the railroad or trolley link to downtown, for he considered suburb and city to be distinct but complementary. Moreover, his commitment to improving life in the burgeoning industrial city was absolute; that is why he was devoted to creating urban parks. He might have lived in the suburbs, but he was also a man of the city.

Olmsted would be disappointed by the decline of our cities and the increasing isolation of our suburbs. As a nineteenth-century gentleman, he would doubtless be appalled at our consumer society. "More barbarism and less civilization," he might say. But the practical planner was never one to despair. "So, you have Walmarts and strip malls and cineplexes. Very well, there is a place for everything. But that is not sufficient. You are obliged to create public places among all this private expansion. Places for all people to mix. You must think big, you know. And you must think far ahead. What is it that you really want the metropolis to become, forty years from now? Because you'll have to start working on it now."

This essay is dated only inasmuch as in a post-9/11 world it is hard to imagine suburban sprawl becoming an election issue. The suggestion that Olmsted was the godfather of sprawl was made tongue in cheek, but the challenge of dealing with sprawl remains and must be faced, not as a malady, but as part of our modern urban condition.

PART THREE

The Art of Building

A Distinguished Failure

The Architecture of Humanism was first published in London in 1914. Its author, Geoffrey Scott, a twenty-nine-year-old British architecture school dropout, had been living as an expatriate in Florence. Scott's book was reprinted in Britain and the United States in 1924. In 1980, a new British edition, with a foreword by David Watkin, appeared, followed in 1999 by an American edition, with a foreword by Henry Hope Reed and an introduction by Paul Barolsky. This minor classic of architectural criticism is well worth reading, for the architectural situation a hundred years ago was not dissimilar to our own. Here, for example, is Scott complaining about the confused state of architectural thinking:

> There may, at the present time, be a lack of architectural taste: there is, unfortunately, no lack of architectural opinion. Architecture, it is said, must be "expressive of its purpose" or "expressive of its true construction" or "expressive of the materials it employs" or "expressive of the national life" (whether noble or otherwise) or "expressive of a noble life" (whether national or not); or expressive of the craftsman's temperament, or the owner's or the architect's, or, on the contrary, "academic" and studiously indifferent to these factors. It must, we are told, be symmetrical, or it must be

picturesque—that is, above all things, unsymmetrical. It
must be "traditional" and "scholarly" . . . or it must be
"original" and "spontaneous," that is, it must be at pains to
avoid this resemblance; or it must strike some happy compromise between these opposites; and so forth indefinitely.

Scott lived during a period of astonishing architectural variety.
The five years leading up to the outbreak of World War I witnessed
the following important buildings: Frank Lloyd Wright's rebuilt
Wisconsin home, Taliesin; Edwin Lutyens's severe and magnifi-
cent Castle Drogo in Devon; Adolf Loos's proto–International
Style Steiner House in Vienna; Walter Gropius and Adolf Meyer's
factorylike glass-and-brick Werkbund exhibition pavilion in
Cologne; Horace Trumbauer's neo-Georgian Widener Library at
Harvard; and Cram & Goodhue's muscular Gothic Revival U.S. Mil-
itary Academy at West Point. That period also saw McKim, Mead &
White's full-bore Roman classical Pennsylvania Station in New
York City, Paul Philippe Cret's Beaux Arts Pan American Union
Building in Washington, D.C., and Peter Behrens's even more
simplified classical AEG turbine hall in Berlin.

Scott championed the architectural principles of the Renaissance, a period that he broadly defined as starting with Brunelleschi in the fifteenth century and ending with the rise of the Gothic
Revival four hundred years later. In *The Architecture of Humanism*, he went about his task in an unusual way, for he devoted the
bulk of his book not to a defense of classicism but to an examination of current architectural attitudes. He challenged four general
points of view, which he provocatively called the Romantic Fallacy, the Mechanical Fallacy, the Ethical Fallacy, and the Biological Fallacy.

The Romantic Fallacy referred to attempts to adapt a poetic and
literary sensibility to architecture. This attitude, engendered by the

Gothic Revival and the subsequent writings of John Ruskin, produced buildings such as Fonthill, a millionaire's country mansion made to resemble a medieval abbey, with the requisite cloister and a towering spire over the living room. The problem with this approach, according to Scott, was that an image in a poem and an image in a building are different. In literature, the content might be romantic, but the form—the language—follows traditional conventions. "The 'magic casements' of Keats," he wrote, "have their place in a perfectly formal and conventional metric scheme that displays their beauty, and are powerful over us because they are imagined. But the casements of the romantic architecture, realized in stone, must lack this reticence and this support. They were inconvenient rather than magical, and they opened, not on the 'foam of perilous seas,' but, most often, upon a landscape-garden less faery than forlorn." By attempting to introduce poetic meaning into buildings, the Romantic movement distorted architecture, Scott argued, rendering it chiefly symbolic. Architecture "ceases to be an immediate and direct source of enjoyment, and becomes a mediate and indirect one." Were Scott writing today, he might use the term "Disneyfication," in which what a building represents is more important than what it actually is—stagecraft rather than architecture.

In the chapter on the Mechanical Fallacy, Scott attacked the assumption that construction could be used as the basis for judging architecture. "The art of architecture studies not structure in itself, but the effect of structure on the human spirit," he wrote. Influential theorists such as Viollet-le-Duc admired medieval cathedrals because their pointed vaults, flying buttresses, and clustered piers were seen as a direct expression of the weight they carried. Conversely, they judged Renaissance buildings to be inferior, because their domes were often reinforced by hidden chains and their vaults were routinely strengthened by iron tie-rods. This casual approach to structure made the Renaissance architects appear clumsy. Scott retorted that this attitude was intentional:

> The Renaissance grasped this distinction between the several elements of architectural design with extreme clearness. *It realised that, for certain purposes in architecture, fact counted for everything, and that in certain others, appearance counted for everything. And it took advantage of this distinction to the full.* It did not insist that the necessary fact should itself produce the necessary appearance. It considered the questions separately, and was content to secure them by separate means.

In other words, it is important to distinguish between the mechanical art of building and the aesthetic art of architecture, that is, between fact and fiction. An example of this difference is Christopher Wren's great dome of St. Paul's in London. The exterior dome is a wood structure, designed to be seen from afar; the interior wood and plaster dome is part of the interior experience of the cathedral; while the structure that actually supports the heavy lantern is hidden, a conical stone dome. On the other hand, the piers that carry the great weight of the entire structure are massive, probably more massive than strictly required by engineering.

In *The Stones of Venice*, Ruskin criticized Renaissance architecture because he considered it immoral and corrupt. He hated the sensuousness, and what he called the pagan roots, of classical architecture. Ruskin introduced what are, in effect, ethical standards to architectural criticism. Henceforth, it was not sufficient for buildings to be beautiful; they also had to be righteous. Scott took issue with what he called the Ethical Fallacy.

> It was a Puritan revival, but with this difference: the fervour of Puritanism was now active in vindicating the value

of art. It insisted that architecture was something more than a mechanical problem. It gave a human reference. But, unluckily, this Puritan attack, far from clearing the path of criticism, did but encumber it with fresh confusions no less misleading than the logic of inhuman science. Art was remembered, but the standards of art remained forgotten.

According to the Puritan view, which was later espoused by most architectural modernists and is still in favor today, buildings that conceal their structural parts, as does St. Paul's, are less "honest" than those that expose their columns and beams. The pilaster, a flattened column that was the staple of Renaissance architecture, is considered deceitful because it serves no structural function. Faux finishes, common in eighteenth-century interiors, are likewise disdained. Conversely, if a building is "truthful," if it exposes its structure and avoids adding extraneous elements, it has perforce to be beautiful. Scott argued that this was a simplistic view. One should consider the overall goal of the architect in arriving at a judgment. In any case, he denied that morality had a place in making aesthetic decisions; in his opinion, the artistic end—in the case of architecture, the experience of the building by its occupants—justified the means.

The fourth fallacy was to consider the changing architecture of the past analogous to biological evolution, a view held by many art historians at that time and still influential today.

The object of "evolutionary" criticism is, *prima facie*, not to appreciate but to explain. To account for the facts, not to estimate them, is its function. And the light which it brings comes from one great principle: that things are intelligible through a knowledge of their antecedents. *Ex nihilo nihil fit*; the nature of things is latent in their past. The myriad forms of architecture fall, by the compulsion of this principle, into necessary order.

The Renaissance is often described as following a course that began with youth (Brunelleschi), reached maturity (the so-called High Renaissance of Bramante and Raphael), and finally succumbed to decline, old age, and decay (the Baroque and the rococo). Scott, who particularly admired Baroque architecture, argued that focusing on the sequence of styles missed the point. "The first condition of aesthetic understanding is to place ourselves at the point of vision appropriate to the work of art: to judge it in its own terms," he wrote. Thus, Brunelleschi did not know that he would be followed by Bramante, any more than Bramante could imagine Bernini. Each should be judged on his own merit rather than as an episode in an imagined evolution, a view echoed by James S. Ackerman in his influential essay "A Theory of Style."

Scott was an aesthete. He wrote in the tradition of Walter Pater and Oscar Wilde, describing the Italian Renaissance, with some exaggeration, as "an architecture of taste, seeking no logic, consistency, or justification beyond that of giving pleasure." The "humanism" of his title referred to a theory that had been developed by the contemporary German aesthetic philosopher Theodor Lipps, whose *Ästhetik* influenced Bernard Berenson as well as the critic and novelist Vernon Lee. Lipps's theory of empathy (*Einfühlung*), as Scott adapted it to architecture, meant that people experience buildings with reference to themselves. The essence of architectural aesthetics, Scott insisted in a passage that anticipates Siegfried Giedion's *Space, Time and Architecture* by twenty-seven years, is the position of the human body with respect to the material organization of space:

To enclose a space is the object of building; when we build we do but detach a convenient quantity of space, seclude it and protect it, and all architecture springs from that necessity. But aesthetically space is even more supreme. The architect models in space as a sculptor in clay. He designs his space as a work of art; that is, he attempts through its means to excite a certain mood in those who enter it.

Scott used the example of a spire, which, if it is well designed, is often described as "soaring," even though it actually exerts downward pressure. We identify with its upward thrust, just as we identify with "springing" arches, "stretching" roofs, or "muscular" columns. According to Scott, these are not merely metaphors of speech but a profound reflection of how we actually experience architecture.

The insights in *The Architecture of Humanism* owe much to the author's firsthand experience. Geoffrey Scott was born in Hampstead in 1885, the youngest son of a successful flooring manufacturer, and was sent to Rugby, then one of the best public schools in England, and to Oxford, where he took Greats. His social life interfered with his studies, but he distinguished himself in his final year at New College by winning a prestigious prize for his essay "The National Character of English Architecture." This success led him to enroll at the Architectural Association in London. Finding the practical courses uncongenial, however, he left after a few months. Although he had a small allowance, he needed a job. For a time, he accepted a position as the traveling companion of a wealthy young American on a tour of Italy. Then, for several months, he worked in Paris as an assistant to Ogden Codman Jr. compiling a catalog of French châteaus. Codman, an architect, was the co-author with Edith Wharton of *The Decoration of Houses*, a leading book of its type, and Scott later became close friends with Wharton and with Elsie de Wolfe, America's leading interior decorator.

These early experiences exposed Scott to architectural influences, but they did not set him on a career. That impetus was provided by Bernard Berenson's wife, Mary. While still a student,
Scott had been the Berensons' summer houseguest at I Tatti, their
Fiesole villa. Mary, who might have fallen a little in love with the
personable young man, took him under her wing. It was she who
introduced him to Codman and Wharton. In 1907, the Berensons
invited Scott to return to Italy to help organize Berenson's library
and to assist in improvements to their villa. This work, which
eventually included laying out the large garden, was done in association with Cecil Pinsent, an English architect whom Scott had met
some years before. They established an architectural partnership
and over the next four years, in addition to I Tatti, realized several
architectural commissions for members of the Anglo-American
community in Florence.

Thus, in 1913, while he was writing *The Architecture of Humanism* (which is dedicated to Pinsent), Scott had the benefit of several
important influences. He was working as an architect and living in
surroundings that put him in daily, intimate contact with some of
the best Italian Renaissance architecture. He had traveled extensively in France and Italy. Most important, he was in close contact
with Bernard Berenson, the foremost Renaissance art scholar of
the day. Berenson's circle at I Tatti included his neighbor Vernon
Lee, whose intellectual influence Scott also acknowledged.

The Architecture of Humanism was a critical success. Edith
Wharton called it "brilliant and discriminating" in *The Times
Literary Supplement*. Scott, who had just turned thirty, seemed
destined for great things, and he immediately planned a sequel, a
history of architectural style. Medically unfit for military service,
he spent most of World War I in Italy, but the second book never
materialized. Instead, he frittered away the next ten years with a
variety of odd jobs, including an unpaid position at the British embassy in Rome. Scott, who came to terms with his homosexuality

only late in life, had an unhappy marriage to Lady Sybil Cutting, a wealthy English aristocrat, and several inconclusive love affairs, notably a two-year liaison with Vita Sackville-West.

Years later, Virginia Woolf wrote of Scott in her diary, "He was tall, & dark & had the distinguished face of a failure; reminded me a little of . . . other 'brilliant' young men, who remain 'brilliant' & young well into the 40ties & never do anything to prove it." Woolf didn't like Scott, and she obviously wasn't impressed by his architectural writing, but her characterization, while not entirely off the mark, was too harsh; although he gave up architecture, he did do something—more than once. In 1925, he published *The Portrait of Zélide*, a slim biographical essay on Madame de Charrière, an obscure eighteenth-century novelist and wit, who is also remembered for her liaisons with James Boswell and Benjamin Constant. Once again Scott scored a critical success, gaining plaudits from reviewers and winning the James Tait Black Memorial Prize, the Booker of its day. Soon after, he was appointed editor of the newly discovered Boswell papers (after T. E. Lawrence had turned down the position). The long-lost papers had come into the possession of an American, Ralph Isham, and Scott spent the next year and a half in New York City. In 1928, he published the first three volumes to great acclaim, becoming a minor celebrity and signing a lucrative contract for a biography of Boswell. Less than a year later, after returning to New York from a visit to England, Scott, always sickly, caught pneumonia and died. He was forty-five.

"Architecture, simply and immediately perceived, is a combination, revealed through light and shade, of spaces, of masses, and of lines," Scott wrote in *The Architecture of Humanism*. This definition, which anticipates Le Corbusier's "Architecture is the masterly, correct and magnificent play of masses brought together in light" by almost a decade, is surprisingly abstract and disregards his emphasis on subjective experience. Yet Scott was hardly a trailblazer for architectural modernism, which in 1918 was just around the corner. "Humanism has two enemies," he wrote, "chaos and inhuman order." They were just around the corner, too. The inhuman order of industrialized building, mass production, standardization, and the other paraphernalia of the International Style would have appalled him, as would have its aesthetic puritanism and moral posturing. If there is one early modernist architect that Scott might have approved, it would probably be Mies van der Rohe. For Mies, as for Scott, appearance counted for everything; Mies never believed in form merely following function. A building such as the Seagram Building, with its neoclassical sense of composition and detail, is morally neutral. Its elegant facade hides as much as it reveals.

As for chaos, there is no doubt what Scott would have thought of the work of our contemporary architectural avant-garde: whether Thom Mayne's shifted tectonic plates, Coop Himmelb(l)au's jagged collisions, or Zaha Hadid's nervous compositions. "Fantastic architecture, architecture that startles and delights the curiosity and is not dominated by a broad repose, may sometimes be appropriate," Scott wrote. "But it is unfitted, aesthetically, for the normal uses of the art, for it fatigues the attention; and architecture once again is insistent, dominating, and not to be escaped."

The architectural historian Reyner Banham once characterized *The Architecture of Humanism* as "the aesthetic hand-book of the neo-Georgian and Playboy phases of English architecture." Banham was taking a swipe at the work of contemporary architects who design in the classical style and for whom Scott is something of a hero. There is no doubt that Scott's architectural taste was classical. His designs in Florence were classically inspired: the villa that he and Pinsent built for Charles A. Strong, an American professor, has a triple-arch loggia as delicate as a Brunelleschi arcade. Yet while Scott saw the four-hundred-year-old Renaissance tradition of architecture as an ineluctable fact, I'm not sure that he would entirely approve of the doctrinaire classicism that appears in different guises today. He admired the academic tradition of classicism so long as it was freely interpreted and allied to a living sense of art, for he always rejected academic theory. "My contention is that 'theory'—the attempt to decide architectural right and wrong on purely intellectual grounds—is precisely one of the roots of our mischief," he wrote in *The Architecture of Humanism*.

Scott did not mention any contemporary architects in his book, not Edwin Lutyens, whose Baroque Heathcote was inspired by Sanmicheli, nor Paul Cret, whose simplified version of classicism Scott might have approved. Nor did the author take issue with such modernist proselytizers as Loos or Gropius's partner, Adolf Meyer. Perhaps, sequestered in Florence, he was simply uninterested in current architectural fashions. Or maybe he was being shrewd. By avoiding specific references, he gave his book a timeless quality that partly accounts for its longevity. The chapter on the Romantic Fallacy, for example, can be read as an attack on today's architectural deconstructivism, with its pretentious literary metaphors and romantic, albeit often nihilistic, allusions. (The work of Eisenman and Libeskind provides examples.) The Biological Fallacy continues to be a rebuke to those who promote architecture novelty on the grounds that the new—and only the new—is a proper reflection of our time.

Scott laid out general principles in *The Architecture of Humanism*, but he resisted the impulse to formulate an alternative intellectual theory. "What we feel as 'beauty' in architecture is not a matter for logical demonstration," he wrote. The closest he came to practical advice was to recommend a greater firsthand familiarity with the tradition of humanist architecture. This familiarity would presumably develop one's taste, and taste, as the subtitle of *The Architecture of Humanism* signaled, was at the center of Scott's architectural sensibility. He defined taste as a "disinterested enthusiasm for architectural form." He recognized that to many this would sound capricious and inconsequential; nevertheless, he called for the primacy of aesthetics and for responding to buildings with the eyes and heart rather than with the intellect. In a period such as our own, where architecture is so dominated by intellectual interpretations and theories, by a seemingly endless succession of isms, it is useful to be reminded that buildings are—or should be—made to be experienced and enjoyed. Scott can be maddeningly vague at times, but his love of architecture rings clear and true, and his rewarding insights guarantee that *The Architecture of Humanism* continues to be read almost a century after it was written. Not bad for a distinguished failure.

Show Dogs

In 1955, the French architect Le Corbusier built the chapel of Notre-Dame du Haut in Ronchamp, a remote site in the Jura Mountains near the Swiss border. The building had roughly plastered curved concrete walls and a swelling roof that resembled a nun's coif. These sculptural features challenged the functionalist dogma—to a large extent pioneered by Le Corbusier himself—of the white shoe-box International Style. After Ronchamp, modern architecture was never quite the same.

Frank Gehry's Bilbao Guggenheim is equally iconoclastic. With its ballooning shapes and titanium swirls, its colliding forms and unusual spaces, it has been described as biomorphic sculpture, an intergalactic spaceship, and a silver artichoke. There is a major difference, however, between the museum and the chapel. When I went to Ronchamp in 1964, there were few other visitors. Most, judging by their cameras and sketchbooks, were architectural—not religious—pilgrims, students like myself. Corbu, as we called him, was one of the most important architects in the world, yet his was hardly a household name. Most Americans, pressed to identify a contemporary architect, would probably name Frank Lloyd Wright—who had been dead for five years. People did go out of their way to visit buildings, but they were usually ancient works of art like Chartres Cathedral or historic monuments like the Tower of London. Buildings by modern architects were objects of veneration for architecture students, but they were not paid much attention by the general public.

Today's public definitely knows about the Bilbao Guggenheim; since its 1997 opening, it has attracted almost four million visitors. According to the London *Financial Times*, to date the museum has helped to generate about $500 million in economic activity and about $100 million in new taxes. Now other cities, casting an envious eye on the silver artichoke, decide, "We want one of those."

Seattle got off the mark early. In 1996, before the Bilbao Guggenheim was even complete, the Microsoft co-founder Paul Allen, a Jimi Hendrix fan, commissioned Gehry to design a rock-and-roll museum and performance venue called the Experience Music Project. Gehry delivered a striking building whose bulbous shapes are variously covered in shimmering gold, silver, and purple stainless steel and in red and blue aluminum shingles. These forms resemble the fragments of a giant multicolored broken guitar left over after a particularly violent rock concert.

Two years after the Bilbao Guggenheim opened, the Corcoran Gallery of Art announced that Gehry would build a major addition to its century-old building in Washington, D.C. The new design is a composition of sail-like metallic forms. Construction is slated to begin in 2003, which is probably sooner than the commencement of Gehry's other major museum project: a forty-story Guggenheim on the East River in Lower Manhattan—yet more titanium swirls.* While a Guggenheim museum in New York City designed by Frank Gehry would likely attract millions of visitors, will people really flock to New Orleans to see the Grammy Hall of Fame, a project that has recently been announced and is not yet designed but according to its backers "will have the 'wow' factor not found at the Experience Music Project"? Will the recently opened addition to the Milwaukee Art Museum by the Spanish

---

*Neither the Corcoran addition nor the New York Guggenheim was built.—Ed.

architect Santiago Calatrava, which features a giant kinetic sun-shade resembling a flapping pair of pterodactyl's wings, bring in the throngs? Will the city of Manchester, which will soon have a branch of the Imperial War Museum designed by Daniel Libes-kind, whose Jewish Museum in Berlin attracted 350,000 visitors in two years before it even had any exhibits, be the new Bilbao? Maybe, maybe not. A year after the opening of Seattle's Experience Music Project, attendance is down approximately a third, leading to a layoff of 124 employees. This may be partly because of September 11, but it is worth noting that during the same period the number of visitors to the local art museum increased by more than a third.

Whatever effect the Bilbao phenomenon will have on the way that tourists choose their destinations, it has already had a major in-fluence on the way that clients, especially museums, choose their architects. In 1967, when the National Gallery of Art in Washing-ton, D.C., was planning a new wing, it solicited portfolios from a dozen prominent architects and, after narrowing the list down to four (Kevin Roche, Philip Johnson, Louis I. Kahn, and I. M. Pei), visited their buildings as well as their offices. It was only after the choice was made that the winner—Pei—got down to work. Last year, when the Corcoran went looking for an architect, it too had a short list: Gehry, Libeskind, and Calatrava. While Gehry billows, Libeskind zigs and zags. The Jewish Museum, his first major building, resembles a fragmented Star of David, which seemed to many a stroke of genius, although it turns out that Libeskind is simply partial to spiky, agitated forms; his winning design for the Denver Art Museum was described by *The New York Times* as a "dramatic glass-and-titanium jumble of rectangles and triangles." Calatrava's stylishly engineered structures, by contrast, often re-semble sun-dried skeletons: "techno-Gothic," according to one commentator.

Rather than merely visit the previous work of the three architects, however, the Corcoran commissioned each to prepare a
design. This kind of invited competition, now the preferred way
for choosing the architects of high-profile buildings, resembles a
beauty pageant. With great fanfare, a list of invited architects is
announced. Their proposals are often exhibited, and sometimes
the architects themselves give public presentations. The ranks of
the competitors are culled. The cliff-hanging atmosphere is an
important part of the publicity surrounding the proposed new
building. When the Los Angeles County Museum of Art planned a
major renovation and expansion, it invited five noteworthy architects to submit designs, including the ubiquitous Libeskind, Steven
Holl, who was recently featured as "America's best architect" by
Time magazine, and Thom Mayne, an avant-garde Los Angeles–
based architect. Their projects were eliminated in the first round
of judging, leaving the Frenchman Jean Nouvel, whose best-known
building is probably the Arab World Institute in Paris, and Rem
Koolhaas, a globe-trotting Amsterdam architect. Finally, Koolhaas,
who recently won a competition to design Seattle's new public library, was declared the winner.

I have no objection to architects' duking it out, and I think it's
great that architecture is attracting so much attention. But I'm
skeptical that designing in the full glare of public competitions en-
courages architects to produce better buildings. The charged atmosphere promotes flamboyance rather than careful thought and
favors the glib and the simplistic over the subtle and the nuanced.
Architects have always entered competitions, but they have usually honed their talents doing commissioned work. Today, young
architects such as Libeskind, Nouvel, and Koolhaas have built
their reputations almost entirely on participating in competitions;
"competition show dogs," a friend of mine calls them. And show
dogs are rarefied breeds, often refined and styled to the point of
caricature.

Some years ago, in *Learning from Las Vegas*, Robert Venturi, Denise Scott Brown, and Steven Izenour differentiated between buildings whose architectural image was chiefly the result of surface ornament applied to structures shaped by their functions and those whose image was the result of unusual forms. They called the former "decorated sheds" and the latter "ducks" (a reference to a Long Island roadside stand that sold poultry and was shaped like an actual duck). Italian Renaissance palazzi, for example, which are essentially relatively straightforward buildings with exquisitely ornamented exteriors—and interiors—are decorated sheds, whereas Gothic cathedrals, with their flying buttresses, pinnacles, and steeples, are ducks. The point was not that one approach was better than the other—*Learning from Las Vegas* allowed that "both kinds of architecture are valid"—but that, historically speaking, ducks are few and far between. Venturi and his co-authors argued that clients were better served by decorated sheds than by dramatically modeled buildings, no matter how exciting. After all, it is the former approach that has produced some of our most memorable public buildings: John Russell Pope's National Gallery of Art in Washington, D.C., Carrère & Hastings's New York Public Library, and McKim, Mead & White's Symphony Hall in Boston—all decorated sheds.

Yet clearly it's ducks that are in season. Ironically, Venturi himself has fallen victim to this fashion. Some years ago, his firm was commissioned to design a new concert hall for Philadelphia. The result was a sensible design with an attractive performance space but a relatively modest exterior. However, as more and more cities announced the construction of trophy buildings, the Philadelphia concert-hall backers decided that a decorated shed simply would not do. They dismissed Venturi Scott Brown, increased the budget from $60 million to $265 million, and hired the New Yorker Rafael Viñoly, who delivered the requisite "wow factor": an immense glass vault.

Viñoly's concert hall, known as the Kimmel Center for the Performing Arts, illustrates another aspect of the Bilbao effect. Show-dog architecture, especially in a signature style, is unlikely to pay much attention to its surroundings. Venturi's design was carefully inserted into its site on Broad Street, and its conservative exterior suited Quakerish Philadelphia, his hometown. Viñoly's glass vault, however dramatic, is an alien presence. The devaluing of context is even more flagrant in international competitions, in which architects are expected to add major civic monuments to cities they barely know on the basis of one or two brief visits.

One of the greatest American architects of the twentieth century was Louis I. Kahn. His best work, such as the Kimbell Art Museum in Fort Worth, the Salk Institute in La Jolla, and the Yale Center for British Art, was always directly commissioned. Kahn entered several design competitions but never won, and in later life he avoided competitions altogether. Competitions did not suit him, for he developed his designs slowly, refining them in the process, and his early sketches bear little resemblance to the final building. Moreover, the qualities that make his architecture so good are poorly communicated in drawings and models; the architecture has to be experienced in the completed buildings.

Kahn's spiritual successor is the Japanese architect Tadao Ando, whose accomplished designs earned him the 1995 Pritzker Prize. His first public building in the United States, the Pulitzer Foundation for the Arts in St. Louis, opened last year. Ando is a minimalist whose modest buildings depend on modulated natural light falling on simple materials, particularly concrete, which in his hands acquires a silky, sensuous texture. The forms of his buildings are uncomplicated; this is not eye-popping architecture. Benjamin Forgey, architectural critic of *The Washington Post*, wrote of the Pulitzer Foundation that "it is almost dumbfounding in the

United States to find an art museum whose interiors possess both the austerity and serenity of a Zen garden."

Emily Rauh Pulitzer, the founder and president of the foundation, has said that the choice of Ando was purely aesthetic. Undoubtedly, other architects were considered, but no design competition was involved. The choice was who should be the architect; the design came later. Indeed, the site of the museum was not yet finalized when Ando was commissioned. (Incidentally, his building—despite being abstract and minimalist in appearance—responds to its urban context very well.) To a degree that is not well understood, remarkable architecture is almost always the result of a dialogue between architect and client. Cut loose from this sort of creative conversation, few architects do their best work. The British architect Sir Edwin Lutyens once said, "There will never be great architects or architecture without great patrons." The ideal project, from the architect's point of view, is not one with an absent magnanimous client; it is one with a *thoughtful* magnanimous client. In the Pulitzer Foundation, Ando not only had a thoughtful client; he also worked with Richard Serra and Ellsworth Kelly, two of the three artists whose works constitute the permanent collection of this tiny museum. "My goal was to take to the limit the relationship between the works of art and the volume of the building's space," the architect has said.

The Pulitzer Foundation for the Arts is a small building for a private client; obviously, it was not meant to attract a vast public. Yet it would be nice to think that it signals, if not an end, at least an alternative to the influence of Bilbao. The chief aim of architecture should not be to entertain, titillate, or shock. After the third example of swirling titanium and colliding prisms, the effect begins to wear thin. Le Corbusier understood this, which is why he never repeated the sculptural effects of Ronchamp. Once was enough. Of course, beauty, along with function and structure, has always been the concern of architects. But architectural beauty has a particular nature: calm and considered, standing slightly to one side of fast and furious fashion. After all, buildings are built for the ages. They are not one-night stands, like blockbuster movies—or blockbuster art shows. Art shows are eventually dismantled; buildings last for centuries. That's why architecture should be conservative in its instincts. The "wow factor" may excite the visiting tourist and the junketing journalist, but it is a shaky foundation on which to build lasting value. Great architecture carries many messages, about society as well as individuals, about our values and our dreams. It should have more to tell us than merely "Look at me."

My 2002 prediction that what came to be known as the Bilbao effect would wane was incorrect. Museums, opera houses, and libraries continue to hold high-profile competitions, and the show dogs dominate the architectural world more than ever.

When Buildings Try Too Hard

In a devastated real estate market, builders and developers are cling-
ing to an ambitious word with magical properties. In Tribeca, a
proposed fifty-six-story luxury residential tower, designed by the
Pritzker Prize–winning Swiss architects Jacques Herzog and Pierre
de Meuron, though as yet unbuilt, already claims to be "iconic." In
Brooklyn, a condominium high-rise with a textured facade of jagged, light- and dark-colored glass designed by SOM, the same
firm that designed Chicago's Sears Tower, promises "iconic design
within reach." A Seattle developer, taking no chances, has named
his forthcoming residential tower simply the Icon.

Apparently, everyone wants his building to be an icon, but it's
not that easy. Traditionally, a building is an icon when it is a popularly recognized symbol of something larger than itself—like the
White House, the Eiffel Tower, and the Empire State Building.
Architectural icons are generally anointed by the public, sometimes a long time after they are built. So why do developers think
that they can create instant icons? Frank Gehry and the Bilbao
Guggenheim, that's why. The Guggenheim Museum in Bilbao, an
industrial city in northern Spain, opened in 1997. Using innovative computer technology, Gehry designed and built a structure of
striking originality and formal inventiveness. The swirling shapes
covered in highly reflective titanium were astonishing, unlike any
other building that people had ever seen. Moreover, unlike most

avant-garde creations—one thinks of atonal music or Nouvelle Vague cinema—the Bilbao Guggenheim was *fun*.

The Bilbao museum is not the first modern architectural icon; it was preceded by the Sydney Opera House. Jørn Utzon's stunning waterside building, which reminds many people of sails or seashells, became an international sensation when it was completed in 1973. Gehry has been quoted as saying that his Basque clients wanted the Guggenheim "to do for Bilbao what the Sydney Opera House did for Australia." In fact, Gehry's museum succeeded so well at attracting visitors—millions of them—that the phenomenon of iconic architecture acting as a tourist draw became known as the Bilbao effect.

However you interpret Gehry's museum, as billowing sails, an extraterrestrial object, or a silver artichoke, it has unquestionably become an internationally recognized icon—for travel to Spain and for tourism generally. It is the built equivalent of Niagara Falls or the Grand Canyon: a place that you must visit at least once. That is the chief promise of the Bilbao effect, whether for a concert hall hoping to attract patrons, a downtown luring tourists and conventioneers, or a real estate developer looking to draw buyers: people will come.

Despite the success of the Bilbao Guggenheim, the Bilbao effect has not proved easy to replicate, not even for Frank Gehry. His Experience Music Project for Paul Allen, the Microsoft billionaire, was supposed to put Seattle on the architectural map. Despite its unusual architecture, consisting of colorful, rounded forms said to be inspired by electric guitars, the museum of rock music and Jimi Hendrix memorabilia has not proved to be a success. Attendance has been poor, and recently a part of the building was converted into a science fiction museum. The Massachusetts Institute of Technology, which had not built a significant modern building since Eero Saarinen's Kresge Auditorium, commissioned Gehry to add a landmark to its campus. The Stata Center is an eye-catching structure, all slipping and sliding shapes, but the intended iconic effect has been severely compromised by a public furor (and a lawsuit) over cost overruns and functional failings. Daniel Libeskind is another architect who, following his universally acclaimed Jewish Museum in Berlin, was considered to have the Midas touch when it came to iconic buildings. Yet his recent crystalline addition to the Denver Art Museum has failed to attract the expected number of visitors, and another crystalline—and slightly scary-looking—extension to the Royal Ontario Museum in Toronto has not exactly set the architectural world on fire. None of this bodes well for cities that are counting on instant icons to save them in a looming recession.

Perhaps the Bilbao effect should be called the Bilbao anomaly, for the iconic chemistry between the design of the building, its image, and the public turns out to be rather rare—and somewhat mysterious. Herzog & de Meuron's design for Beijing's Olympic stadium is ingenious, for example, but instead of the complex engineering it was the widely perceived image of a bird's nest (a nickname that did not originate with the architects) that cemented the building's international iconic status; the woven steel wrapper seemed to symbolize both China's ancient traditions and its rush to modernization. The so-called Water Cube, housing the Olympic pools, also became an instant hit, although, because the illuminated box is chiefly effective at night, it is something of a one-trick pony, and it will be interesting to see how long its iconic effect lasts. But for every Bird's Nest, there are scores of costly iconic failures, buildings that fail to spark the public's imagination. Of course, failed icons don't go away, which is a problem. Because the Bilbao effect teaches—I believe, mistakenly—that unconventional architecture is a prerequisite for iconic status, clients have encouraged their architects to go to greater and greater lengths to design buildings that are unusual, surprising, even shocking. But the shock will inevitably wear off, and a hundred years from now all those iconic wannabes will resemble a cross between a theme park and the Las Vegas strip.

Although the term "iconic" is increasingly used to mean simply prominent or attention-getting buildings, architectural icons embody specific messages. The White House, for example, symbolizes the office of the presidency, just as that other iconic big house, Buckingham Palace, represents the British monarchy. During the Cold War, the Kremlin, a walled citadel on the Moscow River, stood for the Soviet regime—and gave us "Kremlinology." Icons are not only national. Some, such as the Empire State Building and the Eiffel Tower, symbolize cities; "Black Rock," the spooky granite skyscraper in New York that is the headquarters of CBS, represents a corporation; so did the Chrysler Building and Lever House. Icons can have more than one meaning; the Washington Monument, for example, not only commemorates the first president but also symbolizes the capital city that bears his name and, because it's overlarge and self-confident, Americanness itself.

The Washington Monument is an obelisk, a traditional commemorative device that dates back to ancient Egypt, so we know it's a memorial, but the relationship between the form of an architectural icon and its meaning is not always direct. The fairy-tale onion domes of the Kremlin have always struck me as an odd symbol for a totalitarian regime. The Argentine presidential palace, the Casa Rosada, or Pink House, was given its color and its name by a nineteenth-century president, but some buildings have become icons by accident. Because the porous sandstone walls of what was originally known as the Executive Mansion in Washington, D.C., were painted with a protective coating of whitewash, people started calling it the White House. The name was formally adopted—by Theodore Roosevelt—only in 1901. The Pentagon got its nickname from its unusual five-sided plan that was the result of an awkward site; in another location, it might just as easily have been a square or a rectangle, and we would not have the delicious irony of the Department of Defense being symbolized by a secret cabalistic sign.

The famous clock tower of the Palace of Westminster, popularly known as Big Ben after its main bell, is a widely recognized symbol that also happens to be part of an important work of the British Gothic Revival. The White House, on the other hand, which was modeled on a Georgian mansion in Dublin, is handsome enough, but it breaks no new architectural ground. I've always liked the iconic Empire State Building, but it's a less interesting skyscraper than the rambunctious Chrysler or the soaring RCA Building at Rockefeller Center. As for the Pentagon, it has few architectural merits and is impressive chiefly for its great size—and, of course, its shape. The truth is that great icons don't have to be great architecture.

When the Museum of Modern Art in New York opened in 1939, Philip Goodwin and Edward Durell Stone's design, with its white walls, ribbon windows, and perforated roof canopy, was hailed as the fresh harbinger of the forward-looking International Style. Not quite an icon, perhaps, but definitely a portent of the future. Two years later, the National Gallery of Art in Washington, D.C., opened its doors. Its architect, John Russell Pope, had died a few years earlier, so he was spared the scorn and ridicule that modernist critics heaped on his neoclassical design. "The last of the Romans," they called him. Yet, sixty-seven years later, it is the restored facade of the Museum of Modern Art that looks quaint— nothing ages faster than today's idea of the future—while Pope's pile of Tennessee marble looks as grave and implacable as the year it was built.

Most people would call the National Gallery a "classic," referring not to its style but to its stylistic durability—that is, its quality of timelessness. Colleges and universities, in particular, are concerned with architectural longevity and with extending—not compromising—their built legacies. That was presumably why Yale picked Robert A. M. Stern to design two new residential colleges. Stern has built student residences at Columbia, Georgetown, and the Hotchkiss School, all in distinctly traditional styles. His dormitory at the Taft School, in Watertown, Connecticut, is part of a campus designed in the early twentieth century by Bertram Grosvenor Goodhue in the Arts and Crafts Gothic style and later added to by James Gamble Rogers, who built many of the Gothic Revival colleges at Yale. Stern's building at Taft, which exhibits his characteristic "hearty material physicality," in Vincent Scully's happy phrase, deploys a large-scale high-collegiate Gothic vocabulary of red brick, limestone trim, slate roofs, and leaded windows to great effect.

At Williams College, Boston-based William Rawn was commissioned to design a new center for theater and dance. While the architects of putative icons concentrate on exterior effects, Rawn was more circumspect. "We usually tell our clients that they can choose three or four special things to spend extra money on," he says. Following consultations with the college, these "special things" turned out to be the main performance space, a dramatic glass-enclosed dance studio, and a striking wood-lined lobby facing the town's main street. These highlights take their place in a nuanced composition of glass, brick, limestone, and wood that feels vaguely Scandinavian. While iconic buildings stand apart, the Williams theater and dance center is visually connected to its surroundings, contributing to a broader sense of place.

Another example of a building that responds to its setting is Toronto's new opera house, the Four Seasons Centre for the Performing Arts, designed by Diamond & Schmitt Architects. The traditional horseshoe-shaped auditorium is situated within an unprepossessing blue-black brick box whose chief feature is a glazed lobby facing one of the city's main streets, University Avenue:

dramatic, but hardly iconic. "It's easy to do an iconic building," says Jack Diamond, "because it's only solving one issue." The Four Seasons Centre addresses several issues: on the exterior, the building responds to a busy downtown site with transparency and openness; on the interior, it creates a multiuse lobby that includes an informal performance space and a remarkable all-glass stair; and in the two-thousand-seat hall, it provides intimacy, excellent sight lines, and exemplary acoustics. At $150 million, the cost of the Four Seasons Centre is relatively modest as opera houses go, but more important is how the money was spent—on the hall and the interiors rather than on exterior architectural effects. There is something very Canadian about this hardheaded reticence.

Buildings such as the Taft dormitory, the Williams College arts complex, and the Toronto opera house seek to fit in rather than stand out and to enhance rather than overwhelm their surroundings. While hardly shy, they don't stand there shouting, "Look at me!" Being in it for the long haul, they approach fashion gingerly, leaning to the conservative and well tried rather than the experimental. They are handsome, beautiful even, but they don't strive to knock your socks off. Anti-icons, you might call them. Or just good architecture.

The Unreal America

Ada Louise Huxtable is well-known to readers of *The New York Times* for her early advocacy of historic preservation. During the almost twenty years that she was the newspaper's architecture critic, she did as much as anyone to inform—and, I dare say, educate—the public about the necessity of preserving the rich architectural heritage of American cities. The Pulitzer Prize–winning journalist lost several famous battles, notably the fight to prevent the demolition of Manhattan's Pennsylvania Station, but there is no doubt that she was instrumental in winning the war.

Victory has left Huxtable dissatisfied, however. In *The Unreal America*, she takes historic preservation to task. Attempts to recreate the past, such as the renovation of the immigration halls at Ellis Island, strike her as overly sanitized. She is disturbed by the intrusion of commercialism into historic landmarks such as Boston's Faneuil Hall. Above all, she abhors the notion of authentic reproduction. "What the perfect fake or impeccable restoration lacks," she writes, "are the hallmarks of time and place. They deny imperfections, alterations, and accommodations; they wipe out all the incidents of life and change . . . they are hollow history."

Her concern with what she considers to be architectural pretense goes far beyond preservation, however. She visits Disneyland, the Mall of America, and Las Vegas and finds their celebration of make-believe symptomatic of a widespread condition. "Surrogate experience and surrogate environments have become the American way of life," she proclaims. "Distinctions are no longer made, or deemed necessary, between the real and the false; the edge usually goes to the latter, as an improved version with defects corrected—accessible and user-friendly—although the resonance of history and art in the authentic artifact is conspicuously lacking."

This gives a good idea of the style of this short book: assertive rather than reasoned, sweeping in its condemnations, and full of thinly veiled sarcasm. *The Unreal America* is based on a lecture delivered to the American Academy of Arts and Letters. It must have been a rousing evening, afire with righteous outrage and lectern-thumping wrath. But overheated rhetoric should not be pondered too closely. Read in the cold light of day, Huxtable's harangue wears thin. Reflecting on the above passage, for example, I thought to myself, What on earth is surrogate experience? Climbing a stair, watching someone climb a stair, and reading about someone climbing stairs are certainly different—but all are experiences. And what is wrong, after all, with correcting defects? Are accessibility and user-friendliness really that bad? Finally, what is the relationship between art and authenticity; something can be historically authentic, but, forgeries aside, what does artistic authenticity signify?

Artistic authenticity is never defined, for this is a poorly argued book. It brims with inconsistencies. On one page, the author claims that it is not her intention to prove anything right or wrong; on another, she does exactly that. She characterizes the union of culture and consumerism as uniquely American—as if the French had not invented the department store in the nineteenth century and the *hypermarché* in the twentieth. She maintains that she only writes about buildings she has personally visited but includes an extended discussion of the new Disney community of Celebration that appears to be based entirely on promotional brochures.

Huxtable's polemic leans heavily on the writing of European intellectuals such as Umberto Eco, André Corboz, and Jean

Baudrillard. They provide a shaky support, consisting chiefly of academic jargon: "surrogate experience," "artificial environments," and "simulacra." Such pseudoscientific terms are intended to lend credence to a thesis that is, at its core, unconvincing. It presumes that the public—except you, wise reader—cannot tell the difference between what is real and what is not, that we live in a sort of perpetual haze. It strikes me that the people watching the erupting lava outside the Mirage in Las Vegas don't mistake this for a real volcano, any more than the people sitting on the steps of the New York Public Library would mistake the stone sculptures for real lions. The visitors to Sleeping Beauty Castle in Disneyland know that they are in Anaheim and not the Black Forest, just as the commuters who used to hurry across the neoclassical concourse of the old Pennsylvania Station knew that they were in Manhattan and not in ancient Rome.

Make-believe has always played a role in our surroundings, and the relationship between reality and illusion has always been blurred; Pennsylvania Station was simultaneously a surrogate Baths of Caracalla *and* a real place. Such ambiguities do not faze Huxtable, however. She is more interested in using words such as "unreal" and "nostalgic" to depreciate architects whose work she dislikes. These include Jon Jerde, the designer of the Mall of America; the neo-traditional town planners Andrés Duany and Elizabeth Plater-Zyberk; the postmodernists Michael Graves and Robert A. M. Stern; and anyone who has had anything to do with Prince Charles.

Graves and Stern, in particular, are castigated for the hotels that they have designed for Walt Disney World and Disneyland Paris. Indeed, the Disney Company is the Great Satan of this jeremiad. The author refers darkly to the "Disneyfication of architecture." This sounds ominous, but exactly what does it mean? Shouldn't an architect designing a resort hotel incorporate make-believe? Shouldn't amusement parks be frivolous? Leisure and

fantasy have often gone hand in hand. When the Georgian architect John Nash was commissioned by the Prince of Wales to design the Royal Pavilion at Brighton, he concocted a gaudy Hindu
palace, not one of his normally sedate classical designs. Is it Disneyfication when the Disney Company hires critically acclaimed architects such as Frank Gehry, Arata Isozaki, and Aldo Rossi to
design its office buildings? Apparently not, because these are three
designers whom the author admires.

The final chapter of *The Unreal America* describes the work of
Gehry, Isozaki, Rossi, and a number of other architects practicing
what the author calls "the new architecture . . . the best-kept secret
in the arts." This is a curious claim. Several of these architects—the
late James Stirling, Fumihiko Maki, Álvaro Siza, and Christian
de Portzamparc, as well as Rossi and Gehry—are the recipients
of the highly publicized Pritzker Architecture Prize (on whose
jury Huxtable sits). Most have received prestigious commissions
such as institutional buildings and art museums. Museums, particularly, are very much in evidence; apparently, the "new architects"
don't concern themselves with anything as mundane as shopping
malls or resort hotels. What these architects do generally share is a
commitment to architecture that is abstract, fashionably minimalist,
austere, and undecorated. Judging from this assortment, with the
exception of the buildings of the effervescent Gehry, artistic authenticity is not much fun.

The author remains an unrepentant modernist. "I cannot think
of anything more ludicrous than the idea that modernism somehow got off the track and was a monstrous mistake that should
simply be canceled out," she writes. "Revolutions in life and technology can never be reversed." But if the late twentieth century
has taught us anything, it is precisely that revolutions *can* be reversed, as they have been in the Soviet Union, in central Europe,
and in large part in China. And, sadly, monstrous architectural
mistakes *were* made in the name of revolution. In that regard,

historic preservation is clearly reactionary. It reflects the public's intense skepticism of the architectural avant-garde whose misbegotten theories were responsible, in part, for the devastation wrought on American cities in the name of urban renewal. Many of the inhumane public housing projects of that era are now being demolished. Would that we could as easily remove the overblown performing arts complexes (Lincoln Center), the unpleasant civic centers (Boston City Hall), and the dysfunctional civic spaces (Philadelphia's Independence Mall).*

The historian Vincent Scully called historic preservation "the single most significant architectural movement of the past twenty years." It is part of a general fascination with the past that is also reflected in publishing, television, and films. But it is also evidence of a broad change in the consciousness of the American public. We have discovered that old buildings and old neighborhoods—like old music—are not merely of antiquarian interest; they are a continued source of pleasure. Is this nostalgia? Of course it is. For the moment, we have had it with novelty and experimentation. We miss the easy familiarity with buildings and urban places that our forefathers took for granted. And, Ada Louise Huxtable's protestations notwithstanding, we will have it back.

In hindsight, I was perhaps a little hard on The Unreal America, *which was, after all, based on a lecture. But the author's rhetorical pronouncements and disdainful judgments called for a response.*

---

*Between 1998 and 2004, Independence Mall was rebuilt according to a different design.

The Story King

The new parking structure at Disneyland in Anaheim, California, holds ten thousand cars. It must be one of the largest garages in the world; it is certainly one of the handsomest. Harry Wolf's stylish design is light, white—and serious. Except for the discreet drawings of Minnie Mouse, Goofy, and the like that identify each of the six parking levels, cartoon characters are nowhere in evidence: no jokes, no wizard hats, no mouse ears.

Perhaps sensing an unspoken question, my guide, Timur Galen of Walt Disney Imagineering, explains. "Mickey lives over there," he says, pointing to the spires of Sleeping Beauty Castle visible in the distance. "He doesn't come out this far." We are on a long escalator leading from the second level down to the ground. The shading roof above is a cocoon of fabric stretched on a lightweight steel frame. "This building is about structure, movement, and concrete," says Galen. "It's architecture. Over there it's not architecture. It's scenography."

"Over there" is the Imagineers' latest project, a major expansion to Disneyland. Galen, who is the general manager of the work and has taken time off from what he calls the "death march to the opening" to talk to me about the planning of the five-year, $1.4 billion project, emphasizes that this is not a simple undertaking. What started as a bermed theme park surrounded by parking lots has been turned into a full-fledged resort. The exercise in complex urban design involves major infrastructure improvements in collaboration with city, county, and state agencies: adding new ramps to I-5, depressing a city street, improving surrounding city streets, and replacing parking lots with the titanic parking structure. In addition, Disney has built a brand-new theme park called the Disney California Adventure, created a thirty-thousand-square-foot entertainment and shopping district, refurbished two existing hotels, and added a 750-room hotel and conference center.

The Grand Californian Hotel is the work of Peter Dominick of the Urban Design Group of Denver, who designed Wilderness Lodge for Disney in Orlando, Florida. Because the Grand Californian is in effect inside the new theme park (a first for Disney), it was imperative that the building complement the California theme. The roadside googie architecture of L.A. excepted, there are only two widely recognized native California architectural styles: Spanish Colonial Revival and Arts and Crafts. Disney chose the latter. Dominick created a pleasantly old-fashioned hotel with low, spreading wings, skillfully weaving together elements from several related architectural traditions: Bay Area Shingle Style, Maybeck, early Wright, and even hints of such British Free Style designers as Voysey and Mackintosh. The chief inspiration, however, was the work of Greene & Greene, whose famous Gamble House is in nearby Pasadena. The architecture of the Grand Californian is fussy and obsessive—even the room numbers are boxed in perfect little crafted frames. But then I tend to find the work of Greene & Greene fastidiously over-detailed, so the fussiness is really a measure of the hotel's stylistic finesse.

The soaring lobby is a dramatic space, reminiscent of the great national park hotels of the early twentieth century, but with polished finishes, fine woods, and articulated details. The line between architecture and scenography is sometimes blurred. For example, the complicated timber beams and the massive boulders are faux, and while the furniture recalls Stickley, it is mass-produced in factories. On the other hand, much of the ironwork, pottery, and stained glass is the work of contemporary American craftsmen, the carpets incorporate real William Morris patterns, and exquisite cabinetry abounds.

I stayed in the hotel the first day it officially opened, and dozens of young men and women were prowling the corridors, clipboards in hand, ticking off checklists, making sure that everything was *perfect*. It was, but that brings up my only reservation about this beautiful building: the Arts and Crafts movement was not chiefly about perfection. What the hotel lacks is the sense of conviction that is visible in Mackintosh's disciplined interiors or in the young Wright's devotion to craft. Those architects sought beauty, but they also wanted to challenge prevailing taste by proposing a way of living that was simpler and more natural. The Grand Californian does not challenge but seeks only to please, which makes it an admirable hotel but not exceptional architecture.

My room overlooked Downtown Disney, a collection of restaurants, music clubs, shops, and cinemas. This area is immediately adjacent to the theme parks and is open to the public; indeed, it is intended to be a nighttime destination for Anaheim residents, as well as an amenity for Disney guests and conventioneers. I walked down the rambling promenade one evening. Though not yet officially open, the place was already crowded, lines forming outside Ralph Brennan's Jazz Kitchen and couples strolling among the fountains and attractive ficus trees, overlooked by rooftop restaurant terraces. Downtown Disney is an eclectic mix of architectural styles. Arts and Crafts next to—and under—the hotel; slightly farther away, Art Deco. Many buildings are distinctly scenographic: the balconied Jazz Kitchen looks like something from New Orleans, a flamboyant Cuban nightclub is a Miami transplant, and Rainforest Cafe resembles a Mayan temple. On the other hand, ESPN Zone, the multiplex, and a monorail station are abstract contemporary designs, more in the architecture category.

This eclectic mix of buildings is loosely arranged along a land-scaped pedestrian promenade in an informal but highly considered manner. I had expected a tightly themed version of Main Street, a staple of many Disney parks. "This is not a shopping mall, nor is it like the downtown of Celebration," says Jaquelin T. Robertson, who was a consultant on the project. Robertson encouraged Michael Eisner, Disney's CEO, to go to Copenhagen and visit the Tivoli Gardens. Tivoli's magical combination of fountains, lights, and landscaping became the chief inspiration for Downtown Disney's twinkling, garden-esque atmosphere.

The promenade ends in a large plaza outside the entrances to the theme parks. I spent an afternoon walking around the fifty-five-acre site of the Disney California Adventure accompanied by Barry Braverman, the leader of the creative team for the park, and a group of his colleagues—an architect, a landscape architect, and two art directors. Walt Disney Imagineering has a staff of two thousand and designs or oversees the design of theme parks, resorts, hotels, stores, ships, and office buildings—"everything that isn't movies," according to Braverman.

I had never been in a Disney park before, and I was impressed. While architects often talk about creating "environments," we are mainly interested in making buildings. Not so here—every de-tail of the surroundings is designed, including sounds and smells. Braverman points out the reddish tinge to the asphalt road that leads us through an area called High Sierras, the result of an ag-gregate that is characteristic of that mountainous region. The landscaping, carefully chosen to survive Southern California's dry heat, completes the illusion. We traverse seamlessly to Cannery Row, a funky group of waterside sheds. The water level in the pu-tative tidal canal, which functions as the overflow reservoir for a nearby water ride, rises and falls realistically. On to Paradise Pier, a re-creation of a Southern California seaside amusement park, where the booming surf crashes against the pilings, thanks to a hidden wave machine.

The premise of this park is as convoluted as a Ray Bradbury novel. It is about California, of course, but past and present bear upon each other in complicated ways. The buildings of Pacific Wharf, for example, appear to be rehabilitated fish canneries, in one case housing a working sourdough bread bakery, in another, a tortilla factory. Elsewhere, a "street" of fake facades turns out to be really fake because it is intended to recall a disused set in a Hollywood movie back lot. A restaurant located inside a television shooting stage incorporates settings that a devoted viewer of daytime soap operas would recognize, or so Braverman assures me. Aerospace, an important industry in California, is commemorated by Condor Flats, an "abandoned" airstrip whose buildings appear to have been converted to contemporary uses. The Taste Pilots' Grill, for example, is shoehorned into a jet-engine testing workshop, with Chuck Yeager's Bell X-1 suspended over the entrance; elsewhere, the restrooms are in a pilots' shack; and a ride called Soarin' over California is housed in what appears to be an old hangar. Braverman insists that we go in. I generally avoid amusement park rides, but this one, thanks to a Disney-developed cinematic projection process called Omnimax, is truly breathtaking.

Jean Baudrillard once visited Disney World and wrote archly about "simulacra" and "hyper-reality." What would he make of this park? It is both about California and in California, it refers to the past yet is about today, it contains a portion of real vineyard and a real bakery next to a fake oceanfront and a simulated—but geologically accurate—mountain. It would all be grist for Baudrillard's intellectual mill, no doubt, but I imagine that the public, used to flipping TV channels and surfing the Internet, will love it— all of it, the fake, the real, the half fake, the half real, and everything in between.

As Galen emphasized, the buildings in a theme park are sceno-graphic. That does not make them any less real: there is a techno-logically sophisticated three-thousand-seat Broadway-style theater on the Hollywood back lot whose handsome interior was designed by Hardy Holzman Pfeiffer. But scenographic buildings have a different relationship to reality. Architecture is about itself—or, in the case of so-called signature buildings, about its maker. A build-ing in a theme park is always subservient to the Story. Talking with the Imagineers, I learned that storytelling is at the heart of the Disney corporate culture, no doubt the result of roots in ani-mated films such as *Fantasia* and *Snow White and the Seven Dwarfs*. Everything begins with a storyboard. When I asked Braverman about the function of stories in his project, he insisted that they are primarily a creative tool, a technique for coordinating the work of hundreds of designers and technicians and ensuring that everyone involved grasps the underlying premise. He assured me that it was not important for the public to follow the plot. However, as we talked, it became clear that the stories *are* meaningful. Not that all parkgoers experience these stories the same way—how many people will recognize the reddish asphalt, for example? Probably no more than will identify the smell of wine must in the Robert Mondavi film theater. What storytelling does is provide the park experience with greater depth, allowing a variety of perceptions on the part of the visitor, deep as well as shallow.

Storytelling is not entirely foreign to architecture, of course. Ever since the Renaissance, classicism has told and retold the myths of antiquity. Gothic Revival buildings, whether they are churches or college dorms, recount tales of medieval abbeys and cathedrals. Both offer the opportunity to read the story in the de-tails as well as in the whole. Indeed, the experience of a classical or Gothic Revival building is vastly enriched by being both literary *and* architectural. Even early modernism contained a narrative— of ocean liners, fresh air, and technology—although the heroic harbingers of the new machine age hardly saw themselves as story-tellers. But then they never went soarin' over California.

Soarin' over California simulates a five-minute hang-glider flight over the Golden State, complete with motion, dangling feet, breezes in your face, and the smells of sagebrush, orange groves, and ocean mist. I can only imagine what Baudrillard would have made of it. I loved it.

A Good Public Building

The 1970s and 1980s were the decades of building museums. The international boom is easy to understand: the public's interest in art was fueled by blockbuster exhibitions, the well-publicized extravagances of the art market, public-television programs, including Kenneth Clark's *Civilisation* and Robert Hughes's *Shock of the New*, and the museums themselves. It appears that the 1990s are going to see another boom in cultural building—one that is less predictable. Not new museums—new public libraries.

Los Angeles is currently spending more than $250 million to renew and expand its public library, and San Francisco is building a new 377,000-square-foot main public library. Denver recently held an architectural competition, won by Michael Graves, for a $65 million central library, and San Antonio is undertaking a similar project. Even Las Vegas, not known as a book town, has built a new public library, designed by that southwestern firebrand Antoine Predock. In Canada, Vancouver has chosen Moshe Safdie as the architect of its new public library. The French have begun work on an immense new national library, which Parisian wags have already christened the TGB, for *très grande bibliothèque*—a pun on TGV, the high-speed train. The portentous composition of four glass towers has become the focus of public controversy because the books are exposed to light and the public reading rooms are in the basement.

Chicago has also built itself a new public library. Some library! The Harold Washington Library Center, which opened to the public on October 7, 1991, is the largest municipal library in the country, and the second-largest public library in the world, after the British Library, in London. The $144 million, 756,000-square-foot building occupies a full city block on State Street in the South Loop. Perhaps "possesses" would be a better word, because the sturdy ten-story monolith lays claim to its place in this city of famous architecture in such a forceful manner that it already looks as if it had been there forever.

No doubt this impression is exactly what the architect intended. "It's a building of memories," Thomas Beeby of Hammond, Beeby & Babka told the *Chicago Sun-Times*. Beeby, who headed the design team, is a native-born Chicagoan, and his fellow citizens will easily recognize in the library bits and pieces of many of their favorite Chicago buildings. The cyclopean granite base is an obvious reference to the Rookery Building, designed by Burnham & Root and completed in 1888. The thick brick walls recall the same firm's massive Monadnock Building of 1893, which stands just around the corner. The arched entrances repeat those of Adler & Sullivan's 1889 Auditorium Building. The huge pediments on the roof and the composition of the main facade are derived from the classical front of the Art Institute, a Beaux Arts landmark on Michigan Avenue designed by the Boston firm of Shepley, Rutan & Coolidge. And some of the metal ornament is based on the same botanical forms that inspired Louis Sullivan's exuberant Carson Pirie Scott Store. Although most of the references are to nineteenth-century buildings, the back of the library—and its steel-and-glass curtain wall—is a nod to Chicago's modernist Miesian tradition.

This makes the library sound like a collage. But this is not one of those buildings that deconstruct the architectural past in order to reassemble it in some bizarre, skewed fashion that delights the architecture critics and confuses everyone else. Nor is it, like

Robert Venturi and Denise Scott Brown's recent addition to the
National Gallery in London, a clever, tongue-in-cheek rendition
of a classical building. Beeby and his colleagues take their classicism seriously. Their use of traditional elements avoids the shallowness of much postmodern architecture, because instead of
merely aping the classical style or, worse still, parodying it, they
are attempting to revive a classical attitude. If this sober and rugged building looks old-fashioned, it is because its designers are
concerned with old-fashioned architectural virtues: civility, clarity, utility, and beauty.

The new library has no windswept plaza with a forlorn Calder or
Henry Moore sculpture, no dried-up reflecting pools, no concrete
planters with dying evergreens and paper litter. The building
springs straight up from the sidewalk just as all downtown American buildings used to do, before architects adopted the building-
in-a-plaza approach. The Harold Washington Library reaffirms
the older tradition, and it's a reminder that cities are made up first
of all of streets and that the prime function of urban buildings is to
define these streets.

The exterior of the library, like that of all well-designed buildings, conveys several messages. Its heavy walls proclaim solidity
and permanence. The monumental scale suggests a civic building
of some importance. The different materials—metal and glass on
top, brick for the main body, and stone at the base—are not arbi-
trary choices but express the need to support heavier and heavier
loads. The tripartite organization also reflects what is going on inside: the base houses special facilities (lobby, bookstore, film and
video center, a children's library), the brick body contains six floors
of book stacks, and the top houses special public rooms and the
administrative offices.

If the interior of this mammoth building feels familiar and

unintimidating, that is probably because it resembles a traditional department store, with social sciences on one floor, literature on another. As in a department store, the public is transported from floor to floor by escalators as well as elevators. Each of the library floors consists of book stacks among which the public can freely browse. There are plenty of reading tables and, along one side, a series of intimate alcoves that resemble the carrels found in university libraries. The Chicago library incorporates a wealth of technical gadgetry, including an electronic directory system that displays floor layouts, book locations, and information on special events such as readings and lectures; a computerized reference system; and banks of freely accessible computers and printers.

The main lobby is a bland, characterless space that is a letdown after the robust exterior. Its focus is an art installation by Houston Conwill that incorporates text from Mayor Harold Washington's speeches, but the intent of the art, which conveys neither wisdom nor joy, remains obscure. The winter garden, however, a glass-roofed space at the top of the building, is spectacular. Perhaps too spectacular. What was intended to be a public room furnished with benches and trees remains largely empty; it appears to have been co-opted by the city administration for civic galas and is also being rented out for private social events. Too bad.

A great deal of credit goes to a municipal administration that insisted on high-quality construction, inside and out, figuring that flimsy materials would only increase maintenance costs later. The Napoleon red granite of the base looks thick because it is thick; the entrance doors are bronze; the interior walls are hand-plastered metal lath, not wallboard; and the old-fashioned, comfortable courthouse chairs in the reading areas are maple. Parenthetically, the solid craftsmanship was realized concurrently with the most modern of construction techniques: "design-build." In design-build, a developer, a contractor, and an architect form a team that undertakes to design and build a project within a fixed period of time and within a fixed budget—no cost overruns. In the case of the Chicago library, the building was built within the budget and delivered only one month late.

In his recent book *Architecture: The Natural and the Manmade*, the historian Vincent Scully repeats the old architectural adage that "one should decorate construction, never build decoration." Scully is referring to the use of decoration to give character to buildings, contrasting this with striving for individuality by making the shape of each building different. It's not surprising to learn that Scully was on the jury for the 1987 architectural competition that chose the Hammond, Beeby & Babka design. The building is a large box that derives its architectural character from the use of applied decoration.

The library is the first large American public building since the 1930s to incorporate figurative ornament. There are cast-stone festoons between the windows and medallions with puff-cheeked faces, drolly personifying the Windy City. Window spandrels are decorated with sheaves of cornstalks that terminate in a head of Ceres, the Roman goddess of agriculture, and a ribbon with Chicago's motto, "Urbs in Horto" (City in a Garden). The most dramatic ornaments were designed by Raymond Kaskey for the perimeter of the roof. Huge cast-aluminum barn owls, backed by spreading palm leaves, appear at the corners of the building, and the center of the main facade, on State Street, is marked by a huge horned owl, wings spread, clutching a book.

"Classicism is an architectural language that is highly developed and understood by most people," Thomas Beeby says. But do the sweatshirted and baseball-capped teenagers who use the library know who Ceres was? Can they read Latin? Do they know that owls are symbols of wisdom? Probably not. And they won't know that the chain-patterned band of cast stone that surrounds the building's base is called a guilloche or that the frieze along the pediments represents swords and shields. That will not necessarily stop them from deriving pleasure from the decorative shapes, the puff-cheeked faces, and the wise owls. In any case, the function of architectural ornament is not only symbolic. Ornament provides buildings with scale, or rather with many scales. Modernist buildings without decoration can be handsome structures, like Mies van der Rohe's Seagram Building or Louis Kahn's Salk Institute, and can make their powerful presence felt at a distance. But what happens when one approaches? Nothing. There is no finer grain, no detail, except perhaps a neoprene window gasket or a bolt head. Seen close up, the abstract shapes of the bronze mullions and flat concrete surfaces are one-dimensional, dull, uninteresting.

In 1982, Michael Graves built the Portland Building, a municipal office building in Portland, Oregon; it was the first large public building by a postmodern architect. After the Portland Building, critics of postmodernism, of whom there were many, could no longer dismiss it as a fringe movement; it had joined the mainstream. Will the Chicago library, a more accomplished piece of design and a more prominent building, do the same for modern classicism? That is unlikely. The spread of postmodernism in the 1980s, like deconstructivism today, was driven by architectural magazines, museum exhibitions, and schools of architecture, none of which appear to be interested in classicism. Although *Progressive Architecture* magazine did single out the design of the library for a citation in its 1989 awards for excellence, since then no classical work has been so honored. And students in schools of architecture (with the sole exception of a fledgling program at the University of Notre Dame) are not being taught the classical vocabulary but being encouraged to find their own personal languages of architectural expression.

Beeby has stubbornly refused to develop a personal style and has preferred to adapt his buildings to their contexts. Several years ago, he built a children's camp in Connecticut for Paul Newman and took his cue from the rugged log-cabin vernacular of the Adirondack camp. A ranch house he recently designed outside Santa Fe, New Mexico, is built in adobe. And in London, Beeby is part of an Anglo-American team that is replanning and rebuilding Paternoster Square, a seven-acre area around St. Paul's Cathedral, in conformity with its original Georgian roots.

It's unlikely that there will ever be a recognizable Beeby style, just as there was no Thomas Hastings style, to name an accomplished classical architect of the turn of the century. With John Carrère, Hastings built Spanish Revival hotels in St. Augustine, Florida; French-classical stately houses on Long Island and in the Berkshires; and—their masterwork—the New York Public Library, a building as ambitious, grand, and technologically advanced in its day as the Harold Washington Library Center is in ours.

New York built its public library almost a hundred years ago, and to some people the idea of building a large downtown library might seem an anachronism. They would argue that the grand public library, like the majestic railroad terminal or the opulent city hall, is a relic of the nineteenth century; surely the money would be better spent on strengthening branch libraries, on developing outreach programs, on promoting literacy, and on purchasing books and periodicals. This position is bolstered by the fact that technology has in great part done away with the need for central libraries. The banking machine has replaced the stately bank, so why shouldn't a computer terminal, which could be anywhere—in the office, at school, at home, or even in one's car—replace the grand public library?

Decentralization may yet come, but although we need reading programs, and neighborhood libraries, and books, we need civic

monuments, too. Civic monuments enshrine values that we hold
dear, and publicly proclaim these values to us and to our children.
It is surely no coincidence that the boom in building public libraries coincides with a serious public effort to combat illiteracy and to
promote reading. "I do think that the library stands as a symbol
that the life of the mind is still vital," says John B. Duff, the com-
missioner of the Chicago Public Library. Just so.

I spent several hours in the Harold Washington Library Center.
The atmosphere was different from that in other public buildings.
Unlike a museum, it had no price of admission, and the security
guards were unobtrusive; the stacks were open, and the books were
there to be picked up and leafed through. There was also a more
mixed crowd than one finds in a museum or a concert hall: groups of
teenagers, elderly men and women, college students, street people.
In a period when even art museums are beginning to resemble
shopping malls, this library stands apart. It didn't make me feel
like a consumer, or a spectator, or an onlooker; it made me feel like
a citizen.

Most striking of all, the library makes not the slightest effort
to entertain the people who use it. Too many of our public places
(shopping malls, airports) are either selling us something or attempting to keep us amused. The Chicago library takes itself, and its
users, seriously, and through an architecture that is calm and measured, it resolutely communicates this sense of purpose: that books
and reading and knowledge are important.

*I was correct to observe that Beeby's library did not signal a new classi-
cal revival; on the other hand, it was not a flash in the pan. In 2003,
the Richard H. Driehaus Prize in classical and traditional architecture
was established at the University of Notre Dame. The subsequent decade has seen significant classical public buildings such as Robert A. M.*

Stern's Nashville Public Library, David Schwarz's Schermerhorn Symphony Center in the same city, and Beeby's own Federal Building and Courthouse in Tuscaloosa. Classical, or at least traditional, buildings have also appeared on campuses, at Harvard, Brown, Princeton, Penn, Rice, and Yale.

A Blight at the Opera

The most talked-about Canadian work of architecture of the last decade is located not in Canada but in France: the new Opéra Bastille in Paris, designed by the Toronto architect Carlos Ott. From the beginning, the Opéra Bastille was the subject of lively controversy. For one thing, critics were skeptical about the whole idea of a new opera house because Paris already had two venues for lyric performances, the Opéra Comique and the famous Paris Opera, also known as the Palais Garnier. The Garnier, an 1875 Second Empire building, does have some technical drawbacks, but it is widely admired and loved. There were also those who maintained that the new opera had been built in the wrong place, that it should have been located where Pierre Boulez wanted, as part of the new music complex at La Villette, rather than being shoehorned into the cramped and awkward site of an old railway station in a working-class district, beside the Place de la Bastille.

However, other than town-planning considerations had led to locating the new opera on this historic spot that every year is the site of a popular street festival. When the idea of building a new opera house had been proposed to the government in 1981, it was argued that the Palais Garnier was an old-fashioned, elitist institution and that there was a need for a more progressive *opéra populaire*, hence the symbolic (cynics would say public-relations) import of the Bastille site.

The idea of a people's opera probably appealed intellectually to the socialist president Mitterrand, even though he is not known to be an opera lover, but the concept is a mushy one. It's true that French opera could do with a boost—it does not currently rank high with the French public—and since 1945 the Paris Opera has slipped from the first rank to mediocrity. But would a new hall really make a difference? Wouldn't that be like trying to save a corporation from bankruptcy by building a new headquarters? And just because the Palais Garnier has chandeliers and gilt, does that really make it elitist? After all, in Italy, where opera has a mass following, it's presented in neoclassical buildings like Milan's La Scala, which was inaugurated in 1778, or Venice's La Fenice, which opened in 1792. In any case, judging from the international celebrity of star opera singers like Beverly Sills and Luciano Pavarotti and the prominence of opera on public television, opera—that is to say, classical opera—is arguably the most popular of the fine arts. This raises another contradiction: the proponents of a "people's opera" have argued that it would present a more modern repertoire and would not rely on the international star system, yet it's precisely the nineteenth-century operas and the superstars that the general public desires.

If Parisians were lukewarm to the Opéra Bastille, it might also have been because of a growing sense of exasperation. It was not merely a question of the building's cost, which the government now admits was not $540 million but at least $775 million. The Opéra Bastille was ill-starred from the start. In 1984, for two months, Jacques Chirac, the right-wing mayor of the city of Paris, refused to grant a building permit for the left-wing president's new opera house. In 1985, the newly appointed artistic director, Jean-Pierre Brossmann, resigned, apparently unwilling to bend to one of the exigencies of a people's opera—fewer rehearsals and more performances. In July 1986, the building site was shut down completely for two weeks; political wrangling had broken out again between Chirac, newly elected as prime minister, and Mitterrand, and it threatened to scuttle the opera completely. In 1988, Mitterrand won a second term as president, the socialists were returned to power, and a plan to build a reduced version of the Opéra was revived—it remained to complete the building for its opening on Bastille Day, July 14, 1989, the bicentennial of the French Revolution. Then, in January 1989, the Israeli conductor Daniel Barenboim, who had been named artistic director only two years before, was abruptly fired; his programming ideas had been judged too "elitist" (Barenboim had proposed Mozart!). His dismissal caused an international stir: prominent conductors such as Herbert von Karajan, Zubin Mehta, and Sir Georg Solti said that they would have to reconsider their association with the Paris Opera; Pierre Boulez, the director Patrice Chéreau, and the singer Jessye Norman (who was to sing at the inaugural) all resigned in protest. "What's the difference between the *Titanic* and the Opéra Bastille?" went a Parisian joke. "The *Titanic* had an orchestra."

Well, the Opéra didn't sink, and it did acquire a new conductor, albeit not a famous one: Myung-Whun Chung, a young Korean-American previously best known as the younger brother of the violinist Kyung-Wha Chung. But Parisians were still not satisfied. I had the feeling that what most disturbed the people I talked with about the new opera house was the architecture itself. On this there was general agreement: the Opéra Bastille was too big for its site, it was an awkward composition, it lacked style and grace (*Le Monde* had called it "a rhinoceros in a bathtub"), it was, in a word, *moche*—ugly.

I went to see for myself. There is no question that the site chosen for the new opera is too small. The Place de la Bastille, a historic spot but not a very attractive urban space, lies between the Marais, a seventeenth-century quartier that has recently been restored,

and the twelfth arrondissement, a gritty working-class neighborhood. The massive Opéra in this residential landscape resembles a
beached supertanker. The chief feature of the main facade facing
the Place de la Bastille is a colossal curved wall, partly of glass and
partly of stainless steel panels. The main entrance is located in the
middle of this wall and is approached by a large exterior staircase.
The staircase, as well as a forbidding square arch sheathed in black
granite, is slightly askew to take into account the commemorative
Colonne de Juillet in the center of the circular Place de la Bastille.
(The column commemorates the Parisians who fell in the popular
uprising of July 1830, which led to the downfall of Charles X, not
the destruction of the notorious prison, which occurred in July
1789.) From the Place, the building stretches back along the rue de
Lyon for more than two hundred meters, an undistinguished collage
of columns, office-building-type glazing, and blank walls, interrupted by a curved volume that marks an experimental performance
space that is as yet unfinished.

So tight is the site that there is no space from which the new
building can be seen to advantage, except perhaps from the base of
the column, were one courageous enough to brave the hazardous
traffic. To make matters worse, the main facade of the Opéra is
partially obscured by a small, undistinguished building housing a
brasserie. At the time of construction, historians believed that
a nineteenth-century building on this site had originally been a
seventeenth-century neighbor of the Bastille prison. This turned
out not to be the case, but by then the building had been torn down,
so a replica, based on an old engraving, was built in its place.

What about the architecture of the Opéra? Carlos Ott has described it as "a functional project which is not essentially aesthetic." Indeed, as much as such a thing is possible, Ott has reduced
the aesthetic experience to a minimum. This is a building in which
everything that is not granite is stainless steel, everything that
is not white is black, and everything, absolutely everything, is

obsessively arranged according to a square grid—the window mullions, the seams of the granite slabs and the stainless steel panels, the joints of the paving, even the supports of the railings. The same graph-paper motif and the same palette, if one can call it that, are continued in the interior.

The lobbies are located immediately behind the curved glass wall and take advantage of the view in a manner common to many modern concert halls like Place des Arts in Montreal and Roy Thomson Hall in Toronto. But neither of these buildings enjoys much of a view. At night, the homely Place de la Bastille achieves a magical quality with its spotlit column topped by a gilt Hermes, and Ott's chief architectural conceit becomes apparent: to establish a dialogue between the building and the square by emphasizing the transparency of this huge building. I hadn't much liked the Opéra during the day, but nighttime improved it; if not magical like the Place, it at least managed to appear dramatic.

The heart of an opera house, at least for the audience, is the hall itself. The greatest constraint on the design of any performance space is its size: the greater the number of seats, the more difficult it is to achieve visual and acoustic intimacy. Some postwar opera houses, like Berlin's Deutsche Oper, which was built in 1961, have limited their capacity to fewer than two thousand seats, which happens to be about the size of La Scala (2,015) and the Palais Garnier (1,991). At the other end of the scale are enormous modern halls like New York's Metropolitan Opera, which can accommodate 3,800 persons. At 2,700 seats, the Opéra Bastille steers a middle course. Although there are several tiers of loges, the layout, unlike the horseshoe-shaped La Scala or the Palais Garnier, is predominantly frontal, with two steep balconies.

I attended a performance of Arthur Honegger's dramatic oratorio *Joan of Arc at the Stake*, a moving if necessarily lugubrious work, whose gloomy atmosphere was heightened by the sight of drably attired actors and singers slogging across a stage that was

covered ankle-deep in what appeared to be mud. The music, however, was glorious, and with an expanded orchestra and an eighty-
five-voice choir it easily filled the cavernous space. From the first
balcony, where I was sitting, the stage was far away, but the sound
was good, at least to my amateurish ears. (I have been told that
there are some acoustical blind spots among the front rows in the
orchestra.) I asked Arthur Kaptainis, the music critic of the Montreal *Gazette*, what he thought of the acoustics. "The Opéra Bastille
has what you could call a modern sound: clear but not especially
resonant," he said. "I thought that the sound lacked warmth," he
added, "but perhaps that's a psychological reaction."

What Kaptainis was referring to is the cool decor: the walls
covered in gray granite and black wood, an undulating ceiling of
white glass, and seats upholstered in black fabric. It's true that
decor matters little when the lights are out, but an opera house
should not merely function as a background to the spectacle; it
should create an atmosphere of anticipation. To say that "the place
looks like a gymnasium," as the soprano June Anderson remarked
after singing at the opening, is perhaps ungenerous, but the interior of the Opéra is distinctly impersonal—imperturbable and
sleek in a corporate-boardroom sort of way, which perhaps reflects
the architect's previous experience as a project manager for a real
estate developer.

The Opéra Bastille is obviously intended to be a modern re-
thinking of the traditional opera house, but in turning away from
la grande cuisine bourgeoise of the Palais Garnier, Carlos Ott has
eschewed *nouvelle cuisine* and instead has provided the Parisian
public with the architectural equivalent of bread and water. Moreover, because many of the details are crude and the workmanship
is sloppy, the bread is not even a crusty *baguette*; this is American-
style sliced bread.

If truth be told, American style, or at least American expertise,
is what the jury that picked Ott's project as one of three finalists

from among 756 entries in an international architectural competition thought it was getting. According to Michèle Audon, director general of the state body that oversaw the Opéra Bastille project, several of the jurors voted for the Ott project assuming that its anonymous author was the renowned American architect Richard Meier, to whose retro-modern style Ott's entry did bear a superficial resemblance. (Meier has since built the Parisian headquarters of a cable television company; the result suggests that a Meier opera house would probably have been just as monochromatic but carried out with a lighter touch than Ott's unwieldy design.) In fact, Meier had entered the opera competition but was eliminated in the first cut, together with other architectural stars such as Charles Moore, Kisho Kurokawa, and the Miami firm Arquitectonica. As designers often do, these architects had taken liberties in interpreting the competition program. The French bureaucrats who had originally promoted the idea of a modern people's opera and who were advising the jury were having none of that. The bureaucrats had written a 423-page competition program minutely describing the new opera (including a schematic plan of the building), and they expected it to be slavishly followed. That is what Ott—and he alone—had done.

In the end, the French got what they wanted: not the most beautiful opera house in the world, but the biggest (despite its smaller seating capacity, the Opéra Bastille complex is three times larger than the Met) and technologically the most advanced. The French continue to have an abiding faith in new technology—which they often invent with considerable skill—and what is most innovative about the Opéra Bastille is not the architecture but the engineering. More than half of the Bastille site is taken up by enormous backstage facilities, which include not only a rehearsal hall, a mobile orchestra pit, a turntable, and a mobile stage that is also an elevator but also eleven ancillary scenery stages on two levels, joined together by an automated system of motorized trolleys. The

purpose of all this space and machinery is to permit the rapid rota-
tion of different operas: while one is being performed, another
can be in rehearsal, and scenery for a third can be made ready on
the lower level. It is a marvel of engineering, and despite some
opening-night mishaps it all does appear to function as intended.

Whether such complexity is really required in an opera house is
another story. Moving scenery around at dizzying speeds was supposed to provide a larger repertoire and a more varied program—a
different opera every night, as many as 450 performances annually! But, as Maryvonne de Saint-Pulgent, a French journalist,
points out in her fascinating account, *Le syndrome de l'opéra*, in
1990 Parisian concert halls were trying to sell twelve thousand
tickets nightly to an operagoing public that barely exceeded thirty
thousand persons, each of whom would have had to go to a concert three times a week to keep the halls full. Hugues Gall, a Frenchman who was the director of Geneva's Grand Théâtre, called the
Opéra Bastille "the wrong answer to a problem that doesn't exist."
(Now the wrong answer is Gall's problem, too; earlier this year, he
replaced Chung, who was fired as music director after months of
well-publicized wrangling with the Opéra's chairman.) There are
already signs that in practice the people's opera house will not
function in a manner much different from opera houses in New
York, Berlin, or Milan, except that so far it has presented fewer
operas and fewer performances. After a 40 percent price hike in
1990, the price of a ticket is as expensive as it had been at the Palais
Garnier; there's an increasing reliance on stars (the leading role in
Joan of Arc at the Stake was taken by Isabelle Huppert, a popular
film actress); and the second season included *The Magic Flute*—
pace Barenboim.

The Met, La Scala, and Covent Garden are merely opera houses—
the Opéra Bastille is a *grand projet*. The Big Projects—there are

nine of them—refer to a series of monumental architectural works in Paris undertaken by Mitterrand since his election in 1981. Mitterrand, the impact of whose presidency on the city has been compared to the *grand siècle* of Louis XIV, is an enthusiastic builder of somewhat erratic taste whose ambition vastly exceeds that of his immediate predecessors. Charles de Gaulle rebuilt Paris after the war but added little that was new except the donut-shaped Maison de la Radio, a broadcasting center; Georges Pompidou built highways along the Seine and replaced the market of Les Halles with the Centre Pompidou, which today, paint peeling and steel rusting, resembles an oil refinery more than ever; and Valéry Giscard d'Estaing converted the vast Gare d'Orsay into a polyglot museum of the nineteenth century. So far, in addition to building the new opera house, Mitterrand has moved the Ministry of Finance out of the Louvre and into a new building, renovated the Louvre itself, and endowed Paris with something called the Arab World Institute. At La Villette, on the northeast edge of the city, he has had built a music center and a park of architectural follies, and at La Défense, in the northwestern suburbs, he has erected an office building in the shape of an arch, a modern counterpart to the Arc de Triomphe. Construction has recently begun on an enormous new national library, a controversial building that will add over $1 billion to the $3 billion that has already been spent on the *grands projets*.

If ever there was an argument against the hoary notion that each generation must feel an obligation to make its own distinct architectural contribution "symbolic of its time," the Big Projects is it. With the exception of I. M. Pei's elegant glass pyramid in the courtyard of the Louvre, and some of the historic restorations at La Villette (which were begun by Giscard), Mitterrand's *grands projets* are not great architecture. The grandiose library will resemble four half-open books, a banal and simpleminded concept; the Parc de la Villette is a collection of silly-looking pavilions set amid arid landscaping; the new Ministry of Finance is an exercise in the kind of monumental modernism that has long been discredited elsewhere; and the bombastic government office building at La Défense is less like a triumphal arch than a huge, marble-clad coffee table. Unfortunately, Mitterrand is not Louis XIV, or rather, his architects haven't lived up to the standards set by Claude Perrault's east front of the Louvre, Jules Hardouin-Mansart's Dôme des Invalides, and André Le Nôtre's Tuileries Garden.

Or even to the standards of Charles Garnier, the designer of the old opera house. Garnier, like Ott, came out of nowhere to win an architectural competition for a new opera house and likewise did so at a tender age—both were thirty-six—and with little previous experience. Garnier also had to navigate the treacherous shoals of French politics in order to see his ideas realized, although it took him somewhat longer—thirteen years compared with Ott's six-year odyssey. But Garnier's was a different time. His opera house included innovations such as a cast-iron roof structure and an unusual foundation, but these were hidden behind a marble architecture of eclectic richness. In the nineteenth century, going to the opera was chiefly a social occasion, and Garnier devoted considerably more space to sumptuous, mirror-lined lobbies and a grand staircase than to the hall itself. Technical efficiency was given distinctly second place: the backstage areas are spartan, and a quarter of the seats have an inadequate view of the stage. Nevertheless, it is a building that, while it was criticized at first, eventually captured people's affection. "I remember being disarmed by the warm, comforting acoustics of the Palais Garnier," recalls Kaptainis. "The sound, at least in the good seats, was magnificent." Perhaps one day, the Opéra Bastille, too, will evoke such sentimental reminiscences—time can be the architect's best friend—but I wouldn't count on it.

•

The much-loved Palais Garnier was merged with the Opéra Bastille, and following a complete restoration it is used for ballet and occasional operas, especially seasonal favorites such as La Cenerentola. As The Wall Street Journal *observed, audiences "tend to dress up more for performances at the Garnier than at the twentieth-century granite and glass opera house at Bastille."*

Sounds as Good as It Looks

The story of the new Seiji Ozawa Hall at Tanglewood reads like a Hollywood movie—a movie by Frank Capra, not Oliver Stone. A famous big-city symphony orchestra decides to build a concert hall at its rural summer facility. An architect must be found to create a beautiful building, not just one that looks good, but one that also sounds good. A long list is drawn up. It consists of the most celebrated practitioners in the country but also, because this is an orchestra that practices blind auditions for unseasoned musicians, several young up-and-comers. Finally, seven architects are invited to be interviewed. (Here is an opportunity for several cameo roles. Let us cast Brian Dennehy, who was the convincing star of Peter Greenaway's *Belly of an Architect*, as well as Richard Gere, who also once wielded a T square.) Gruff and rumpled, handsome and Armani-suited, trailing assistants carrying portfolios bulging with photographs of impressive museums, dramatic corporate headquarters, and, of course, eye-popping concert halls, they make their presentations to the orchestra committee.

Surprisingly, one of the unseasoned newcomers is among them. (Tom Hanks has the Jimmy Stewart role.) He is hampered by never having built a concert hall, so he shows his latest project instead—affordable housing on the waterfront! Then he makes an impassioned speech about the rural site of the new hall—its landscape, its spirit, its ambience. He talks about the kind of building he thinks the orchestra needs: open, informal, yet reflecting the intensity of the music. It shouldn't overpower the place, he warns; he calls it a background building. (This is a fine set piece: the earnest and impassioned architect confronting the attentive but skeptical committee of civic leaders, retired businessmen, wealthy socialites.) Finally, our hero—Hanks is always the hero—returns to his small office. He is dejected. The committee appeared interested, but what chance does he have against the architectural stars?

Meanwhile, back at the symphony the committee deliberates. Everyone has his or her own favorite. The chairman suggests that they have an informal poll, each member to write two names on a slip of paper. When the ballots are read, there is general surprise at discovering that only one candidate appears as the first or second choice on every single ballot—Hanks. There is more deliberation, and the final choice is made. It is, of course, our hero. As in every Capra movie, the outcome is predictable, but that is precisely the appeal of the genre.

The movie is not over. The concert hall must be built. The architect travels to Europe to visit famous concert halls. Together with the acoustician (Charles Grodin in a co-starring role), he develops a design. The building goes up. It certainly looks impressive, but how will it sound? After the rehearsal, the musicians seem happy. "It's going to be fine," says Grodin. But that prognosis is based on an empty hall—how will it sound with an audience at the opening gala? More to the point, how will it sound to the influential music critics? On opening night, we see the critic of *The New York Times* among the concertgoers (it is Edward Rothstein, playing himself). The music starts. The critic sits concentrating intently, his brow furrowed. He looks slightly irritated. During the intermission, he gets up and moves to another seat. We start to get nervous—will this be a movie with a fashionably unhappy ending? (Hanks, elsewhere in the hall, is *really* nervous; Grodin is merely "trepidatious.")

The next day, Hanks and Grodin read the music review.

They—and we—can relax. "Precisely what a concert hall should be," Rothstein writes. "It is rare for a new hall to begin its career with such a mature, seasoned character." The movie closes with a reprise of the closing of the gala concert and the music of Randall Thompson's *Alleluia*, an unaccompanied chorus. The audience joins in. The camera pulls back from the stage and moves across the heads of the singing people and through the great doors that open the rear of the hall to the outside lawn, where more people sit and sprawl on the grass. As the camera rises, we can see the dark silhouettes of the rolling Berkshire Hills on the horizon. Below us, the warm glow of the light spilling out of the doors identifies the concert hall. The patch of light glows smaller. The credits begin to roll.

I am sitting with William Rawn, the architect, who is telling me about that July 7, 1994, concert. His office is in downtown Boston, and outside the window I can see the historic Granary Burying Ground. A dusting of snow covers the grass between the crowded grave markers (Samuel Adams, John Hancock, and Paul Revere lie here). It is a bleak sight in December, but this would be a sobering prospect at any time of year—and an odd view to have from your workplace. But William L. Rawn III is a serious man. He doesn't look anything like Stewart or Hanks (though he is exceptionally tall), but he does have that affecting combination of gravity and guilelessness that both actors have often brought to the screen.

"After one of the first rehearsals, several of the musicians came up to me and told me how happy they were with the sound of the hall," Rawn says. "I think I knew then that we had something good. Still, we were concerned about the reaction of the media. The first reviews will stick in the public's mind. Not that there haven't been halls that initially got bad reviews and were eventually considered to be excellent."

The critical reception of the acoustical qualities of Seiji Ozawa

Hall has been consistently positive, although Rothstein did have a quibble about "too much being shaved off the top frequencies." After the first season, Rawn's acoustician, R. Lawrence Kirkegaard, ordered an eighth inch of the absorptive cellulose fiber that covered the ceiling to be removed. The sound is judged to be improved. Such tinkering is not uncommon in a new hall. What is unusual is for the sound of a new concert hall to be so widely praised, for the reaction to new halls has frequently been lukewarm, if not downright hostile. It is usually the old halls that are loved and admired.

That is certainly the case with Boston's venerable Symphony Hall. It was built at the end of the nineteenth century and designed by McKim, Mead & White, working in its full-blown Italian Renaissance mode. Symphony Hall is generally held to be the first hall in whose design the new science of acoustics played a role, for the architects had the assistance of Wallace Clement Sabine, a professor of physics at Harvard and the father of modern architectural acoustics. The music critic of the *Boston Evening Transcript* was not impressed, however. After the inaugural concert, he wrote that "the tone was beautifully smooth . . . but it had no life, there was nothing commanding and compelling about it." Nevertheless, Symphony Hall has become known precisely for its exceptional sound. "Even the first time that I conducted there, I was struck by its acoustics," said Bruno Walter; "it is the most noble of American concert halls." Herbert von Karajan was even more effusive, and even went so far as to say that for much music Symphony Hall was even better than the Grosser Musikvereinssaal in Vienna. Now, that was saying a lot because the Musikvereinssaal is considered by many to be the best hall in the world.

Of course, "the best hall in the world" is a slippery concept, because the setting for music—and hence music itself—has changed considerably over time. Baroque orchestral music was played in small rooms with relatively short (less than 1.5 seconds)

reverberation times. Reverberation time refers to the length of
time that sound gives the impression of lingering in a room, the
result of being reflected by the surrounding hard surfaces. Short
reverberation times are ideal for intimate and highly defined music.
Much sacred music, like Bach's fugues, was written to be performed
in private chapels whose reverberation times are also relatively
short. Bach's major choral works, on the other hand, were usually
staged in churches and took advantage of the larger, more rever-
berative spaces. During the classical period, the music of Haydn
and Mozart was performed in what were the first concert halls.
Although these halls were small by modern standards and sat only
several hundred people, the reverberation times were longer, 1.5 to
1.7 seconds. The second half of the nineteenth century saw a new
generation of larger concert halls that reflected the popularity of
orchestral music. The Musikvereinssaal, for example, opened in
1870 and has 1,680 seats. Such halls have longer reverberation times
(1.9 to 2.2 seconds), fuller tones, but slightly lower definition,
which complements the music of Romantic composers like Brahms,
Tchaikovsky, and Richard Strauss. The music of the twentieth
century is more varied in its demands.

A contemporary hall, in which works ranging from Bach to
Górecki are performed, must always, to a certain extent, be a compromise. Nevertheless, there is a surprising amount of agreement
about which are the best-sounding concert halls. Most musicians,
critics, and concertgoers would probably include not only Vienna's
Musikvereinssaal and Boston's Symphony Hall but also Amsterdam's Concertgebouw and New York's Carnegie Hall. A system-
atic study of these and other halls is contained in *Concert and Opera
Halls: How They Sound*, a vastly revised and enlarged edition of the
now-classic study *Music, Acoustics, and Architecture* (which was
originally published in 1962). The author is Leo L. Beranek, a
Cambridge, Massachusetts–based acoustician who is co-founder

of one of the world's leading firms of acoustical consultants—Bolt, Beranek & Newman.

Beranek's top rating is "Superior," and it is accorded only to the Musikvereinssaal, Symphony Hall, and the Concertgebouw. An additional six concert halls are described as "Excellent": Basel's Stadt-Casino, Berlin's Konzerthaus (formerly Schauspielhaus), Cardiff's St. David's Hall, Tokyo's Hamarikyu Asahi Hall, Zurich's Grosser Tonhallesaal, and Carnegie Hall. The rest of the halls are consigned to lesser categories, although Beranek diplomatically does not give a detailed ranking of all the halls. An amateur musician, he visited sixty-six famous concert halls and ten opera houses around the world, listening to performances, measuring reverberation times, and studying blueprints. He polled concertgoers and talked to music critics. He also interviewed musicians, including Charles Munch, Leopold Stokowski, and Leonard Bernstein, as well as von Karajan and Walter. Eugene Ormandy told him, "In my many years as a conductor, this is the first time anyone has come to me to ask my opinion about acoustics."

Why do old halls sound better than new ones? To a large extent, it is a question of their shape. The Musikvereinssaal (1870), the Concertgebouw (1888), and Symphony Hall (1900) all have what is known as a shoe-box shape. (So do four of the six halls in the "Excellent" category.) In a typical shoe box, the orchestra is at the narrow end, and the seats are on the floor and in one or two galleries that extend along the long sides and across the rear. Sound is reflected to the listener from the two parallel walls (which are about sixty to eighty feet apart) as well as from the ceiling. Because the concertgoer is relatively close to the musicians, the atmosphere is intimate, visually as well as acoustically.

The majority of concert halls during the twentieth century have departed from the successful shoe-box formula. Why? One reason is the requirement for greater seating capacity (as well as enlarged standards of comfort and safety). Basel's Stadt-Casino has 1,448 seats; many contemporary concert halls, especially in America, where orchestras lack government subsidies and rely on box office receipts, approach 3,000. To bring the rear seats closer to the stage, halls have been made wider, or fan shaped. This sacrifices some of the acoustical qualities of the shoe box, especially the ability to reflect bass notes from the side walls. Audience capacity may not be the only reason, however. After all, Boston's Symphony Hall, the largest of the shoe-box types, accommodates as many as 2,630 concertgoers. This is about the same as Lincoln Center's Philharmonic Hall, but Philharmonic Hall, which opened in 1962, adopted a distinctly untraditional shape. So perhaps size is not the whole story. Maybe some architects' willful desire to reinvent the wheel is also part of the explanation.

The acoustician R. Lawrence Kirkegaard, who was responsible for the 1989 renovation of Carnegie Hall, has a sound respect for tradition. Originally Harvard-trained as an architect, he apprenticed with Bolt, Beranek & Newman precisely at the time that the firm was struggling with the acoustical shortcomings of Philharmonic Hall—"Beranek's Waterloo," Kirkegaard calls it. (The acoustics of Philharmonic Hall proved so bad that the interior was gutted, and a new hall—Avery Fisher Hall, a classic shoe box—was put in its place.) Because Ozawa Hall was to be small, it could follow the tried-and-true models. "The shoe-box shape was identified very early," Kirkegaard says. "The Boston Symphony loves its hall, and all their favorite concert halls were that shape." On his European tour, Rawn had been especially impressed by the architectural presence of the Musikvereinssaal and Berlin's Konzerthaus (another nineteenth-century shoe box, designed by the great neoclassical architect Karl Friedrich Schinkel), so it did not take much prodding from Kirkegaard for him to adopt the shoe box as the model for the new hall. Ozawa Hall is 65 feet wide, 130 feet long, and 50 feet high, about the same size as the Musikvereinssaal; like

Symphony Hall, it has two galleries. One feature of Ozawa Hall is unique, however: the rear wall consists of a fifty-foot-wide door that permits another two thousand concertgoers sitting on the gently sloping lawn outside to listen to the music.

Beranek's *Concert and Opera Halls* concludes with three general observations: small halls generally sound better than large halls; halls built for a single purpose are superior to multipurpose halls; and old halls sound better than new ones (all three of the "Superior" halls were built by 1900, as were four of the six halls rated "Excellent"). These insights obviously influenced the design of Seiji Ozawa Hall. From the beginning, the Boston Symphony decided that the new hall should be small, the audience not to exceed twelve hundred. Because the new hall was being built as a replacement for a wood structure (built in 1941 by Eliel and Eero Saarinen) that served for both opera and orchestral music, the initial plan was for the new hall to likewise accommodate both types of music. However, "as the design progressed, Bill Rawn slowly but firmly steered us to the conviction that a hall designed uniquely for music was the best solution," recalls Daniel R. Gustin, the assistant managing director of the orchestra. This was not only a question of avoiding the complexity—and the cost—of an orchestra pit, a stage house, and backstage facilities. Opera houses require relatively short reverberation times to ensure the intelligibility of the human voice, which inevitably compromises the acoustical qualities required for orchestral music. And, as we shall see, an orchestra hall can benefit from the lack of a proscenium stage.

Another lesson that old concert halls teach concerns construction. Their walls and ceilings were usually plaster applied directly to brick or stone; there was relatively little wood. Heavy massive walls sustain a low-frequency bass response, unlike hollow walls or lightweight wood paneling, which tends to reflect only the treble notes. Although the interior of Ozawa Hall has a lot of exposed wood—teak—it is confined to the seats and the gallery railings;

the walls are stucco over foot-thick masonry, and the ceiling consists of heavy concrete coffers. The result is a reverberation time of about two seconds and, as Rothstein put it in his review, "a resonant, warm space that comes to life with sound."

The enjoyment of music in a concert hall is not only the result of construction, dimensions, and shape, however; architecture, too, plays a role. If Ozawa Hall is traditional in its overall internal arrangement, it is much less so in its decor, for Rawn's respect for the past does not extend to the use of the classical architectural language. There is no figurative ornament here, no statuary as in Symphony Hall, no caryatids supporting the galleries as in the Musikvereinssaal, no crystal chandeliers as in the Stadt-Casino. On the other hand, this is definitely not a coolly abstract modernist interior like the recently constructed Opéra Bastille.

Some have likened Ozawa Hall to a Quaker meetinghouse or a New England town hall. There is certainly an air of gathering here, for in doing away with the proscenium that is a feature of so many American concert halls, pulling the stage into the main body of the hall, and placing some of the audience beside and even behind the musicians (as in the Concertgebouw), Rawn has given concertgoers the feeling of being participants rather than merely spectators. The teak grilles that make up the gallery railings reminded me of yacht gratings, and the seats, which are mostly movable chairs, recalled the deck furniture on a cruise ship. So, if this is a meetinghouse—and there is a sense of Quaker artlessness in the unembellished forms—it is one whose frugality is tempered by hints of boating, and leisure, and summer vacations. My only quibble is that the decor is almost too refined; one misses the makeshift, camp-like quality that is a feature of the other buildings at Tanglewood.

On the exterior, the general shape of the building recalls McKim, Mead & White's Symphony Hall, except that the roof is gently curved instead of pitched, and the lower flanking wings are open porches instead of solid buildings. Because the main hall is brick and the structure of the porches is heavy timber (recycled from old wharves and trestle bridges), the overall effect is of an industrial building, the kind of nineteenth-century mill, say, that one can still see in many small Massachusetts towns. That sounds unusual, but Tanglewood itself is an odd combination of urban culture in a country setting, of intensity and informality.

Before I leave Bill Rawn's office, he shows me one of the sketchbooks he kept during his European tour of concert halls. All architects keep such visual diaries. What struck me about Rawn's sketchbook was that while there were many thumbnail drawings, there were also pages and pages of written notes. Obviously, he had been looking, but he had also been listening and thinking. Contemporary architecture can represent a range of qualities: refinement, excitement, even—in the case of much deconstructivist work—angst. It is rare, however, to come across an architect whose work can be described, first and foremost, as intelligent. I think this is probably what impressed the Boston Symphony Orchestra committee and led it to make what must have seemed, at the time, a risky choice. A bold client, an intelligent architect, and a perceptive acoustician—that is a Hollywood script, indeed.

In the 2004 edition of Concert and Opera Halls, *Leo Beranek ranked Ozawa Hall the fourth-best American concert hall ever built, after Boston's Symphony Hall, Carnegie Hall, and the Morton H. Meyerson Symphony Center in Dallas (designed by I. M. Pei). Rawn and Kirkegaard have since collaborated on several music halls, notably the Music Center at Strathmore for the Baltimore Symphony and Weill Hall at Sonoma State University, both shoe-box designs.*

The Biggest Small Buildings

I happen to live in the neighborhood where Robert Venturi built the now-famous Vanna Venturi House for his mother. I occasionally pass by the building on my morning walks. A long driveway leads down the narrow lot to the front facade, which is almost completely hidden by shrubs and trees in the summer but visible during the winter months. Whenever I stop and look, I remember the first time that I was here, in the summer of 1965. This was only a year after the house was built, although I didn't know that then. Indeed, I had never heard of Venturi. I was in Chestnut Hill to visit a nearby house by Louis Kahn—already celebrated as the architect of the Richards Medical Building. On the way, I passed the Venturi house. It's chastening to admit that I didn't give it a second glance. I was still an architecture student, and I had been taught that proper architecture had white walls and flat roofs—like the Kahn house—not taupe-gray walls and what looked suspiciously like a gable roof. Little did I suspect that I was ignoring what Vincent Scully would later call "the biggest small building of the second half of the twentieth century."

It's striking how many important works of early modern architecture have been houses. The long list includes such masterpieces as Wright's quintessential Prairie house, the Robie residence, the Villa Savoye, in which Le Corbusier introduced the chief elements of what would become known as the International Style, Aalto's masterful Villa Mairea, and Fallingwater, unsurpassed in Wright's later oeuvre and after more than sixty years still the best-known modern house in America. The prosperous postwar period saw many innovative residences built in the United States. Mies van der Rohe designed the Farnsworth House and Philip Johnson the Glass House, Richard Neutra built the Kaufmann House, and Charles and Ray Eames built the influential Case Study House No. 8. Postmodernism, too, has had domestic landmarks, not only the Vanna Venturi House, but also Charles Moore's weekend cottage in Orinda, California. Then there's Richard Meier's Smith House, Frank Gehry's own house in Santa Monica, and Peter Eisenman's House VI.

There have been so many significant houses that it would be easy to compile a convincing history of twentieth-century architecture illustrated solely by residences. There are several explanations for this curious fact. The simplest is that it is easier for a talented young architect to receive a small private commission than a large public one. And if a client is not forthcoming, a tyro with time on his hands can strut his stuff by building his own home, as Johnson, the Eameses, Moore, and Gehry did.

An architect who lacks the opportunity—or the means—to build for himself has another recourse: Mom and Dad. The most famous example of familial patronage is the Vanna Venturi House, but there have been others. One of Charles-Édouard Jeanneret's first built works was a house for his parents, and after he left Switzerland for Paris and metamorphosed into Le Corbusier, he designed a retirement home for them beside Lake Geneva. The long narrow plan influenced my first house—for my parents—beside Lake Champlain. Richard Meier built his first large house for his parents, although not in the white neo-Corbusian style that would make him famous. Charles Gwathmey was still an architecture student when he built his first house—for his painter father. The striking house and studio in Amagansett, Long Island, not only

introduced modern architecture to the Hamptons but also launched
Gwathmey on a prolific career as a designer of homes for the rich
and famous.

A house, even a small house, is programmatically more chal-
lenging than a small store, say, or a small office. It incorporates
sufficient spatial and programmatic complexity that it can convincingly serve as a miniature vehicle for a range of ideas. The transparency and structural rationalism of the Farnsworth House, for
example, were architectural concepts that Mies would explore for
the rest of his career. Moore's own little barnlike Orinda house
consisted of only one room, but it was a persuasive demonstration
of how modernism could be fused with traditional domestic and
regional motifs, a theme that would reappear on a larger scale in
his better-known Sea Ranch project. Finally, a house is always a
house. It is a timeless problem against which a neophyte—or, in
the case of Fallingwater, a master—can measure himself.

During the Middle Ages and the Renaissance, architectural
ideas developed slowly, and large public buildings such as cathedrals and churches could advance the art. Modernism places a
high value on being avant-garde. But if architecture is to be avant-
garde, it must be experimental, and if a building is truly experimental, there must be a chance of failure. Most responsible corporate and
public clients are by nature conservative; only a private individual—
adventurous, or rich—will normally assume such a risk. Thus,
as Aalto explained when he was designing the Villa Mairea, "it is
possible to use the individual architectural case as a kind of experimental laboratory."

The motivation of the innovating architect is obvious, but I
wonder about the client. What drives a person to experiment with
something as personal and lasting as a home? Is it a craving for
notoriety? Is it a sign of social climbing or merely thumbing one's
nose at the establishment? Or is it the traditional desire to assume

the role of patron of the arts? No doubt, what attracted some clients to figures like Aalto and Wright, and continues to bring clients to some of today's celebrity architects, was the desire to be associated, if only for a time, with greatness. The line between patron and groupie is a thin one.

Many avant-garde houses are second homes (the Villa Savoye, the Farnsworth House) or are inhabited by only one or two people (the Venturi house, the Glass House). In such circumstances, functional requirements are greatly simplified. There is no need to deal with the clutter and confusion of family households, and the designer is free to pursue aesthetic concerns to the limit. As a consequence, the aesthetic innovations in many of these houses have little to do with their function as dwellings. This may be why houses that have been architectural milestones have not necessarily been influential domestic models for the general public. Indeed, some distinctly bizarre houses have been elevated to the architectural pantheon, which puzzles—and sometimes alienates—the public. What is one to make of Eisenman's House VI, with its upside-down staircase and unconventional (leaky) rooftop window? There are notable exceptions. The open plan and horizontal lines of the Robie House inspired American home builders for decades. Fallingwater was much too unconventional to be influential, but the house in Palm Springs that Edgar Kaufmann commissioned from Richard Neutra in 1946 became the prototype for several generations of spread-out, open (and heavily air-conditioned) Southern California houses.

Do experimental houses make good homes? Many don't. The Farnsworth House lacks screen doors and with only one small operable window is oblivious to normal domestic well-being. A single long kitchen counter is unsuitable for serious cooking; there is a guest bathroom, but no guest bedroom if someone wants to sleep over. Because the walls are of primavera wood, it is impossible to hang pictures without defacing the elegant material. I have similar reservations about other experimental houses. I wonder if the Savoye family finally tired of the stark interiors of their home. They surely were fatigued by continually going up and down the ramp and stairs. Didn't the rigidity of the plan of Rudolf Schindler's groundbreaking reinforced-concrete Lovell Beach House feel confining? Doesn't one get tired of picking up after oneself in the pristine but antiseptic interiors of the Smith House?

Vanna Venturi lived the last decade of her life in her home and is said to have loved it. Postmodernism has come in for much criticism, yet its ability to blend styles and integrate a variety of furnishings makes it particularly amenable to the demands of everyday life. Aalto's Villa Mairea, too, strikes me as comfortable and livable as well as beautiful. So does the Robie House, although I could do with a little more headroom. These last two houses have something else in common. They are both large family homes, and they are both the work of seasoned designers. By the time Aalto came to design the Villa Mairea, he had a busy decade of public work under his belt, including the extraordinary Paimio Sanatorium. Wright was an experienced house designer when he undertook the Robie residence and had also built the Larkin Administration Building and Unity Temple.

Whether or not architectural experimentation produces good homes, I'm not sure that it always produces better architects. What I mean is that avant-garde houses tolerate a degree of personal expression that is out of place in most buildings. Neutra never produced a public building as interesting as his best houses; the Glass House remains Philip Johnson's best work. I've always admired Charles Moore's houses, but I find his quirky public buildings less compelling. When Richard Meier amplifies and extends the architectural elements that infuse his houses with a retro-modern charm into large buildings, the effect can be deadening, like listening to a Chopin étude that never ends. House experiments do not always translate well into larger civic buildings that are required to speak a different language, a common language that is understood by a large number of people. They are public, not personal, statements. This difference is something that architects such as Wright and Aalto understood instinctively. That is why they were able to design great public buildings as well as great houses, and great houses that were also good homes.

Palladio in the Rough

The suburbs of Charleston, South Carolina, resemble those of any other modern metropolitan area: strip malls line highways and drive-through restaurants mask a leafy interior of residential subdivisions with such names as Sweetgrass, North Creek, and White Gables. Most of the romantic-sounding names are developers' inventions, but one—Otranto—is an exception. The name belongs to an antebellum indigo plantation that was subdivided in the 1960s. The original plantation house, which dates from the end of the eighteenth century, still stands—a low, rambling structure surrounded by deep verandas that recall Margaret Mitchell's description of Tara.

The recent houses of Otranto are pleasant if unremarkable— brick ranches with two-car garages and basketball hoops in the driveways, clapboard split-levels, commodious bungalows with Low Country–style porches. One of them, a house on Leone Crescent, is different. Its facade is distinguished by a large classical portico of the sort that most people associate with small-town banks. Bulky square columns support the portico, and the plain, ocher-colored walls are rudely plastered and have tall windows with green shutters. The house is on one floor but is surprisingly massive, its ponderous simplicity suggesting great age, an impression reinforced by the lack of contemporary details and the roughness of its finish. Like the old plantation house, it seems to have stood here forever.

In fact, this is the newest building on the block. Alan and Julia Johnson moved into their house three summers ago. He is a high school science teacher; she's a hospice nurse. They have two teenage boys, Julian and Eric. An SUV and a Saturn sedan rest in the driveway; a riding mower stands in the garage. In most ways a not unusual family. Nor do they inhabit the house in an unusual way. Their living room, which home builders would call a great room, is divided into several areas: couches in front of the fireplace, Julia's upright piano at one end, and a television-watching area at the other. The furniture is comfortable but not particularly fashionable. There are lots of bookshelves. A compact kitchen overlooks the dining area, which is visible from the living room. The arrangement of kids' and parents' bedrooms and bathrooms and a compact study is also not unusual.

But theirs is not exactly an ordinary house. You enter the living room through large arches supported by ten-foot-tall classical columns capped by imposts, or capstones, in the shape of rough boulders. Arches crisscross the foyer. An open-air courtyard in the middle of the house provides light as well as a private outdoor space; its half columns and arched openings make it resemble a Roman atrium. Then there is the scale. The living room has a sixteen-foot ceiling, the front doors are ten feet tall, and the bedroom windows, which appear small from the outside, are equally tall. The exterior columns measure thirty inches on each side, as big as telephone booths.

How did the Johnsons come to build this new/old house? "We'd lived in our previous house for fifteen years, and it no longer worked for us," says Julia, "so we wanted to move." They decided against buying an old house, because old houses in the South often have mildew and other environmental problems that might trigger their allergies and asthma. Books of house plans didn't turn up anything suitable.

One of Julia's brothers, George Holt, is a builder, so from time to time they would show him plans, and he would comment on them. One day, he showed up with some sketches of his own. "I really didn't want to take it on," he says. For the last twenty years, he had been renovating and building houses in downtown Charleston, and suburbia wasn't his territory. But Julia was his younger sister, and George wanted to help. She was delighted. "Every house that George builds is different, so we knew that it would be something special. I trusted his judgment."

Holt started by asking what she and Alan didn't like in their old house. The list was long. They didn't like living on two floors— Julia has a problem with her knees—and they didn't like the way the house was cut up into small rooms. With her medical background, Julia was concerned about the lack of handicapped access. She'd always wanted a walk-in pantry and a real laundry room, Alan lacked a study, and they needed space for his elderly parents. "They wanted a lot," Holt says, "but they didn't have enough money, so the plan kept growing and shrinking. It took me a year to finish the design."

Holt is a small, wiry man in his mid-forties. Though he has lived in Charleston most of his life, he has no trace of a southern accent. He was born in Madrid, his mother Spanish, his father a sailor in the U.S. Navy. For the next fifteen years, he lived on a series of naval bases in the United States, Europe, Turkey, and Latin America. In 1974, his father, a master chief petty officer who had served in World War II and Korea, was transferred to Charleston. Three years later, he retired from the navy and settled down— in Otranto—to sell real estate. Holt found living in an American suburb an odd experience. He eventually attended the College of Charleston, and although he didn't much like studying, he did enjoy living downtown. He rented a coach house from a local architect, who, he says, "used to show me drawings, models, books." It was Holt's first exposure to architecture, and although he was interested, he never thought of formal study. "I liked history and old buildings. What would I have learned in architecture school?"

After dropping out of college and working a year on the front desk of the Drake Hotel in Chicago, Holt returned to Charleston. "It was my starving-artist period," he says. "I wanted to be a painter." After two years as a bohemian, he gave in to his parents' entreaties, joining them in their real estate business. He got his Realtor's license, but the experiment failed; he disliked everything about it—the houses, the suburbs, the job. In one year, he sold only three houses. "What do you really want to do?" his patient father asked. Holt, now twenty-five, said he wanted to buy an old house in downtown Charleston, fix it up, and sell it.

It was hardly an original idea. In 1931, Charleston was the first American city to adopt a historic district zoning ordinance, and downtown has been a thriving place ever since. But Holt had his eye on a run-down neighborhood outside the traditional historic area. With a friend, Cheryl Roberts, as business manager, and with his father and an air force pilot friend as investors, Holt bought two derelict houses for $35,000. He and Roberts did much of the work themselves. It worked. They lived in the houses for a time, then sold them at a profit. In the time-honored tradition of small developer-builders, they bought more houses, renovated them, and sold those, too.

Holt acted as designer and contractor. He built his first all-new house when the carriage house that he was in the process of renovating was destroyed in September 1989 by Hurricane Hugo. In 1991, with his younger brother, Bob, as an investor, Holt bought a large inner-block parcel of land not far from the College of Charleston. He and Roberts restored one of the houses and built two new ones. It was a rough neighborhood, with crack houses and shootings, so they hired an off-duty policeman to park his squad car out front to discourage the drug dealers. Over the next five years, they bought more land on the same block, assembling three-quarters of an acre in all. They built two private lanes, Tully Alley and Charles Street, and created a mews-like arrangement of twenty houses and apartments. Meanwhile, the neighborhood improved, as they hoped, and real estate values rose. A house that he built in 1995 and sold for $220,000 was resold two years ago for more than twice as much. Holt recently finished a small three-bedroom house on Tully Alley that he put on the market for $595,000.

Holt's company, Historic Renovations of Charleston, builds only a couple of houses a year. He has no intention of expanding and appears uninterested in making a lot of money. A modest man, he dresses unassumingly and drives a beat-up Chevy Tracker that he shares with Roberts. "I don't need a lot of stuff," he says. He employs eight laborers, whom he has trained himself, and says construction is not an easy business. "It's not like *This Old House.* That's fantasyland. Nothing real ever happens on the show, like a subcontractor not showing up, or a carpenter getting arrested for cocaine. Everything always runs smoothly," he says. "And all those fancy tools! Norm's home workshop is better equipped than my cabinetmaker's."

Most of the buildings on Tully Alley are plain-vanilla Colonials, but mixed in among them are more exotic houses with colorful stucco walls and stepped gables that recall Amsterdam rather than Charleston. At the end of the alley is an industrial shed that looks like a down-at-heel body shop. This is Holt's own house. He built it in the mid-1990s, when the neighborhood was still a dangerous place, and purposely made the exterior unassuming. Not the interior. When you enter, you are brought up short, not just to avoid falling into the swimming pool, but also because of culture shock. The room is a cross between an early Christian catacomb, a Byzantine church, and the set of a Douglas Fairbanks movie. Think *The Thief of Baghdad.* The pool is flanked by arched colonnades supported by stained wooden columns, barely visible in the murky light that filters down from a narrow skylight. Holt explains that the room was much brighter when the entire roof was covered in fiberglass, but all that was destroyed by Hurricane Floyd, and the current roof is a temporary replacement. "It's supposed to be like an outdoor courtyard, with muslin draped across the rafters," he says. A couple of Venetian lanterns dimly illuminate the cracked plaster walls and the cracked flagstones. Everything looks faded, shabby, timeworn.

"People come in here, and they usually ask me what this place was originally," he continues. "They assume it must be old. It's not just the columns and the arches but also the roughness of the materials, which seem to be from another time." Holt works hard to achieve this quality. He's had to argue with plasterers, for example, who want to make everything perfectly smooth. "I love a sense of crudeness," he says. He points out that some of the columns are intentionally slightly out of plumb. Large doors, which are not quite centered on the wall, lead to the main room of the house. This astonishing space is about twenty feet square and capped by a tall dome supported on pendentives, triangular vaults that transmit the weight of the dome to the arches below. Arches springing from elaborately carved imposts atop wooden columns carry smaller domes at the four corners. A chandelier in the form of a huge bowl made out of what looks like carved stone hangs from the ceiling. The fireplace, covered with lacy carved decorations, takes up most of one wall. Light enters from two sides through tall, triple-arched windows. In addition to a small drafting table, a couple of easy chairs, a sofa, and a chaise longue complete the furnishings. The room is rather messy and unkempt, cluttered with books and drawings. It manages to be both theatrical and oddly religious and reminds me of the Venetian palazzo of the Art Nouveau designer Mariano Fortuny.

Holt can't understand why all architects don't design their own houses, saying he would never push his theories on someone else if he hadn't tried them on himself. It took two years to finish his house. There are two small bedrooms, one of which opens onto a tiny courtyard—an air shaft, really—with a fishpond and a trickling fountain. There is a minuscule kitchen (he obviously doesn't cook), two small offices, and a separate suite of rooms where Roberts lives.

Holt describes the style of his house as tenth-century Byzantine. He mentions this matter-of-factly, the way someone else might say Federal or French Provincial. Byzantine architecture has a rich heritage. The Byzantine Empire, the late Roman Empire's eastern portion, was founded in the fourth century and lasted more than a thousand years. Its buildings were characterized by a masterful use of dome construction, low-relief decoration, and colored-glass mosaics. Although there are some exceptional European examples, such as the church of San Vitale in Ravenna and the Basilica of San Marco in Venice, there has never been a Byzantine revival. Which is a shame, according to Holt, who describes Byzantine as a young person's architecture. "People react differently to my house," he says, "but the people who really, really like it are the college students." I'm not sure how my own students at Penn would react. Ivy League schools of architecture are wedded to the avant-garde, but in a narrow-minded, conformist fashion, and Holt's eccentric exploration of historical themes would probably strike them as bizarre.

"When I became interested in Byzantine architecture, I couldn't find any books in local bookstores," he says. "This was before the Internet. So a friend borrowed them from the Clemson library, and I spent hours at Kinko's photocopying." While designing his house, he thought he should study the real thing, so he went to Istanbul. He had not been in the city since he was five years old, and he loved its seedy, dirty, slightly run-down quality, its state of disrepair. He saw many Byzantine buildings, including the great church (now mosque) of Hagia Sophia, which he calls "my No. 1

favorite building in the world, no question." The visit encouraged him to continue with the Byzantine design of his house.

Travel appears to be one of Holt's few indulgences, other than his house. He and Roberts try to spend a month in Europe every year. He looks at buildings and sometimes collects details that he can use in his work, but mostly they "just hang out," as he puts it. They generally go to Mediterranean cities, although he also likes Ireland, "not Georgian Dublin, but the rough Celtic architecture." They return over and over to Rome and Istanbul.

Despite his newfound enthusiasm, Holt didn't design a Byzantine house for his sister. "It would have been too gimmicky in that neighborhood," he says. "The corner lot is rather prominent, so a Palladian villa seemed like the thing to do." The great Renaissance architect Andrea Palladio is another of Holt's obsessions. Palladio's country houses are distinguished by their nobility, their beautiful proportions, and their inventive use of classical elements. They are also marked by a canny practicality, for Palladio was trained as a stonemason and was first and foremost a builder—like Holt.

Starting with Thomas Jefferson at Monticello, many American architects have been influenced by Palladio, but American Palladianism was filtered through eighteenth-century British eyes. In the process, it became a rather delicate architecture of brick and white-painted wood, characterized by carefully proportioned moldings and classical details. By contrast, Holt's robust villa in Otranto is Italian in inspiration, a little cruder, a little less refined. It recalls Isabella Stewart Gardner's 1903 Fenway Court in Boston's Back Bay, which has the same idiosyncratic mix of sources, rough edges, and the mossy atmosphere of old Venice.

Holt's design for his sister is not based on a specific Palladio villa, although the Renaissance master did design several suburban houses. Palladio's villas usually had a raised basement containing the kitchens and service areas, as well as an attic; the Otranto house has neither. Yet the recessed central loggia and the temple front are unmistakably Palladian. "I was concerned that the temple front would look pretentious," Holt tells me. "Square columns seem cozier to me than round columns." "Cozy" is not the word I would use to describe these massive piers. They are modeled on the rusticated bases of the colonnade of Palladio's Palazzo Pretorio in Cividale.

Holt's approach to Palladio is refreshingly unacademic and not dissimilar to Palladio's own attitude to the past. Palladio studied ancient Rome, then put it through the wringer of his own fertile imagination. He admired Roman temples, but because he was designing country houses, he grafted old forms onto new. Holt loves Palladio, but he loves Byzantine architecture, too, so he happily combined them. Hence the arches in the living room, which are supported by columns whose impost capitals are based on originals he saw in a Justinian cistern in Istanbul. The imposts are concrete but made to look like roughly carved stone. "I wanted the rough capitals to tone down the interior and keep it from looking too polished," he says. In fact, the house is much less rough than his own, though the tight budget has kept the details simple. This doesn't bother Holt. "I love fabulous moldings," he says, "but if a room is well proportioned, it will look good without all that ornament." Because he has manipulated the scale of the rooms, they appear larger than they are, but they feel good because they are smaller than they look.

Holt was able to roughen things up on the exterior, especially in the portico. The columns are made out of stacked-up pieces of precast concrete, each about a foot thick. Instead of using one standard mold, however, he made a dozen molds, each very slightly different in size. Before he cast the concrete, the interiors of the molds were coated with a mixture of sand and vegetable shortening, which produced a rough-finished surface. The dye that colored the concrete was also varied from batch to batch. Finally, the finished columns were painted with three coats of linseed oil, "which tends to soak in unevenly, and livens up the color." The variations in size and hue are barely perceptible, felt rather than seen. The subtle effect is similar to the slightly splotchy surface of the cement plaster on the walls.

Holt frequently incorporates flaws and blemishes in his work. "I really like the handmade quality of older buildings," he says. But his penchant for flaws is not simply a desire to simulate the wear of age. He talks about visiting Santa Maria in Cosmedin in Rome. This church dates from the sixth century, after the fall of Rome, when the early Christians were trying to reclaim the lost art of building. When he first saw the building, he was dismayed by what appeared to be a coarse and ill-formed imitation of ancient Roman architecture. But when he returned a second time, he realized that the lack of finesse and the crudeness were endearing. "You could see that the builders had put a lot of love into their work. It's as if they were trying to do something and weren't sure exactly how to do it."

Roughness and imperfection distinguish Holt's work, not only from modernist buildings, which celebrate precision and accuracy— the machine aesthetic—but also from the architecture of so-called modern classicists such as Allan Greenberg and Robert A. M. Stern, whose designs, while they use an architectural idiom derived from the past, exhibit a similar machinelike precision. "The problem with many modern houses is that they are too perfect, and perfection can be intimidating," Holt says. Of course, most architecture is intended to intimidate, or at least to impress. What makes Holt's houses unusual—and appealing—is the air of hesitation that he imparts to his designs. "For me, architecture is always an emotional experience," he says. And the emotion one feels most strongly in his buildings is, oddly enough, a sense of human frailty. Which makes these houses, despite their ancient roots, very modern indeed.

•

I recently visited another Palladian house designed by Holt with his partner Andrew Gould. The tiny (870-square-foot) version of the Villa Saraceno, no larger than the original's portico, is squeezed onto an in-fill group of houses in the center of a block on Ashley Avenue in downtown Charleston.

PART FOUR

Place Makers

The Master

The summer of 2001 saw a spate of architectural exhibitions. In New York City, there were two shows on Ludwig Mies van der Rohe, one at the Whitney, the other at the Museum of Modern Art, as well as a Frank Gehry exhibit at the Guggenheim Museum. In addition, the Philadelphia Museum of Art held a major retrospective of the work of Robert Venturi and Denise Scott Brown.

These exhibitions underline the fickle nature of architectural fame. Robert Venturi rattled the cage of modern architecture when he built an iconoclastic house (for his mother) in 1962 and followed it with *Complexity and Contradiction in Architecture*, "probably the most important writing on the making of architecture since Le Corbusier's *Vers une Architecture*," according to Vincent Scully. For the following two decades, Venturi was architecture's most influential theorist. He advocated buildings that were rich in meaning and awareness of history, and he ridiculed formally monumental buildings, which he called "ducks," proposing to replace them with "decorated sheds." Two famous—or rather infamous—decorated sheds of the 1980s were Michael Graves's gift-wrapped Portland Building and Philip Johnson's Chippendale-topped AT&T office tower. What came to be known as postmodernism was all the rage, but it didn't last; Graves went on to a sort of stylized classicism, and Johnson just went on—and on. As for Venturi and Scott Brown, their ironic combination of flattened decoration and mannered modernism never really caught on. Although they built some striking campus buildings and several high-profile museums, including the handsome Sainsbury Wing of the National Gallery in London, they also lost prominent commissions, notably the Staten Island ferry terminal and the new Philadelphia concert hall. They stuck to their guns, but it turned out that ducks—or rather titanium artichokes, in the case of the Guggenheim Museum in Bilbao—not decorated sheds, were what clients and the public wanted.

Frank Gehry is, of course, the architect du jour. The Guggenheim in Bilbao is not only at the cutting edge of architectural design but also a hit with the public. Hundreds of thousands of people have flocked to an obscure Basque industrial city, attracted by his extraordinary sculptural confection of titanium curves. If the new Guggenheim that he has designed for New York City is built, it will likely be a great success. Currently, Gehry occupies a unique position in the architectural world: he is a popular avant-gardist, or an avant-garde populist, I'm not sure which. This is unusual. All too often in the last seventy-five years, the architects most admired by other architects and the critics did not find favor with the public, which was unimpressed by bare concrete, unadorned brick walls, and steel-pipe railings. On the other hand, the crowd-pleasing works of Raymond Hood, architect of Rockefeller Center, Morris Lapidus, of Miami Beach hotel fame, and I. M. Pei, whose East Building of the National Gallery of Art is the most visited site in Washington, D.C., were pooh-poohed by the architectural cognoscenti.

Mies van der Rohe never achieved popularity. On the other hand, he had an architectural following, and the so-called Miesian style, in vogue throughout the 1950s, produced such distinguished offspring as Gordon Bunshaft's Lever House, Philip Johnson's Glass House, and Eero Saarinen's General Motors Technical Center. However, by the time that Mies died in 1969, less really did seem a bore, as Venturi cheekily put it, and Mies's brand of architectural minimalism was out of fashion. But fashion in architecture is no different from any other kind—it swings. The attention paid to Mies last summer is revealing. As a younger generation of architects works to reinvent modernism, it is the taciturn Mies—rather than the mercurial Corbusier, the flaccid Gropius, or the obscure Kahn—who stands out as the beau ideal.

This interest does not herald a return to Miesian architecture, however. Although every designer of a skyscraper owes a debt to Mies's steel-and-glass high-rise buildings, his brand of Platonic idealism will not be taken up again by real estate developers, as it was in the 1950s. That moment has passed. Mies will continue to be venerated, and his buildings will be admired both for their beauty and for their pioneering influence, but already only thirty-two years after his death he is slipping into history. A hundred years from now the Seagram Building will still be a brooding presence on Park Avenue, and its architect will be remembered, the way that H. H. Richardson, say, or Louis Sullivan is remembered today. But what about three hundred years from now? The Seagram Building may survive—its curtain wall is, after all, bronze—but if Mies van der Rohe is remembered at all, it will likely be by historians, not by the general public, who will have forgotten what "Miesian" meant.

For a durable architectural reputation, consider the long-lived influence of an architect who lived at the end of a very different revolutionary architectural period. Andrea Palladio, whom Paul Johnson has called the last of the true Renaissance architects, died in 1580. Thirty-three years after *his* death, there was no museum retrospective, but there was something much more important—a revival. Inigo Jones visited the Veneto, saw Palladio's churches, palazzi, and villas, and as a result introduced Palladian classicism to Britain. Jones was a genius, and although only eight of his forty-six completed buildings have survived, masterworks such as the Banqueting House in Whitehall and the Queen's House in Greenwich mark him as one of the world's great architectural talents. More than a hundred years later, there was a second Palladian revival, led by Lord Burlington and architects such as Colen Campbell and William Kent. Its imprint on British architecture, particularly on country houses, was indelible, and a columned portico in the center of a house facade became the quintessential image of a country retreat. Meanwhile, Palladian buildings were springing up all over Europe, not only in his native Italy, but in Germany, the Netherlands, Poland, and Russia. And a hundred years after that, when Thomas Jefferson was asked for architectural advice by a Virginia neighbor, he responded, "Palladio is the Bible. You should get it and stick to it." Jefferson, whose entry in the architectural competition for the new President's House in Washington, D.C., was a faithful rendition of a Palladio house—the Villa Rotonda—was a great admirer, as was George Washington, who included a beautiful Palladian window in Mount Vernon. Nor did Palladio's influence stop there. The great Edwardian architect Sir Edwin Lutyens considered himself a Palladian, and Palladian motifs reappeared in twentieth-century classical buildings such as the National Gallery of Art in Washington, D.C., the Frick Collection in New York City, and the Tennis House in Brooklyn's Prospect Park. And every American Colonial house with a pedimented porch, whether it is the Ewings' fictional spread at Southfork or a suburban bungalow, owes a debt to Palladio.

The architect who wielded this long-lived influence lived and worked most of his life in Vicenza, a small city in the Venetian Republic. With the exception of two prominent churches in Venice—San Giorgio Maggiore and Il Redentore—most of Palladio's surviving work is either in Vicenza or, in the case of villas, scattered in far-flung locations in the Veneto countryside.

Although Jones and Lord Burlington—and thousands of architects since—made pilgrimages to Palladio's buildings, his designs
and ideas became known chiefly as the result of his book, *I quattro
libri dell'architettura* (*The Four Books on Architecture*). Palladio was
hardly the first Renaissance treatise writer—he was preceded by
Alberti, Filarete, Serlio, and Vignola, to name only the most prominent authors—but he had the greatest influence. This was due to a
number of factors. *Quattro libri* is written in simple language. Its
author was a seasoned practitioner who emphasized practical advice and avoided abstract theory. Above all, the book is full of images; almost every page contains an illustration. Architecture is a
visual art, and Palladio provides abundant visual information: plans
of buildings, elevations, sections, details, all carefully drawn and
dimensioned.

Palladio's first book describes the rudiments of architecture,
not only construction techniques, but especially the five orders
that form the basis of the classical style. The second and third
books document his own designs for residential buildings and
bridges. The fourth book is devoted to ancient temples. Palladio
was not only an exceptional designer; he was an expert on ancient
Roman architecture, and he devoted almost half of his treatise to a
catalog of his surveys and reconstructions of ancient monuments.
This was an invaluable source of information for any architect interested in studying the prototypes of classicism.

Book 2 had the greatest architectural influence. It is a catalog
of fourteen palazzi and twenty-three villas. Although these are
not theoretical projects but actual commissions that Palladio had
built—or was in the process of building—they amount to an architectural manifesto. Palladio was a designer of enormous invention but also endowed with a sharp analytical mind. His buildings
consisted of discrete elements—columned porticoes, curved log-
gias, pedimented porches. In the hands of a skilled architect like
Jones, they could fuel designs that were entirely original and yet

still recognizably Palladian. It is as if Palladio had magically unearthed an architectural gene that could be spliced and respliced by others to make apparently endless permutations. Moreover, he was a magician who explained his tricks. *Quattro libri* is full of simple formulas for laying out rooms (Palladio recommended seven pleasing shapes), calculating ceiling heights, and spacing columns. For generations of gentlemen amateurs, as well as professional architects, Palladio's treatise served as dictionary, primer, and pattern book. The first American to own a copy was Thomas Jefferson.

Quattro libri was published in Venice in 1570, when Palladio was sixty-two. It was translated into Spanish, French, German, and Russian. There were several eighteenth-century English translations, the most accurate of which was by Isaac Ware, a distinguished Palladian architect. Ware's 1738 edition became the standard English text, since 1965 available in an inexpensive paperback facsimile edition from the redoubtable Dover Publications.

The Ware translation has a number of serious limitations. The language is often stilted, and eighteenth-century spelling and typography make it inconvenient for the modern reader. For example: "If upon any fabrick labour and induſtry may be beſtowed, that it may be comparted with beautiful meaſure and proportion; this, without any doubt, ought to be done in temples." For the sake of convenience in printing, Ware placed the illustrations in groups, losing the concordance between text and drawings that characterized Palladio's treatise. Lastly, he had his engravings copied directly from the original woodblocks, with the curious result that all his illustrations are mirror images of the originals. Because so many of Palladio's plans and facades are symmetrical, this is less disturbing than it sounds, but it means that occasionally a plan shows a staircase on the left when it should be on the right or facing pages do not match. Moreover, Ware's metal engravings have a somewhat spindly appearance compared with Palladio's sturdy woodcuts.

Now, after more than 250 years, a superb new English translation of *Quattro libri* corrects all these defects, breathing new life into the architectural classic. Robert Tavernor, a professor of architecture at the University of Bath, who was a co-editor of a translation of Leon Battista Alberti's *On the Art of Building in Ten Books*, and Richard Schofield, a professor of art history at the University of Nottingham, have produced a model of the scholarly translation. They have augmented the text with a thoughtful introduction, copious notes, a comprehensive bibliography, and a useful glossary. Their translation is more accurate than Ware's and above all more readable. For example, the awkward sentence quoted above is now "If any building should have effort and labor expended on it, so that it is laid out with beautiful dimensions and proportions, then, doubtless, this should be done for temples."

"Ultimately, it is the qualitative combination of purposeful words and readable images that has made Palladio's *Quattro libri* an enduring source of inspiration," Tavernor writes. He and Schofield use facsimile reproductions of the original woodcuts, and, equally important, they follow Palladio's original graphic layout. In the treatise, the words and pictures for a particular project were usually on the same page, and full-page illustrations were arranged in specific sequences. The beautiful drawings of the Basilica in Vicenza, for example, were on facing pages, and small- and large-scale drawings of the same building complemented each other. Palladio was an artist, and reading his book was intended to be a visual as well as an intellectual experience. This translation re-creates the masterful and stimulating mix of words and pictures that their author intended.

There is no doubt that Tavernor and Schofield's translation will henceforth be the standard *Quattro libri* in English. By making Palladio more accessible—and more readable—they have increased the likelihood that yet another generation of architects and lovers of architecture will discover this Renaissance genius. On the other hand, it is also likely that the excellence of this new edition will unintentionally carry on what Douglas Lewis refers to as its "pernicious influences." Lewis, the author of *The Drawings of Andrea Palladio*, gently indicts *Quattro libri* as a guide to Palladio's own architecture on several counts. First, because Palladio regularized—and sometimes idealized—his designs for didactic purposes, the descriptions in the book do not correspond to the actual buildings. Second, the illustrations in the book are black-and-white, whereas Palladio's buildings frequently incorporated color. Third, Palladio's architecture is part of a preexisting context of surrounding buildings and landscape features, which the schematic illustrations in *Quattro libri* do not convey. Lastly, the rather crude woodcuts are a poor medium to communicate the subtle and often delicate quality of Palladio's architecture.

Paradoxically, these limitations accounted for Palladio's enduring appeal. An eighteenth-century rationalist, for example, could see Palladio as a kindred spirit. So could a twentieth-century modernist, who could imagine Palladio to have been a designer of monochrome, object buildings, a Platonic explorer of idealized geometry, of harmonic proportions and "pure" space, unconcerned with his immediate surroundings. Yet Palladio's buildings "are not black and white; they are not flat and boldly outlined," Lewis writes, "they do not sit on pristine, abstract, inviolate Euclidian planes, but instead are jostled and nudged and crowded in dense urban or agrarian contexts, which almost universally have never been measured, drawn, photographed, dated, or otherwise acknowledged to exist."

The authority of *Quattro libri* rests on the incontrovertible fact that it was the book that Palladio himself compiled and whose publishing he oversaw. Whatever its limitations, this was the source of its power, a power that even Palladio's surviving buildings could not dampen. Palladio's buildings should overshadow his book, but they don't. Partly this is because of their frequently remote locations. Moreover, many of his designs—even the Villa Rotonda, arguably the most famous private house in architectural history—were never completed or were completed by others. Not one of Palladio's palazzi was built in its entirety, and even the great church of San Giorgio Maggiore was in large part unfinished at the time of Palladio's death. And many of Palladio's buildings have been destroyed. Only a small portion of the Carità convent, which Goethe considered Palladio's best work, has survived. Of roughly thirty villas, only seventeen are more or less intact. For these reasons, the misplaced notion has arisen that the buildings documented in *Quattro libri* represent the "real" Palladio.

The aim of *The Drawings of Andrea Palladio* is to correct this view. Douglas Lewis is curator of sculpture and decorative arts at the National Gallery of Art in Washington, D.C., and in 1981 he organized an exhibition of more than a hundred Palladio drawings that was shown in the National Gallery and five other American museums. The annotated catalog that accompanied the exhibit has now reappeared in a larger format and vastly expanded form. Because there are no comparable books on Palladio's drawings, it is an invaluable work. Published in a large format, on good-quality paper, the reproductions of the drawings in this splendid book are almost as good as the real thing, because most of Palladio's original drawings are small, generally about eight by ten inches. In addition, the book contains numerous photographs of surviving buildings, floor plans, and illustrations from *Quattro libri* that can be studied side by side with the drawings. An exhaustive bibliography and a particularly thorough index complete the book.

Thanks to English collectors such as Inigo Jones and Lord Burlington, there are about 330 surviving drawings by Palladio, more than for any other Renaissance architect. They are not necessarily a typical cross section of his total output. About two-thirds are drawings of ancient buildings that he was going to use for additional books of his treatise (which he never completed). There are also drawings of early work and a few later projects. There are no construction drawings, however, as these were presumably destroyed through hard use. Some projects are described in preliminary sketches, allowing a glimpse into Palladio's creative process; many others have no backup documentation. The most valuable drawings are of projects that do not appear in *Quattro libri*. Some, like the beautiful drawing of a new facade for the Palazzo Ducale in Venice, postdate the treatise. The palazzo had been damaged by fire in 1577, and Palladio, who was by then the semiofficial architect of the republic, proposed demolishing what remained of the structure and building anew (the Senate decided instead to restore the palazzo to its former state). Other drawings are of buildings, especially villas, that for one reason or another he did not include in the treatise. Such drawings enrich the Palladio oeuvre immeasurably and show that Palladio often reused unbuilt plans and that he developed motifs over the course of several buildings. They also show him to have been concerned with site planning and with fitting buildings to their surroundings. Lewis's lively and opinionated accompanying text points out many interesting and previously ignored aspects of the great architect's work.

Lewis's most important discovery (or, rather, rediscovery, because the drawing was known two hundred years ago) concerns a drawing of the interior of the Villa Godi that Palladio made in 1550. The rooms of the Villa Godi, like so many Palladio villas, are richly frescoed. Architectural historians in the past assumed that these frescoes were entirely the work of the artists involved; some even considered the frescoes to be intrusions on Palladio's architectural vision. "That aesthetic viewpoint has insisted (in broad terms) on a Palladian architecture of pure whitewashed spaces, proportionately conceived, and sparingly (if at all) decorated with stone moldings of rigorously chaste profile," Lewis writes. The Godi drawing, which is in Palladio's hand, shows a design for the fictive architectural elements that the painter Giambattista Zelotti later frescoed on the walls of the main room of the villa. In other words, the drawing establishes that Palladio designed the overall layout of the rich decor. Far from being extraneous, the frescoes were an integral part of his architectural design.

A striking feature of Palladio's drawings, which, though severe, are very beautiful, is their modernity. Palladio used drawing to explore design in much the same way as do contemporary architects (computers excepted). There are thumbnail sketches, back-of-the-envelope diagrams, hurriedly drawn preliminary plans, and rendered presentation drawings. He might have been the last of the true Renaissance architects, but he was also the first modern professional. Unlike most of his contemporaries, Palladio was not trained as a painter or sculptor; he was a stonemason. Skilled in the practicalities of the building arts, versed in history, a student of ancient ruins, he was a zealous advocate of classicism as well as a restless and innovative designer. No wonder his influence was so long-lived.

This essay-review was written as I was working on a book about Palladio, The Perfect House. *I came across Douglas Lewis's book during my research, and I was taken by his approach: although he was an art historian, he described buildings not as isolated works of art but as products of specific conditions, sites, building technology, and clients. I later met Lewis at the National Gallery of Art, where he was a curator, and my own view of Palladio benefited greatly from his firsthand research and from that conversation.*

Corbu

Le Corbusier loved Manhattan. He loved its newness, he loved its Cartesian regularity; above all, he loved its tall buildings. He had only one reservation, which he revealed on landing in New York in 1935. The next day, the headline in the *Herald Tribune* informed its readers that the celebrated architect "finds American skyscrapers much too small." Le Corbusier always thought big. He once proposed replacing a large part of the center of Paris with eighteen sixty-story towers; that made headlines, too.

He was born Charles-Édouard Jeanneret in Switzerland in 1887. When he was thirty, he went to Paris, where he adopted the pseudonym Le Corbusier. Jeanneret had been a small-town architect; Le Corbusier was a visionary. He believed that architecture had lost its way. Art Nouveau, all curves and sinuous decorations, had burned itself out in a brilliant burst of exuberance; the seductive Art Deco style promised to do the same. The Arts and Crafts movement had adherents all over Europe, but, as the name implies, it was hardly representative of an industrial age. Some talented practitioners like Edwin Lutyens in England and Paul Cret in the United States turned to the classical tradition for inspiration. This did not satisfy Le Corbusier. He maintained that a new time deserved a brand-new architecture. "We must start again from Zero," he proclaimed.

The new architecture came to be known as the International

Style. Of its many partisans—Mies van der Rohe and Walter Gropius in Germany, J.J.P. Oud in Holland, Adolf Loos in Austria—none was better known than Le Corbusier. He understood the power of mass media, and he was a tireless proselytizer, addressing the public in manifestos, pamphlets, exhibitions, and his own magazine. He wrote books, dozens of them, on interior decoration, painting, and architecture. They resembled instruction manuals. For example, here is his recipe for the International Style: raise the building on stilts, mix in a free-flowing floor plan, make the walls independent of the structure, add horizontal strip windows, and top it off with a roof garden. But this makes him sound like a technician, and he was anything but that. Although he dressed like a bureaucrat, in dark suits, bow ties, and round horn-rimmed glasses, he was really an artist (he was an accomplished painter and sculptor). What is most memorable about the austere, white-walled villas that he built at this time in and around Paris is their cool beauty and their airy sense of space. "A house is a machine for living in," he wrote. The machines that he admired most were ocean liners, and his architecture spoke of the sun, the wind, and the sea.

Similar nautical imagery has resurfaced in Los Angeles recently, in Richard Meier's Getty Center with its piano-curve facades and miles of steel-pipe railings. Le Corbusier would have hated its corporate sleekness, for by 1950 he had changed course, abandoning Purism, as he called it, for something more robust and sculptural. His spartan, lightweight architecture turned rustic, with heavy walls of brick and fieldstone and splashes of bright color. He discovered reinforced concrete and made it his own, leaving the material crudely unfinished, inside and out, the marks of wooden formwork plainly visible. Concrete allowed Le Corbusier to explore unusual shapes. The billowing roof of the chapel at Ronchamp resembles a nun's bonnet; the studios of the Carpenter Center for the Visual Arts at Harvard push out of the building like huge cellos. For the state capital of Chandigarh in India, he created an acropolis of heroic structures that appear prehistoric. It was as if he had decided that now that there were so many machines in the world, what was needed was more homespun roughness.

Le Corbusier was the most important architect of the twentieth century. Frank Lloyd Wright was more prolific—Le Corbusier's built oeuvre comprises fewer than sixty buildings—and many would argue Wright was more gifted. But Wright was a maverick; Le Corbusier dominated the architectural world from that halcyon year of 1920, when he started publishing his review *L'Esprit Nouveau*, until his death in 1965. He inspired several generations of architects—the author included—not only in Europe but around the world, first with his impeccable white villas and the International Style and then with his rough concrete buildings, which gave rise to the movement known as Brutalism. He was more than a mercurial innovator; irascible, caustic, Calvinist, Corbu was modern architecture's conscience.

Le Corbusier was also a city planner. "Modern town planning comes to birth with a new architecture," he wrote in a book titled simply *Urbanisme*. "By this immense step in evolution, so brutal and so overwhelming, we burn our bridges and break with the past." He meant it. There were to be no more congested streets and sidewalks, no more bustling public squares, no more untidy neighborhoods. People would live in hygienic, regimented high-rise towers, set far apart in a parklike landscape. This rational city would be separated into discrete zones for working, living, leisure, and so on. Above all, everything should be done on a big scale—big buildings, big open spaces, big urban highways.

He called it *la ville radieuse*, the Radiant City. Despite the poetic title, his urban vision was authoritarian, inflexible, and simplistic.

Wherever it was tried—in Chandigarh by Le Corbusier himself or in Brasília by his followers—it failed. Standardization proved inhuman and disorienting, the open spaces were inhospitable, the bureaucratically imposed plan, socially destructive. In the United States, the Radiant City took the form of vast urban renewal schemes and regimented public housing projects that damaged the urban fabric beyond repair. Today, these megaprojects are being dismantled, superblocks replaced by rows of houses fronting streets and sidewalks. Downtowns have discovered that combining—not separating—different activities is the key to success. So is the presence of lively residential neighborhoods, old as well as new. Cities have learned that preserving history makes a lot more sense than starting from zero. It has been an expensive lesson, and not one that Le Corbusier intended, but it, too, is part of his legacy.

Why Wright Endures

Last summer, having accepted a position at the University of Pennsylvania, I was in Philadelphia looking for a house. Leafing through the pages of a real estate agent's directory, I came across a postage-stamp-size photograph that looked familiar. It showed a building that I remembered visiting thirty years earlier as an architecture student on a traveling scholarship. The house was an unusual design, a sort of quadraplex; that is, it was one of a four-unit cluster whose cruciform arrangement ensured privacy for each of the dwellings. According to the directory, the house was located in Ardmore, a suburb on Philadelphia's Main Line. It wasn't where we were intending to live, but I thought the house itself would be worth a visit.

The building was almost completely hidden from the adjacent sidewalk by trees. We went up the short driveway, under a large overhanging balcony that sheltered the carport (which previous owners had partially enclosed to create a study), turned right, and faced an unprepossessing front door. Once inside, we were in the corner of a room that unexpectedly rose to a sixteen-foot height, and two of whose tall walls were entirely glass. The garden, which seemed like an extension of the room, was full of foliage that screened us from the street. There was a deep fireplace in one corner and a cozy built-in settee in the other, and the brick walls were lined with built-in cupboards and bookshelves. The floor was polished concrete. The owners were in the process of moving out, but even empty this was a beautiful, serene space.

The modest materials, and the profusion of built-in furniture throughout, reminded me that when it was built—in 1938—this was intended to be an affordable starter house for young couples. Each twenty-three-hundred-square-foot unit, which cost $4,000 to construct, consists of a master bedroom and two additional bedrooms ("Boys" and "Girls") with bunk beds. The house is on three levels, with two large roof terraces that augment the outdoor space of the small garden and make the upper rooms feel like penthouses—the development was originally called Suntop Homes.

A narrow stair led from the living room to an eat-in kitchen that was on a balcony overlooking the living room and the garden beyond. Additional light was provided by an ingeniously designed clerestory window. The table was flanked by a built-in banquette. The compact bathroom (which reminded me of a Pullman sleeper), the master bedroom, and a tiny nursery were also on this level; the two children's rooms were above. The kitchen was conceived by the architect as a kind of command post "where the mistress of the house can turn a pancake with one hand while chucking the baby into a bath with the other, father meantime sitting at his table, lord of it all, daughter meantime having the privacy of the front room below for the entertainment of her friends."

Frank Lloyd Wright, the architect of Suntop Homes, wrote this in 1948. One can excuse the author his misogynist views—after all, he was born in 1867—but there is nothing old-fashioned about the Ardmore houses. The only thing that may be dated is the example of someone of the stature of Wright—then the most famous architect in the United States—applying himself to the mundane problem of the small suburban house. Famous architects today seem to be too busy building museums and corporate offices; Wright built those, too, but he never lost his concern for the common man. That generosity and breadth of vision explain why, thirty-five

years after his death, Wright and his work maintain such a strong
hold on the public imagination.

Even by the frenetic standards of contemporary architectural
publishing, which churns out illustrated monographs on individual architects—living and dead, famous and obscure, gifted and
hacks—by the score, last year's flurry of books on Frank Lloyd
Wright is impressive. Rizzoli, in conjunction with the Frank
Lloyd Wright Foundation, is issuing a multivolume series of the
celebrated architect's collected writings that has, so far, covered
the period from 1894 until 1939. The editor of that series, Bruce
Brooks Pfeiffer, once a Wright apprentice and now director of the
Wright Archives, has also written the text that accompanies the
lavish photographs of thirty-eight Wright buildings, including
several lesser-known houses such as the Auldbrass Plantation in
South Carolina and the Zimmerman House in Manchester, New
Hampshire. Alvin Rosenbaum, a planner who grew up in a Wright-
designed house in Alabama, has produced an uneven memoir titled *Usonia: Frank Lloyd Wright's Design for America*, and this year
Pedro Guerrero, who was Wright's photographer for twenty years,
published *Picturing Wright*, which includes some charming pictures
of the architect at home. Academics have always found in Wright a
rich lode to mine, and there are two new studies of Wright's international influences: Kevin Nute's examination of the role of traditional Japanese art and architecture in Wright's work, and Anthony
Alofsin's fascinating analysis of Wright's European travels between
1910 and 1922. Then there is William Allin Storrer's valuable *The
Frank Lloyd Wright Companion*, a comprehensive guide to the almost
five hundred buildings that Wright realized during his fruitful life.
About three hundred of these buildings are still in existence, carefully maintained by their owners or restored by corporate or individual effort, and Storrer provides a useful index of street addresses
for the interested traveler. This year, fueled by a comprehensive

retrospective that has just opened at the Museum of Modern Art, one can anticipate ever more Wrightiana.

The public interest in Wright's work has always been sustained by the personality of the man himself. "He is a fascinating, adorable, and utterly irresponsible genius, full of magnetism, selfish to the extent of violating all the conventions if he sees fit; and an artist to his finger tips," wrote his friend Frederick Gookin in 1919 in as good a capsule description of Wright as anyone has provided since. The melodramatic contours of the famous architect's life, which are recounted in two recent popular biographies, by Meryle Secrest and Brendan Gill, are well-known, but they are worth summarizing. The rube from Wisconsin, whose domineering mother has told him that he will be a famous architect, comes to Chicago, catches the eye of an old master—Louis Sullivan—at whose feet he learns the rudiments of his profession. Impatiently, the youngster soon strikes out on his own, and almost immediately—effortlessly—he begins to produce work that bears his own individual stamp. His career blossoms, the clients come, the commissions multiply. And then, willfully, he throws it all overboard—wife, six children, flourishing practice—and runs away to Europe with the wife of a client. They return, and though they are the subjects of scandal, they live together in a beautiful country house of the architect's design. He resumes his practice and attracts new clients. Then, tragedy: a deranged servant kills Wright's mistress and her two children and burns the beautiful house to the ground. However, the architect is unstoppable. He rebuilds the house—it is even more beautiful than before. He remarries, and he produces more masterpieces. By the age of fifty—not old for an architect—he has already built three great buildings: the Larkin Administration Building in Buffalo, Unity Temple in Oak Park, and the Robie House in Chicago. He takes up with a young Montenegrin ballerina, they have a child out of wedlock, and as a result of the ensuing scandal (he is threatened with indictment under the White Slave Traffic Act) he almost goes to jail and is driven to the edge of bankruptcy. He is now sixty, but there are still thirty-one years of the saga to go. Thirty-one years during which he will design some of his best—and best-known—buildings: the Fallingwater house, the Johnson Wax Building, and the Guggenheim Museum, as well as his own remarkable desert retreat in Arizona. He lives to be ninety-one, a grand old man surrounded by young acolytes, making oracular pronouncements, the most famous architect in the country, just as his mother promised.

The only other twentieth-century American architect who stands comparison with Wright is Louis Kahn. (Mies van der Rohe's buildings are predominantly in America, but their roots—and their essence—like their transplanted maker, are European.) Kahn's talent flowered late. Nevertheless, among the handful of buildings that he completed before his death in 1974, there are some major masterpieces, like the sublime Kimbell Art Museum in Fort Worth, Texas, and the great capital complex in Dhaka, Bangladesh. But Kahn never achieved the public recognition that was accorded to Wright. For one thing, his buildings, despite their cool beauty, are intellectual exercises in minimalism of a sort that architects find attractive but that often leaves the layman unmoved. The unplanted, paved courtyard of the Salk Institute in La Jolla, California, for example, drew plaudits from critics, even though it provides an uncomfortable setting where a shaded and welcoming garden was surely called for. Kahn's architecture, which is characterized by monumental forms based on abstract geometry, is often described as "timeless," but it could as well be termed "placeless." His designs look equally at home—or not at home—in Bangladesh as they do in a Texas suburb or in a Southern California industrial park. This placelessness gives Kahn's work a mysterious, almost mystical air, which may explain why, although his influence in the United States was short-lived, his ideas have taken root in India, where they continue to be explored by gifted architects like B. V. Doshi and Anant Raje.

In Wright's buildings, the American public recognized a home-grown product. This set him apart from almost all of his contemporaries and from succeeding generations of American architects. Classicists like John Russell Pope, John Carrère, and Paul Cret were every bit as skillful, but their skill derived directly from the Parisian École des Beaux-Arts; eclectics like Stanford White and Horace Trumbauer met the demands of their East Coast clients by manipulating the historical architectural styles of Europe. The influence of Europe was equally strong in the first generation of immigrant modernists—not only Mies van der Rohe, but also Walter Gropius, Richard Neutra, and Marcel Breuer—who dominated the American architectural scene in the postwar years and whose successors—Paul Rudolph, Eero Saarinen, and Philip Johnson—followed in their footsteps. To modernist architects, Wright—who had known such historical figures as Louis Sullivan and Daniel Burnham but who continued to practice until the end of the 1950s—appeared to be an anomaly or, at best, a leftover from the past. "America's greatest nineteenth-century architect," quipped Johnson, in an ill-disguised attempt to put Wright in his place.

The postmodern architecture of the 1970s, which was a reaction against the abstract internationalism of glass-box building, might have signaled a return to a native American architecture. Indeed, the domestic work of Robert Venturi and the late Charles Moore is rooted in the American vernacular, as Vincent Scully has convincingly argued. Moore, especially, was particularly adept at playing with regional styles (California, southwestern, New England) in a series of exuberant houses. Venturi, too, played on American motifs. But the interest of both designers in architectural history also led them to explore European themes; so did Robert A. M. Stern's fascination with early twentieth-century eclecticism. The buildings of Michael Graves, arguably the most talented of the postmodernists, progressively owe more and more to European classicism, especially to the ancient cultures of the Mediterranean.

Nor is Americanness an issue in the work of what passes for the avant-garde today. Not only is the outlook of architects like Frank Gehry and Peter Eisenman international, like their practices, but if deconstructivism has any roots—other, that is, than in the Euro-American world of high fashion—it's probably in the abstract architecture of the Russian constructivists of the early Soviet Union.

As the millennium approaches, it is obvious that Johnson was mistaken: Wright was—is—America's greatest *twentieth*-century architect, not only by dint of his considerable architectural accomplishments, which have proved remarkably durable, but also because of their very Americanness. His buildings belong to America in the same way as Whitman's poems, Faulkner's novels, and Gershwin's music do. Wright's Americanness is not merely a question of style, although style has a lot to do with it. The use of natural materials, the drive to simplify, the fascination with what are often technological gimcracks, the unabashed use of dramatic effects (especially the masterly use of concealed electric lighting), a love of novelty, and a willful evasion of history all add up to a style that spoke—and still speaks—to most Americans.

It isn't just the style of the buildings but also the style of the man. Brash, self-promoting, largely self-taught, individualistic, he also embodies most Americans' notion of the great *artiste*: bohemian in behavior and dress, extravagant, emotional, inspired. The Bauhaus architects dressed themselves up like proletarians in leather jackets and flat caps; Le Corbusier preferred black suits and severe horn-rimmed glasses. Wright, on the other hand, wore striking costumes of his own design and drove in flamboyant Cords and Packards, specially painted in his favorite color, Cherokee red.

Decades before the term came into common use, Wright made himself into a celebrity.

Wright's untutored self-sufficiency—also a part of his Americanness—was carefully cultivated. No European architect had influenced his work in any way, he consistently maintained. This was true inasmuch as Wright avoided explicit references to European classicism as well as to European modernism. Nevertheless, as Anthony Alofsin amply demonstrates in *Frank Lloyd Wright—the Lost Years*, Wright learned many lessons from Europe, especially from the Austrian Secessionist architect Joseph Maria Olbrich and from artists and craftsmen associated with the Wiener Werkstätte. At an earlier moment in his life, Wright was also influenced by Japan, and he developed a style of perspective rendering that was clearly derived from Japanese pictorial art. It may also be, as Kevin Nute suggests, although not altogether convincingly, that Wright drew on Japanese architecture for the open planning of what he came to call his Usonian houses. But while it is possible, and even valuable, to question Wright's blatant assertions of creative autonomy, this does nothing to diminish the extraordinary impact of his work. You don't have to be an architect, or an architectural historian, to appreciate Wright's buildings—their impact is immediate and visceral.

Before Wright, most famous American architects were associated with a particular city or region. H. H. Richardson with Boston and New England, Louis Sullivan with Chicago and the Midwest, Frank Furness with Philadelphia, Bernard Maybeck with the Bay Area. There are more Wright-designed buildings in Illinois and Wisconsin than elsewhere, but he was really a national architect, realizing projects in thirty-seven states. Although Wright did not always alter his architecture to suit different regions—the concrete-block technique that he developed for houses in Los Angeles pops up later in Oklahoma, Ohio, and New Hampshire, and the great sweeping roofs of his so-called Prairie houses show up in Colorado and Northern California—he did develop ways of using local materials that do seem, on the whole, admirably suited to their climate and geography. Heavy stone walls in the Southwest; patterned concrete and flat roofs in Southern California; plant-draped trellises and pergolas in the South; wood walls and protective overhangs in the Midwest.

What makes Wright's architecture American, however, is not only its appearance. Most of his work was residential, and his acceptance—and celebration—of the single-family house is also quintessentially American. Wright did design some grand villas in the British country-house tradition (apart from his own homes in Wisconsin and Arizona, Wingspread is probably the grandest Wright country house). But most of his houses were middle-class homes, and especially after the 1930s projects like the Suntop Homes were intended to be affordable by owners with modest means. These are not scaled-down versions of Tudor mansions or Palladian villas, nor are they adapted Cotswold cottages. They are different from these predecessors not only because of their appearance but also because they are designed to contain a way of life that is different: more casual, more connected to the outdoors, more aware of technical conveniences, that is, more American.

In the popular imagination, a Frank Lloyd Wright house is surrounded by a natural landscape, built on the flank (never the top) of a hill or in the open desert. There were such houses, but more typically they were situated on a street, close by other houses. (This was not always evident in the photographs of his so-called Prairie houses, which were mostly in the Chicago suburb of Oak Park.) Here is, I think, another aspect of Wright's continued popularity: he was America's premier *suburban* architect.

Unlike almost every architect of the twentieth century, Wright did not live and work in a city. For the first sixteen years of his independent practice, his home-cum-office was in Oak Park; later he moved to rural Wisconsin and still later constructed a winter re-treat outside Scottsdale, Arizona. Nevertheless, urbanism did in-terest him, and in 1935 Wright unveiled a theoretical proposal for a new kind of city, as unusual, in its own way, as the earlier *ville radieuse* proposal of his European rival Le Corbusier. Broadacre City, as Wright called it, consisted of buildings in the landscape, linked to each other by a system of roads and highways. The res-idential areas consisted of individual houses—the smallest lots were one acre. Shopping was to be carried out in "wayside mar-kets" and "distributing centers for merchandise of all kinds" that were located at highway intersections. Office buildings, factories, and community centers were scattered. There was nothing resem-bling a downtown in Wright's suburban vision; indeed, his first book on town planning, published in 1932, was titled *The Disap-pearing City*.

Wright continued to tinker with Broadacre City for the rest of his life, but for most architects and planners, whose allegiance was to the traditional city, this proposal was a bit of an embarrassment, an old man's foible. It turned out that the old man was right—or at least mostly right. The latest census confirms that the United States has become a nation of suburbs: more people now live in the suburbs than in traditional central cities. And these suburbs are no longer dormitory communities but self-sufficient metropolitan ar-eas, with retail and entertainment facilities and with employment opportunities. (Nationwide, only 19 percent of worker commutes are from suburb to city, while 37 percent are from suburb to sub-urb.) Moreover, the physical environment of these new suburban cities, or "edge cities," as Joel Garreau christened them, resembles Broadacre City to an uncanny degree.

It seems likely that in one way or another succeeding genera-tions will continue to find their own meanings in Wright's rich oeuvre. For example, his exploration of figurative ornament in the second and third decades of the twentieth century is surely something that current architects, many of whom are, once again, interested in decoration, would do well to study. Wright's use of stained glass, murals, and handmade furniture in his buildings also anticipates a contemporary concern with the crafts. His attempts to develop low-cost building methods for houses, while they may be technologically obsolete, remain a telling reminder that affordability does not have to negate architectural quality. Perhaps most appealing is Wright's ability to combine individualism with a broader sense of humanity. In a period when the individual feels increasingly powerless in the face of corporate and governmental bureaucracy, Wright's valiant protracted struggle to affirm his—and others'—personal worth may be the most moving example of all.

Shortly after this was written, in 1993, Shining Brow, *an opera based on Wright's life, premiered in Madison, Wisconsin. In the subsequent decade, almost twenty titles a year have been added to the sagging Wrightian bookshelf, including a short biography by Ada Louise Huxtable, Neil Levine's magisterial* The Architecture of Frank Lloyd Wright, *Franklin Toker's gossipy* Fallingwater Rising, *and two fictionalized accounts of the architect's scandal-ridden love life. In 2012, following a public outcry, an anonymous buyer paid $2.4 million for a Wright-designed house in Arizona threatened with demolition.*

Call Arup

Behind every great architect, to adapt a familiar adage, there is a great engineer. Or more accurately, behind every great *modern* architect, there is a great engineer, for, until the twentieth century, the two professions were one. The accomplished—and largely anonymous—medieval master masons who built the Gothic cathedrals, for example, were responsible equally for ornament and structure, which may be why it is often hard to distinguish between the two. The pointed arch, as John Summerson observed years ago, is as much fanciful as functional, and what appear to be structural ribs in the stone ceilings are strictly decorative. On the other hand, window tracery, while making a pretty pattern, does effectively resist gravity and wind forces, and although the stone piers that line the nave are designed to resemble bundled columns—a purely visual conceit—their mass is needed to support the great weight of the wall and the stone ceiling above. In a medieval cathedral, architecture and engineering are happily combined.

The architects of the Renaissance, although less interested in structural virtuosity, were equally versed in construction. In his famous treatise, *On the Art of Building in Ten Books*, Leon Battista Alberti devoted one entire book to "construction" and another to "public works," that is, roads, bridges, underground drains, and fortifications, which were all within the architect's purview. The union of architecture and engineering continued for centuries. Christopher Wren designed and built the ingenious triple dome of St. Paul's Cathedral in London, and a hundred years later Thomas Ustick Walter designed the immense dome of the Capitol in Washington, D.C., whose form was modeled on St. Paul's, although it was built of cast iron.

The new material that brought about a sea change in the relationship between architecture and engineering was reinforced concrete. Concrete had been known for centuries: the Romans used pozzolana, a natural mixture of volcanic silica, lime, and fired rubble, as cement mortar and concrete. The manufacture of artificial cement (portland cement) was pioneered in Britain in the mid-nineteenth century. In the late nineteenth century, three French inventor-builders, Joseph Monier, Edmond Coignet, and François Hennebique, independently discovered that concrete—strong in compression but weak in tension—could be reinforced with iron and steel bars. The result, which combined the compressive strength of concrete with the tensile strength of steel, was fireproof and relatively cheap and could be cast in a variety of shapes.

Both Monier and Hennebique built bridges out of reinforced concrete, but it was Robert Maillart, a Swiss engineer and a student of Hennebique's, who is considered the first master of the new material. He built a series of light elegant Alpine bridges whose extraordinary beauty is still impressive, one hundred years later. The largest reinforced-concrete buildings of this early period were built at Orly immediately after World War I by the engineer Eugène Freyssinet: two airship hangars whose thin concrete vaults were three hundred feet wide and two hundred feet high.

The great advantage of reinforced concrete was that the designer could maximize the strength of the material by varying the amount and location of the steel bars, adjusting the precise proportions of the cement-aggregate-water that constituted the concrete mixture, and giving it the most efficient shape. Designing

effectively—and creatively—in concrete required a high degree
of computational and analytical skill. In the early days of reinforced concrete, there were a few accomplished engineer-architects,
such as Eduardo Torroja in Spain, Félix Candela in Mexico, and
Pier Luigi Nervi in Italy, but the training received by most architects did not prepare them for this task. They were obliged to rely
on engineers for the detailed design of the reinforced-concrete
structures that supported their buildings.

Reinforced concrete became the preferred material of most
modern architects. Because their designs usually included exposed
structural elements and dramatic features such as cantilevers and
long, unsupported spans, engineers came to play an increasingly important role in the building design process. This was not necessarily
acknowledged by architects, however, who continued to refer to
themselves as "master builders" and to engineers as "consultants."

Louis I. Kahn, who liked to portray architectural design as an
individual and personal, not to say poetic, act, worked with different
structural engineers, but the one who stands out is August E.
Komendant. Like Kahn, Komendant was a native of Estonia, which
may be why he treated the architect as an equal rather than as a re-
vered master. Whatever the reason, there is no doubt that Komendant's contribution to Kahn's designs was considerable. It is surely
no coincidence that the three buildings that are considered Kahn's
masterpieces—the Richards Medical Building, the Kimbell Art
Museum, and the Salk Institute—all benefited from Komendant's
involvement. In all three, dramatic concrete structure is a major
part of the building's impact—even when the architectural concept
makes the structure illogical, as in the Kimbell vaults that span in
the "wrong" direction. Conversely, in projects where Komendant
was absent, such as the Phillips Exeter Academy Library, the
Bryn Mawr dormitory, and the Yale Center for British Art, while
the architecture remains moving, the structural solutions are less
compelling.

I had a personal experience of Komendant's ability. In 1966, I was a young architect in Moshe Safdie's office, which was building Habitat, the experimental housing project that was part of Montreal's world's fair. Komendant was the engineer for the complicated precast-concrete structure. By the time I joined the office, the design work was done, and the building was under construction. My work involved checking the so-called shop drawings of the precast-concrete fabricators against the architectural drawings, to make sure that everything would fit together as planned. The three-dimensional geometry of the project meant that the exact dimension and location of the parts of the building were sometimes difficult to determine (this was before the widespread use of computers). Whenever I came to a dead end, I would consult the engineering drawings. They were inelegantly drawn compared with the architectural drawings; according to office lore, they were drafted by Komendant himself. Yet in these drawings, I would always find what I needed. The engineer had recorded every critical dimension necessary to construct the building. It was all there.

What do the Pritzker Prize winners I. M. Pei, Richard Meier, Robert Venturi, Renzo Piano, Norman Foster, Rem Koolhaas, Jacques Herzog and Pierre de Meuron, Jørn Utzon, and Zaha Hadid have in common? They have all used the same structural engineer: the London-based firm popularly known as Arup. Arup is responsible for the structural engineering of some of the most striking buildings of our time: innovative office buildings such as the high-tech Hongkong and Shanghai Bank Headquarters, the rocket-shaped Swiss Re Building in London, and the China Central Television Headquarters in Beijing; exemplary museums such as the Tate Modern in London, the Menil Collection in Houston, the Nasher Sculpture Center in Dallas, and the new addition to the High Museum of Art in Atlanta; dramatic stadiums such as the

Olympic stadium in Beijing, currently under construction; and airport terminal buildings at Kennedy and Stansted, as well as the $7 billion Kansai International Airport in Japan. If you are a star architect with an unusual structural problem, you call the people at Arup, and they will solve it for you.

Arup has worked on some exquisite building projects, such as the glass pyramid of the Louvre in Paris, the dramatic new library in Seattle, and the recently opened de Young Museum in San Francisco, but it is not a boutique consultancy. The firm is responsible for the Channel Tunnel Rail Link, the twelve-kilometer sea-crossing Inchon Bridge in South Korea, and the Øresund Bridge, a combination road-and-rail tunnel-bridge that links Denmark and Sweden. Arup is a global organization with more than seven thousand employees in seventy-five offices spread across thirty-three countries. The various divisions deal not only with structures but also with transportation, lighting, telecommunications, water engineering, urban design, and environmental services. The *Engineering News-Record* ranks Arup as the fourth-largest engineering firm in the world (according to income from design services performed outside its home country). Arup is not as large as Bechtel and Kellogg Brown & Root, which are also construction companies, but it is unrivaled in its ability to create superb engineering that is also great architecture.

Arup was founded sixty years ago in London by a fifty-one-year-old Danish immigrant named Ove Nyquist Arup. Though technically a native—he was born in Newcastle (in 1895)—Arup was the son of a Norwegian mother and a Danish father, a veterinarian who had moved to England six years earlier to work as a government inspector of beef cattle. Shortly after the boy's birth, the family relocated to Hamburg. The young Arup grew up in Germany and was sent to Copenhagen to study, where in due course he went to university and graduated with a degree in philosophy. After being turned down for a lectureship, he enrolled in engineering at Copenhagen's Polyteknisk Laereanstalt, did well in his studies, and upon graduating in 1922 secured employment with a large Danish construction firm, Christiani & Nielsen. Christiani & Nielsen was one of a handful of European companies that specialized in the design and construction of reinforced-concrete structures (Rudolf Christiani had trained under Hennebique). The firm built harbor installations, and Arup, who was fluent in German, first was posted to the port city of Hamburg but a year later was transferred to the London office. He would stay in Britain the rest of his life.

Arup's work at Christiani & Nielsen included designing railway bridges, silos, jetties, and deepwater berths. But in the early 1930s, he began to be drawn to architecture, specifically modernist architecture, which he admired. He was invited to join the MARS (Modern Architectural Research) Group, a sort of architectural think tank. Arup, with his knowledge and experience of reinforced-concrete construction, was a welcome addition. His later recollection of this period is characteristically blunt:

> The puzzling part was that these architects professed enthusiasm for engineering, for the functional use of structural materials, for the ideals of the Bauhaus, and all that; but this didn't mean quite what you might suppose. They were in love with an architectural style, with the aesthetic feel of the kind of building they admired; and so they were prepared and indeed determined to design their buildings in reinforced concrete—a material they knew next to nothing about—even if it meant using the concrete to do things that could be done better and more cheaply in another material.

Arup, who by then was working for another Danish engineering firm, collaborated with a number of talented architects in the 1930s. His most fruitful association was with the Russian émigré Berthold

Lubetkin, with whom he built two celebrated reinforced-concrete structures that became icons of early British modern architecture: the dramatic Penguin Pool (1933–34) at Regent's Park Zoo, whose two exceptionally thin intersecting helical ramps were the quintessential expression of the new aesthetic; and a seven-story apartment building, Highpoint I (1933–35), designed with the flat roofs, white walls, and cantilevered balconies of the nascent International Style. Mies van der Rohe, Le Corbusier, and Walter Gropius had built comparable buildings at the famous Weissenhof housing exhibition in Stuttgart, eight years earlier—a reflection of how much British modernism lagged behind its Continental counterpart—but Highpoint's reinforced-concrete structure was unusual: an ingenious system of reusable slip forms into which concrete could be poured, one story at a time.

Lubetkin, whom Arup called his "first real teacher of architecture," was the leading British modernist of the interwar period and exercised a considerable influence on the engineer. At the same time, Arup could be critical of his mentor:

> A wall like the one at Highpoint would have been cheaper to build with bricks, but he claimed it was functional and economic. It wasn't functional at all: it had to be "Modern." Functionalism really became a farce. What is wrong with a sloping roof? *They* can't afford to pay what it costs to make a flat roof really waterproof. Lubetkin didn't care. He just cared for the picture in the architectural magazine.

This was not just a case of a feet-on-the-ground engineer versus a head-in-the-clouds architect. Arup was a multifaceted individual: a trained philosopher and a humanist, he was also a talented pianist as well as an art collector. He was temperamentally a Scandinavian socialist, although his practical Danishness kept him from subscribing to the more extreme political positions of some of his Marxist colleagues. In his new biography, *Ove Arup: Masterbuilder of the Twentieth Century*, Peter Jones provides a colorful description of his subject: an "endlessly doodling, whimsically rhyming, cigar-waving, beret-wearing, accordion squeezing, ceaselessly smiling, foreign sounding, irresistibly charming, mumbling giant." The tall (six-foot three-inch), handsome bon vivant was sociable and outgoing, which helped him to attract clients when he established his own consulting business in 1946, immediately after the end of World War II. (During the war, he built air-raid shelters and underground facilities for the RAF and contributed to the design of D-day's Mulberry Harbour.) Arup had other gifts: he was very good at recognizing, attracting, and keeping talented associates (such as Ronald Jenkins, Povl Ahm, Ronald Hobbs, and Peter Rice); he was not a prima donna but encouraged collegiality and teamwork; and he early saw the global possibilities of his profession—within a decade of its founding, his firm had branch offices in Ireland, Southern Rhodesia, Nigeria, Ghana, and South Africa.

Ove Arup & Partners took on a variety of large-scale engineering projects such as bridges, factories, and warehouses (the latter often with breathtakingly thin concrete shell roofs, an Arup specialty) and was also involved in the development of postwar prefabricated emergency housing. At the same time, the firm developed strong working relationships with architects. Arup's client list included virtually every leading British designer of the postwar period: Jane Drew and Maxwell Fry, Alison and Peter Smithson, Ernö Goldfinger, Leslie Martin, and Denys Lasdun. The firm also collaborated with Basil Spence on Coventry Cathedral, probably the most highly publicized building project in postwar Britain, whose thin concrete shells spanning the nave are a key feature of the design.

Arup's ability to collaborate with architects did not include a willingness to blindly place engineering at the service of architecture, however—quite the opposite. He often challenged the architectural orthodoxy that considered design to be absolute. For Arup, meeting functional and cost requirements was equally important. In any case, he disliked absolutes. "To me, the skill of an Architect, and the excellence of an architectural solution is measured by the ratio between what is obtained, and what is expended," he wrote in a paper titled "Architecture Is Not Only Art." Tongue in cheek, he expressed this ratio as a formula, based on the famous Vitruvian trilogy of commodity, firmness, and delight (notably, he took firmness for granted):

$$\text{Excellence} = \frac{\text{Basic Commodity} \times \text{Excess Commodities} \times \text{Delight}}{\text{Cost}}$$

When I was a practicing architect, I would sometimes run across structural problems that were beyond my limited experience, usually involving a particularly long span. In such cases, I would turn to an engineer friend for advice. After examining the situation, he once asked, "Do you want it cheap or architectural?" What he meant was that the most elegant or attractive solution and the cheapest solution were not necessarily one and the same. Arup likewise differentiated between economy and beauty in architectural structures, and he challenged the belief in structural "honesty" that underpinned modernist theory:

> The idea that the correct functional, the correct structural and the best possible aesthetic solutions are one and the same thing must, I am afraid, be abandoned together with the older philosophers' dream about the harmony and ultimate identity of truth, goodness, justice and beauty.

Arup recognized that while economy of means sometimes produces beauty in large engineering structures such as bridges, dams, and long-span roofs, it rarely does so in buildings.

Jones makes it clear that Arup was an empiricist who considered theories to be provisional hypotheses, subject to continual revision, and was skeptical of what he called "paper-design." "I dislike preconceived ideas or theories about architecture," he once wrote to Philip Johnson. At the same time, he did not think of engineering as a science. "Science studies particular events to find general laws. Engineering design makes use of these laws to solve particular practical problems," he once said in a lecture. "In this it is more closely related to art or craft; as in art its problems are underdefined, there are many solutions, good, bad and indifferent." He was committed to a close integration of architecture and engineering, and his firm eventually established its own in-house architectural division, Arup Associates, headed by Philip Dowson (who was later awarded the Royal Institute of British Architects' Gold Medal).

Jones sums up Arup's lifelong professional concern as a desire "to establish frames of mind, attitudes and organizational structures that would enable architects and their engineers to cooperate from the very outset of a commission." In effect, he wanted to break down the barrier that had grown up between the two professions. The difficulty of achieving this goal was highlighted by one of his largest, and certainly longest-running, projects: the Sydney Opera House. In 1957, an unknown Danish architect, Jørn Utzon, won an international competition to build a large, multi-theater complex in Sydney, Australia. Arup volunteered his engineering services to a fellow Dane and was eventually appointed structural engineer on the project. At this point in his career, Utzon, thirty-eight, while he had won a number of architectural competitions, had built little. This inexperience was evident in the design of the concrete structure of the halls, whose distinctive sail-like roofs looked like huge shells but which were in fact not self-supporting. It was up to the engineers to make it work.

Jones, who had access to the private Arup office archives,

devotes several chapters to the sixteen-year saga of the Sydney
Opera House. He quotes extensively from correspondence between
the engineers and a growingly mistrustful Utzon, who at one point
forbade any direct communication between the Arup firm and the
client. As costs spiraled out of control (the final price was *ten times*
the original estimate), the architect became increasingly isolated.
"I wonder whether you really are master of the situation and can
manage without help except from sycophantic admirers," Arup
wrote to Utzon. "I have often said that I think you are wonderful, but are you all that wonderful?" The building was finally completed, after many delays and controversies that included—halfway
through the process and before construction drawings were
completed—the rancorous resignation of the architect.

The story of the Sydney Opera House has an Ayn Rand–ish
flavor, with Utzon cast as the aggrieved Howard Roark. While
Arup, whose firm stayed on to complete the building, was not assigned the villain's role (despite the architect's well-publicized vil-
ification), he was effectively written out of the plot. In 2003, when
Utzon was awarded the Pritzker Prize, the citation read, "There
is no doubt that the Sydney Opera House is his masterpiece." Yet
the reader of Jones's well-researched account comes away with the
distinct impression that Arup and his colleagues deserve an equal
share of the credit for the building's structural virtuosity.

While the protracted Sydney Opera House episode receives its
due in *Ove Arup*, the book is uneven. Many projects are cursorily
described, and the illustrations—and their captions—bear little
relation to the text (some of the projects pictured are not mentioned
at all). The degree of Arup's personal involvement in specific buildings is not always clear, and although there is a chronology, there
is no comprehensive list of built work. Jones, who is professor
emeritus of philosophy at the University of Edinburgh, is neither a
biographer nor an architectural writer. While his philosophical
background illuminates aspects of his subject's early life, when all

is said and done, Arup was not a philosopher but an engineer—
and arguably an architect manqué. The author writes that his book
"is not a history of engineering or of architecture, or of a firm and
its evolution." Perhaps it should have been. Arup was one of the
leading structural engineers of his time, and while it is diverting to
read about his adolescent romances, his political activities, and his
family vacations, one wants to learn more about his life as an engineer and his specific position in a field to which he contributed so
substantially.

During his long life (he died in 1988, at ninety-two), Arup received many honors: the Gold Medals of both the Institution of
Structural Engineers and the Royal Institute of British Architects,
membership in the Royal Academy, a CBE, and a knighthood.
The architect Richard Rogers, who worked with the Arup firm
on a number of high-profile projects, including the Centre Pompidou in Paris, Lloyd's of London, and a new terminal at Madrid's
Barajas Airport (recently awarded the Stirling Prize), considers
Arup "one of the greatest structural designers of the twentieth
century." According to Félix Candela, Arup was "the only legiti-
mate successor of Maillart, and in several respects he even excels
his predecessor."

A bridge is a true test for an engineer, and Arup designed
several, in Africa as well as Britain. The spans are generally not
exceptional, but the bridges are distinguished by their elegance,
which derives in large part from their evident economy of means.
One of the last projects that Arup designed personally was the
Kingsgate footbridge across the river Wear, in the university city
of Durham. The budget of £35,000 was considered sufficient for
only a short span at the foot of the deep valley. Instead, Arup designed a bridge at the level of the top of the valley, a span three
times longer. Two Y-shaped, 150-ton concrete sections were cast
separately, one on each bank, then swiveled ninety degrees to meet
in the middle. His colleagues in the firm later claimed that it could

have been done even more cheaply, but it is hard to imagine that it could have been done more gracefully, or more beautifully.

Arup continues to work with leading design firms: Foster + Partners on the new Apple headquarters in Cupertino, Zaha Hadid Architects on the London Olympics Aquatics Centre, Gehry Partners on the Dr. Chau Chak Wing Building in Sydney, the Renzo Piano Building Workshop on the London Shard, and OMA on the CCTV Headquarters in Beijing.

Mr. Success

At the time of the recent opening of Cleveland's Rock and Roll Hall of Fame and Museum—or, rather, the I. M. Pei–designed Rock and Roll Hall of Fame and Museum, as it was invariably called—I heard a radio interview with one of the museum officials, who was asked about the famous architect. "Wasn't it odd that Mr. Pei, who is a self-proclaimed lover of classical music and who doesn't listen to rock and roll, was chosen to be the designer?" asked the interviewer. "Not at all," answered the official, "we specifically wanted him because we knew that the Pei name would be recognized and would give credibility to the whole project."

There are not many contemporary American architects who bring that sort of cachet. Philip Johnson, perhaps, or Frank Gehry. But Johnson, despite his celebrity, has never received a commission for a national civic monument; neither (yet) has Gehry. Pei, on the other hand, had designed two of them: the East Building of the National Gallery of Art in Washington, D.C., and the overhaul of the Louvre Museum in Paris. One can debate the architectural merits of both projects, but the East Building is immensely popular with visitors (although less so with the curators), and the refurbished and enlarged Louvre is widely favored by Parisians. Moreover, the glass pyramid that Pei installed in the Louvre's Cour Napoléon seems destined to become a landmark as recognizable as the Eiffel Tower or the Arc de Triomphe.

Yet Pei is not universally admired in the architectural world. Although his office has been the training ground for dozens of talented architects, including William Pedersen, Ulrich Franzen, and James Polshek, as well as Henry Cobb and James Ingo Freed, who became his partners, there aren't any Pei disciples, as there were Mies van der Rohe disciples or Louis Kahn disciples. Nor does there appear to be a Pei philosophy of design. "He's not a design influence," Philip Johnson told Michael Cannell, the author of a new biography of Pei, "he's just Mr. Success." Ralph Lerner, dean of Princeton's architecture school, was even less charitable: "He's irrelevant. There's no body of theory that goes along with his work."

Why is the best-known architect in America, who has been commissioned to build some of the most important buildings here and abroad, not also acclaimed by his peers? Is this a reflection of the shallowness of modern celebrity, or is it, perhaps, an indictment of the rest of the architectural profession, which has grown increasingly estranged from the values of the public it purports to serve and is more interested in a "body of theory" than in accomplished buildings? Pei's buildings are undecorated, sleek, and impeccably detailed—the architectural equivalent of a Mercedes-Benz. Throughout his career, Pei has been a steadfast architectural modernist, even during the 1970s and 1980s, when modernism became distinctly unfashionable. Nevertheless, although postmodern design was supposed to be more accessible and more user-friendly, it was the modernist Pei's buildings that were popular with the public and equally popular with a series of distinguished patrons: Jacqueline Kennedy, Paul Mellon, J. Carter Brown, and François Mitterrand. How does Pei manage to turn cool modernism into such hot stuff?

Cannell struggles mightily with this question, and if he doesn't quite provide a satisfactory answer, he does give the reader many useful and interesting insights into the way that architecture is practiced today. Cannell is a journalist, not an architectural critic, and he sometimes seems unsure of his subject, which causes him to lean on outsiders' opinions as regards Pei's design ability. This produces many one-liners, such as the catty comments cited above, but unfortunately it doesn't produce a coherent analysis of the work.

On the other hand, Cannell is a conscientious reporter, and he describes the actual business of architecture (and architecture at the level practiced by Pei, or any major architect, *is* a business) thoroughly and engagingly. This book provides a clearer description of how large commercial buildings get designed and built than any other I have read. Although Pei will probably be best remembered for his museums, he has also built formidable office buildings, like the John Hancock Tower in Boston and the Bank of China Tower in Hong Kong, currently the world's tallest structure outside the United States.

It was in the hard school of commercial architecture that Pei cut his teeth. Between 1948 and 1960, he was the house architect at Webb & Knapp, the giant real estate company run by William Zeckendorf. This was the period of downtown urban renewal, and Webb & Knapp built apartment and office towers in almost every city on the continent: New York, Chicago, Philadelphia, Washington, Boston, Denver, and Montreal. Pei and his assistants designed them all.

It was not easy to manage a transition from successful commercial architect to high-fashion architect, but Pei managed it as smoothly as he had earlier transformed himself from an effete Harvard professor to Zeckendorf's golden boy. Pei had been a graduate student at Harvard under Walter Gropius, who was so impressed with the young Chinese émigré that he offered him a teaching job. Pei's presence in the United States was something of an accident. Born in Suzhou and raised in Shanghai, Ieoh Ming Pei was the son of a prosperous banker and was sent to America to study architecture. He graduated from MIT in 1940, but by then China had been invaded by Japan, and his father counseled him to stay where he was. He enrolled in Harvard and, when America entered the war, interrupted his studies to volunteer to serve with a wartime intelligence agency. When Pei finally graduated from Harvard in 1945, China was in the midst of a civil war, and he was still stuck abroad. By 1949, with the Communists victorious, it became clear that for Pei there would be no going back. America would be his home.

Pei's professional life has had ups and downs. His decision to work for Zeckendorf marked him in the eyes of many of his colleagues as a talented commercial hack, a reputation he would work hard to reverse. One project, the Kennedy Library in Boston, dragged on for years, the focus of local community protest. The Hancock Tower suffered an embarrassing and well-publicized technical failure (eventually, all the windows had to be replaced). The Louvre commission was a cultural minefield and almost didn't get built. Throughout, the architect persevered. Evidently, Pei is an exceptional person, yet he is so withdrawn and impenetrable— Cannell was given very little access to his subject—that he remains almost a bystander in his own biography. This book is a satisfactory exploration of the background of Pei's professional achievements, but it's "too bad," as Philip Johnson is quoted as saying, "one can't grasp the man himself."

Though officially retired, Pei returned to the public eye in the first decade of the twenty-first century with three acclaimed museums, in his hometown of Suzhou, in Qatar, and in Japan. A revealing 2010 PBS documentary, I. M. Pei: Building China Modern, *features an engaging and almost garrulous nonagenarian, whose cogent explanations of his designs make it clear that while not founded in theory, his work is most certainly grounded in architectural ideas.*

The Unfettered Eclectic

The two dozen houses represented in Robert A. M. Stern's latest bulky monograph, *Houses and Gardens*, are the products of different geographical locations, different sites, and different clients. Many are suburban villas; some are holiday houses by the sea. The largest residences—and some are very large, indeed—have extensive gardens. Country houses in commanding natural settings contrast with urban residences on small lots with close neighbors. Two are what home builders call model homes. Whether large or small, the houses share a distinct sense of place, an elegant resolution of plan, and careful attention to detail. What they don't share is an architectural language.

This collection of houses is a history lesson in the styles that have characterized American domestic architecture over the last hundred years: Colonial, Georgian, Italianate, Norman, they're all here. The diversity is sometimes a response to a distinct regional context: a mountainside in Aspen, a rocky Maine coastline, sun-drenched Southern California. In other cases, the designs are inspired by the local architecture, as in two Mediterranean-style New Jersey villas or a quirky shingled house in San Francisco's Pacific Heights. The French Directoire style of a residence on Long Island is a response to a request by the client. But one suspects that the variety also derives from the architect's encyclopedic knowledge of architectural history, his delight in finding inspiration in the past, and, above all, his restless eclectic taste.

In ancient times, "eclectics" were an independent class of philosophers who did not invent a new school of thought, or attach themselves to any particular canon, but who selected their ideas from many schools. Architectural eclecticism emerged in the nineteenth century, when architects began to build in a variety of historical styles. Modernist historians have treated this period with disdain; Nikolaus Pevsner called it "the fancy-dress ball of architecture." That is a narrow view. In the capable hands of an architect such as Karl Friedrich Schinkel or Stanford White, eclecticism produced many memorable buildings.

In the United States throughout the first half of the twentieth century, it was taken for granted that architects should be versatile in matters of style. Delano & Aldrich, for example, was a distinguished New York City firm that flourished in the period 1903–40 and is generally associated with French-influenced classicism, of which Oak Knoll, a residence in Mill Neck, New York, is an exquisite example. William Adams Delano and Chester Holmes Aldrich were both "Paris men"—École des Beaux-Arts graduates trained in the compositional methods and forms of classical architecture. But, like their contemporaries, they accepted the tradition of vernacular building that included many long-lived regional styles. When circumstances—or clients—demanded, they designed Federal clubhouses, American Colonial country houses, Gothic college buildings, and even a memorable Art Deco marine air terminal.

The dictionary defines an eclectic as someone who is "unfettered by narrow systems in matters of opinion or practice; broad, not exclusive, in matters of taste." "Unfettered" is just the right word to describe the work of Robert A. M. Stern and his partners. Stern calls his approach to design "modern traditionalism" and explicitly likens it to nineteenth-century and early twentieth-century eclecticism. "On a case-by-case basis," he writes, "a Modern Traditionalist decides which architectural language to apply."

At the beginning of a project, Stern's office often gives the client a book that contains images of residential architecture, chiefly from the nineteenth and early twentieth centuries. It is organized according to different styles: Regency Revival, English vernacular, classical French, Spanish Colonial, and so on. The hefty compendium is part primer and part Rorschach test, to uncover what people like—and dislike. Thus, two large residences in Texas, built only a few years apart, can turn out very differently. A house in the River Oaks neighborhood of Houston is a sprawling classical Italian villa that is casually planned in several stepped wings. The relatively spare exterior belies the sumptuously detailed public rooms that would not be out of place in a country palace in Dresden or St. Petersburg. While the guiding spirit here is Italian, that of a house in Preston Hollow, a neighborhood of Dallas, is English. At first glance, it appears to have all the hallmarks of a Georgian mansion: geometrical regularity, red brick, white limestone trim, and slate roofs. While the Georgian style can be dry, this Texas version is rather flamboyant; the columns and pilasters that adorn the facades are stylized Corinthian, and the limestone details are bold and assertive.

Like the River Oaks house, the Preston Hollow house is planned as a series of narrow wings. However, the plan is not casual but highly ordered, an H-shape whose low arms enclose two courts, one overlooked by a breakfast room pavilion, the other by the living room. Low wings containing a garage and a natatorium frame a paved motor court at the entrance. The overall planning strategy recalls Oheka, a large Norman country house designed by Delano & Aldrich in 1914–17. Like his predecessors, Stern uses the H-plan to effectively face the house in several directions and to reduce the visual impact of the twenty-five-thousand-square-foot interior.

The Preston Hollow residence is intended to be a venue for

public social occasions and fund-raising events. But while the house can accommodate several hundred people at a time, it is also required to be a family home for two. The ingenious plan weaves together these apparently opposite demands, providing an intimate library as well as a capacious living room, an informal breakfast room as well as a grand dining room for twenty, and an indoor swimming pool that is like an aquatic family room. Next to the pool is a spa, a gaudy tented interior which recalls that Regency fantasy, the Royal Pavilion at Brighton.

The Regency style reappears in Bel Air, but this time in another guise. The clients wanted a glamorous home, and Stern and his design team concocted a Hollywood-influenced version that is sophisticated and edgy. The lush, monochrome interiors are as much Art Deco as Regency; Paul Poiret meets Sir John Soane. The Soanian exterior is painted brick with implied classical orders, while the composition of the south facade recalls another house oriented to a view, C.F.A. Voysey's Broad Leys on Lake Windermere. The styles are very different, although what Pevsner called Voysey's "Art Nouveau piquancy" also informs this complex design. This is eclecticism carried to a particularly refined level.

One of the regional vernacular styles that remains a Stern favorite is the so-called Shingle Style, which he did so much to reinvigorate in the 1980s. A large, picturesque house at Kings Point, New York, is a collage rather than a tightly ordered composition. Turrets, chimneys, porches, bay windows, balconies, and even a sort of lighthouse jostle each other in unruly disharmony. An unusual kidney-shaped glazed porch curves away from the north side of the house. Classicism appears in the form of an Ionic porte cochere, but it seems to be a last-minute addition. It isn't, of course, for the patchwork composition and the twisting and turning of the plan are integral parts of this carefully contrived design, which is dictated by a desire to frame views, capture the sun at different times of day, and create memorable interior spaces.

A smaller ocean-side residence on Martha's Vineyard also uses a regional style, this time from New England. The main body of the house, under a large gambrel roof, is turned at an angle to face Katama Bay. A screened porch, a circular gazebo, a low wing, and the garage wing shoot off at various angles, almost as if they had been built at different times. The artless composition is casual and unprepossessing, a spinet's tinkling to Preston Hollow's pipe-organ arpeggio.

Starwood in Aspen, built for the same clients who later commissioned the Preston Hollow house, is an interesting example of how classical and vernacular elements can be combined. The entrance loggia is framed by a Palladian arch on Greek Doric columns, yet the mottled granite walls around it, bereft of moldings or other decorations, have the flinty look of a house in the Cotswolds. The Palladian motif reappears in the rear porch, but in rough timber rather than dressed stone. Inside, the rich moldings are classical, as are the rusticated door frames of the entrance hall and the fluted Doric pilasters in the library. On the other hand, the timber and wrought-iron details of the pergola suggest Japan, and there is also a hint of the Orient in the gentle curve of the roof eaves.

The style of the Starwood house is hard to characterize. Unlike many of Stern's designs, it does not have an obvious historical precedent, although the triple-gable entrance is clearly inspired by two famous Edwardian houses, Tigbourne Court and Homewood, both designed by Sir Edwin Lutyens. Lutyens, whom many consider the greatest British architect of the first half of the twentieth century, was an eclectic par excellence. In his earliest houses, he explored the romantic vernacular styles of his native Surrey, which, according to Hermann Muthesius's 1904 classic, *Das englische Haus*, reflected his "attachment to the styles of the past, the charms of which he finds inexhaustible." In later houses, Lutyens found inspiration in the work of classicists such as Christopher Wren, Andrea Palladio, and Michele Sanmicheli. In Abbey House and

Castle Drogo, he developed an "abstracted, military Tudor style," in Gavin Stamp's words, which he deployed to great effect. His largest house, a palace really, is the Viceroy's House in New Delhi, an inventive fusion of European classicism and Mogul architecture on a truly imperial scale.

In a 1969 essay that anticipated the revival of interest in Lutyens, Allan Greenberg described a common feature of the British architect's houses: "Neither the formal and symmetrical massing, nor the elevations express the intricacy of the interior plan." The same is true of the domestic designs of Robert A. M. Stern Architects. In Starwood, for example, the gate to the motor court, the flanking curved pavilions, the entrance loggia, and the vestibule establish a prominent axis. But when one enters the house, the axis is abruptly terminated in the central hall by the solid mass of the chimney. The circulation becomes increasingly labyrinthine until one arrives in the dining room, where the axis reappears, although not, in fact, exactly aligned with the original. It is extended outside, following the length of the swimming pool and ending in a garden overlook.

In these houses, what you see is not necessarily what you get. In a residence at Apaquogue, for example, what appears to be a simple, five-bay center-hall Colonial is anything but. The living room and dining room stretch across the entire garden front, and the stair hall is located immediately behind the entrance facade (which accounts for the presence of a false window). A French country-style house in East Hampton has one central axis corresponding to the front door and another corresponding to the center of the living room, but the axes are offset, with a long entrance hall accommodating the shift. A Palo Alto residence is the most strictly axial of all the house plans, as befits this version of Palladio's Villa Foscari, but an additional wing contains the kitchen, family room, and loggia, which results in a second major axis, a distinctly un-Palladian feature. On the entrance side, the main axis of the house lines up with the temple-front

entrance, while on the garden side it shifts over to a triple-arch loggia overlooking a swimming pool. Even the picturesque, Shingle
Style houses can be deceptive; the rambling Kings Point house, for
example, contains a highly ordered sequence of public rooms. A
final example: the Directoire-style residence in Long Island is one
of the grandest and most strictly ordered compositions in this collection, yet the arrangement of public rooms within is syncopated
rather than classical.

Stern's attitude to house planning is markedly modern and,
incidentally, quite different from the more rigid, Beaux Arts–
influenced approach that informs the work of many of his younger
contemporaries. Early twentieth-century houses were planned for
a way of life that no longer exists. The contemporary American
lifestyle, no matter how grand its setting—and some of these houses
easily bear comparison with the country houses of the Gilded Age—
is more relaxed and informal than in the past. Homeowners want
casual family rooms and eat-in kitchens and place a high premium
on comfort and convenience. These houses are planned to respond to such requirements.

The pragmatism of the layouts is not only the result of functional expediency, however. In the River Oaks house, for example,
the symmetry of the entrance facade is undermined by the presence of a single oval window (lighting a powder room) that has
no counterpart on the opposite side. A villa in Montecito presents
what at first glance appears to be a symmetrical facade to the garden, except that one columned opening is filled in with glass and
the other is an open loggia. The oval dining room of the Bel Air
house is reached by an oblique door that is hidden in the apsidal
end of the gallery. The shifting of axes, the changing lines of movement through the house, sometimes on axis and sometimes off, the
unexpected accommodation of functional needs, produce an architecture that is, in Robert Venturi's famous phrase, "complex and
contradictory."

Stern's earliest houses were directly influenced by Venturi; the
historian Vincent Scully, who had been Stern's teacher at Yale,
called Stern "Venturi's most devoted follower and first serious,
sympathetic critic." Venturi, and the late Charles Moore, greatly
expanded the language of modernist architecture, instilling it with
a regional and historical sense of place. They did not go so far as to
use historical styles, however. Their approach, usually referred
to as postmodernism, was neither completely modernist nor completely traditional. Perhaps for that reason, it did not last long. By
the 1980s, many architects were returning to orthodox modernism,
while others, including Stern, having absorbed Venturi's teaching,
were moving toward a more literal representation of the past. This
shift is visible in two houses illustrated here. A villa at Deal, New
Jersey, still has vestiges of postmodernism in the rather thin trim
and an overscaled thermal window. Sunstone, on the other hand,
which was begun the following year, is unaffectedly vernacular—
an exercise in style rather than stylization.

Stern also abandoned another hallmark of Venturi's and
Moore's work: irony. In this current group of houses, one looks in
vain for exaggerated details, mannered transpositions, and knowing architectural winks, the sorts of tongue-in-cheek gestures that
characterized postmodernism. Stern no longer self-consciously refers to the past, as he did in his earlier work; rather, he confidently
deploys an array of architectural forms and motifs, some old, some
new. But like the best eclectics—Lutyens, Platt, Delano—he does
not merely duplicate the distinctive hallmarks of a historical style;
rather, as Philip Johnson once put it, he uses style as a springboard.

Early twentieth-century domestic architects placed great emphasis
on garden design. Lutyens worked with the great garden designer
Gertrude Jekyll to integrate the house and the garden; at Oheka,
Delano & Aldrich collaborated with Beatrix Farrand and the

Olmsted brothers; Charles A. Platt, one of the greatest American country-house architects and garden designers of the Gilded Age, actually started his career as a landscape painter. All these men and women took it for granted that the function of the man-made landscape was not merely to be a setting for the house but that house and garden should be married to create a cohesive set of aesthetic experiences.

In his early houses, Stern treated the garden in a more or less modernist fashion; that is, he largely ignored it. (With the notable exception of Frank Lloyd Wright, modernist architects have created few memorable gardens.) Apart from ancillary terraces, decks, and swimming pools, Stern's early houses were surrounded either by largely untouched natural landscapes or by lawns. It was the Italianate villa in Deal, New Jersey, begun in 1983, that offered an opportunity to achieve what Stern has called "the highest goal of Classical villa design": the integration of house and garden. The site is an L-shaped two and a half acres, within which Stern had to fit not only a large house but also outdoor amenities and outbuildings. The solution was a tightly packed collection of outdoor rooms, which Charles Platt would have called "garden units." The largest of these is a sunken court off the indoor swimming pool, a device that Stern used in an earlier house. But this court is much more elaborate, turning into a stepped garden with a series of fountains, with forced perspective creating the illusion of distance, even though the boundary wall is only a hundred feet away. The other outdoor rooms contain a flower garden, a swimming pool, a tennis court, and a series of gardens formed by sculpted evergreens. All these spaces are interrelated by axes and cross axes, much like the house itself.

The nine-acre site of the residence in Preston Hollow provides considerable scope for landscape effects, especially as the garden had to be created in its entirety. Here, the geometrical order of the house is extended into the landscape. The paved west court, off the living room, overlooks a rectangular lawn terrace that is flanked by allées of trees; an antique fountain terminates the vista. On the opposite side of the house, the court is planted with crape myrtle and overlooks a parterre *à l'anglaise*. In contrast to these intimate spaces, the south garden is a miniature English park, in scale with the three-hundred-foot-long facade. The picturesque elements popularized by Capability Brown are all here: turf, random clumps of trees, and a pond. A set of broad garden steps leads to the water's edge. The illusion of being on a country estate is complete.

The garden of the residence in Bel Air has a very different relationship to the architecture, a counterpoint rather than a complement. The site is a small but dramatic plateau that provides a spectacular view of the city of Los Angeles, the San Gabriel Mountains, and the Pacific. While the house stretches out to take full advantage of the panorama, the garden is an opportunity to escape the view. The intimate spaces—a sloping lawn, several outdoor rooms, and a picturesque walk—lead down to a long allée of fruit trees that completes the path which connects the house to the tennis court and the swimming pool.

Perhaps the most unusual relationship between house and garden occurs in the Montecito villa. The fifteen-acre grounds were part of a much larger estate, El Mirador, that belonged to an Armour meatpacking–fortune heiress. The surviving Italianate garden was originally laid out in the 1920s by a Pasadena horticulturist, Elmer M. Awl. Its central feature is a monumental allée of deodara cedars centered on a cypress-lined walk that is bordered by stepping boxwood parterres. The cascading water channels descend the walk and terminate in a cross-axis lily pond. The upper end of this dramatic landscape axis was to have been a grand house—which was never built. Stern's Italianate villa carefully completes Awl's composition without upstaging it; indeed, the garden veils the house, providing only glimpses of the main facade but no single, dramatic view. While the symmetrical composition of the south front is dictated by the allée, the house becomes more casual on the east side, where a family room opens onto a swimming pool terrace shaded by a giant stone pine. The fusion of new house and old garden creates a particularly strong sense of place.

Muthesius wrote that Lutyens's designs "always reflect the characteristics that distinguish all he does: a forceful efficiency and a reassuring willingness to get to the heart of the problem facing him." Because Stern can be a rather theatrical designer, and because we have become used to architectural minimalism, the often excessive stylistic expression of these houses can be misleading. It's easy to ignore the careful attention paid to solving functional requirements: a cozy place to eat breakfast in the morning, a way to experience a particular view, a felicitous relationship between one room and another. Or the care lavished on functional details such as concealed doors, kitchen layouts, and special client needs—gift-wrapping cupboards, flower rooms, or rooms to store china. It's also easy to miss the fact that these traditional-looking houses are also modern: modern in their sophisticated—although discreetly hidden—technology, modern in their layered spatial complexity, modern in their openness to the out-of-doors, and, above all, modern in their free eclectic spirit.

Since I wrote this, Stern's eclecticism has expanded to include modernism—in a number of campus buildings and in several office towers, notably the fifty-eight-story, all-glass Comcast Center in Philadelphia. Thus far at least, the residential work remains stylistically traditional, although a number of apartment interiors have been modernist, and with Stern you never know.

A Humble Architect

Montreal's Expo 67 was the last world's fair where architects were treated as stars. The two most impressive national pavilions were Frei Otto's tentlike West German pavilion and Buckminster Fuller's U.S. pavilion, a large geodesic dome. Arthur Erickson's delicate wood pyramid housing Man and Health made up for the rather lackluster Canadian pavilion. But the brightest star at Expo was a newcomer, Moshe Safdie, a twenty-eight-year-old Israeli-born Canadian who, according to legend, had turned his student thesis into the fair's most striking attraction. The British magazine *The Architects' Journal* called Habitat "one of the most advanced housing projects ever conceived and certainly the boldest exercise in industrialized building methods attempted to date."

Safdie did not manage to build a second Habitat—for a variety of practical reasons, the bold exercise proved difficult to replicate—and after a dry decade in the 1970s he reinvented himself as an architect of striking public buildings. A very successful architect: in the last five years alone, he has completed an art museum, a performing arts center, a peace institute, a federal government building, and a courthouse. And that is only in the United States. His Boston-based firm practices globally: airport terminals in Toronto and Tel Aviv, the Yitzhak Rabin Center in Israel, a vast Sikh heritage memorial complex in India, and the spectacular Marina Bay

Sands resort complex in Singapore. He is currently designing a Habitat-like housing complex in Qinhuangdao, China.

Safdie's most talked-about recent project is an art museum in Arkansas. The driving force behind Crystal Bridges is sixty-three-year-old Alice L. Walton, the daughter of Sam Walton, founder of Walmart, which is headquartered in Bentonville. Twenty years ago, she started acquiring paintings by American artists, and she has reportedly spent $1.2 billion on a collection that now numbers more than a thousand works. John Singer Sargent, Winslow Homer, Mary Cassatt, Arthur Dove, Stuart Davis, they're all there. Walton's unsuccessful bid (together with the National Gallery of Art in Washington, D.C.) to buy Thomas Eakins's *Gross Clinic* from a Philadelphia hospital made headlines. The Eakins that she finally did get—from the same hospital—is hardly shabby; *Portrait of Professor Benjamin H. Rand* is considered Eakins's second-greatest work. The medical teacher sits at a crowded desk, intent on his reading, absentmindedly stroking his cat, which stares out intently at the viewer.

Roberta Smith, the art critic of *The New York Times*, called Crystal Bridges "an exceptional if idiosyncratic picture gallery assembled by someone with a discerning and independent eye for paintings." How does someone with a discerning eye, who also happens to be the third-richest woman in the world, choose an architect? Walton is not without personal experience of modern architecture, having grown up in a house (in which she still lives today) designed by the renowned Arkansas architect E. Fay Jones. In a recent public lecture, Safdie recounted how he had been contacted by Walton and invited to Bentonville, where the museum was to be located. "I had never met her before. She had visited some of my buildings incognito," he said, referring to the Skirball Cultural Center in Los Angeles, a complex of museum galleries and community facilities that he has been enlarging over the last twenty-five years. Walton and Safdie walked over the Walton family estate, a large tract near the center of town, looking at different sites and talking about the project. "At the end of the day I said, 'I guess you're starting your architect selection process. How are you going to go about it?' And she said, 'Well, I ended it tonight.' And that was it. It was a wonderful way to start."

I've been invited to a literary festival in Little Rock, Arkansas, which is not far from Crystal Bridges. We drive up Interstate 540 through the Ozark Mountains to Bentonville, a small town in the northwest corner of the state. The site of the museum is a densely forested valley with a stream running through it. Sites are important for Safdie. "For me, the particular is central to the making of architecture," he says. "The particular is about the secrets embedded in the site and how from an understanding of the site a concept emerges." After examining various options, he decided to build close to the stream, damming it to create two pools that are the focus of a ring of connected pavilions. The concept—insinuating the galleries between the water and the forest—gives primacy to the natural surroundings. The general strategy reminds me of Frank Lloyd Wright's compound of Taliesin in Wisconsin, although Safdie's architecture is hardly Wrightian. Or maybe it is. Wright's early buildings are characterized by large sheltering roofs, whose shape often provides the chief theme for his architecture. Crystal Bridges is likewise a building of striking sheltering roofs—curved copper shells that suggest the carapaces of crabs or turtles.

The roofs are the first thing the visitor notices, because the museum is located at the bottom of the valley, seventy-five feet below the arrival area. I gaze down at the pavilions clustered around pools, too, but I am more struck by the visitors queuing up for the elevator. It is a motley mixture of young families with babies in strollers, a busload of retirees in colorful print dresses and plaid shorts, groups of tattooed teens, beer-bellied men in T-shirts and baseball caps. This is definitely not the usual art museum crowd.

Northwestern Arkansas was once the home of a theme park called Dogpatch, USA, and the region is associated in the popular imagination with hillbillies and possum stew, not with John Singer Sargent. Alice Walton's seemingly eccentric decision to locate her museum here was prompted by a desire to give people in her hometown an opportunity to experience art. Of course, Crystal Bridges also hopes to attract art pilgrims from farther afield. The evidence so far is that her gamble is paying off. While the museum initially estimated annual visits of 150,000 to 200,000, in its first five months of operation Crystal Bridges has already attracted 240,000 visitors, a quarter from out of state. The future of the museum seems secure; it already has an endowment four times larger than that of the Whitney Museum in New York.

An elevator—a slightly jarring note—takes us down to an entry courtyard that leads through a lobby to the picture galleries. The inaugural exhibition is arranged chronologically, but it also reflects Alice Walton's taste: for American history, in the earliest painting in the collection, James Wooldridge's *Indians of Virginia* (ca. 1675); for landscapes, such as Asher Brown Durand's iconic *Kindred Spirits* and other examples of the numinous Hudson River school; and for paintings of and by women. The nineteenth and early twentieth centuries are splendidly represented, although the late twentieth-century works in the collection are less impressive, seemingly added merely to close a chronological gap.

The galleries themselves are large spaces, spanned by curved wooden beams. The only jarring notes are rather boxy freestanding walls that seem like clumsy intruders in this barnlike space. A very *dark* barnlike space. The original design provided skylights in all the galleries, but a year before the opening, while construction was under way, a new museum curator was appointed, and, as Safdie wryly told an interviewer, "there were different views and the skylights were removed." Modern curators are highly sensitive to gallery light levels, especially when works on paper are involved, and natural light is notoriously difficult to control. Unfortunately, this turns some of the Crystal Bridges galleries into black boxes, which, especially in such an arcadian setting, is a shame. The dark galleries are offset by brightly lit rooms in between, many equipped with comfortable seating and low tables piled with art books, where one can relax, read, and admire the natural surroundings.

Of the eight pavilions at Crystal Bridges, the most dramatic are a gallery and a museum café that both span the pool, and the Great Hall that juts out into the water. Their shell-like roofs are formed by curved laminated wood beams that are supported not on columns but on cables draped from abutments at each end, as in a suspension bridge. Safdie claims to have been inspired by traditional suspended footbridges that he saw while trekking in Bhutan. Working with the engineers of BuroHappold, he created dramatic spaces whose all-glass walls provide views of the water on both sides, while alternating bands of wood and glass in the roofs allow light to enter from above. It is like being under a giant upturned wooden hull. There is a lot of wood in the building as well as stone floors and smooth concrete walls, whose coldness is relieved by inlaid horizontal strips of cedar, a nice detail on the interior, although on the exterior the strips are beginning to stain and weather unevenly.

Details, whether they are slick or rough, complicated or simple, prominent or discreet, rich or austere, are evidence of an architect's intentions. Renzo Piano's exquisite construction details are like perfect little engineering sculptures; Norman Foster's minimalist details, by comparison, manage to appear severe and luxurious at the same time. Safdie's attitude is more casual; although he does not hide how things are made, his details don't attract attention, and they often have a spartan simplicity. There are a few places where the details in Crystal Bridges strike me as a little too casual, although it is unclear whether the poorly finished concrete and awkward junctions are due to the inattention of the architect or of the contractor. But on the whole, Safdie's approach seems right for Crystal Bridges, where overrefined details would be out of place. He avoids the bread-and-water asceticism that drives many people away from modern design, and it is one of the charms of this friendly building that despite its structural virtuosity it is never intimidating. Colorful shorts and baseball caps fit in just fine.

Safdie designed an unusual museum for Alice Walton. It is not an idiosyncratic sculpture, like the Experience Music Project that Frank Gehry built in Seattle for the Microsoft billionaire Paul Allen, nor is it like the coolly sophisticated "machine for looking at art in" that Renzo Piano devised for the collectors Hildy and Ernst Beyeler near Basel. Like Richard Meier, Safdie has created a campus, but unlike Meier's Getty Center in Los Angeles, Crystal Bridges is not a heroic acropolis. Instead, it snuggles into the hillside, close to the ground, among the trees, over the water. The proximity to natural surroundings and the loose arrangement of pavilions were influenced by a museum that Safdie and Walton visited during a European tour. The Louisiana Museum of Modern Art near Copenhagen houses the private collection of Knud W. Jensen. In 1958, Jensen commissioned two young architects, Jørgen Bo and Vilhelm Wohlert, to transform his nineteenth-century country house into a museum. Over the next thirty-three years, the museum was enlarged several more times until it became a loose circle of pavilions connected by glazed corridors. Unlike at the Louisiana, the pavilions of Crystal Bridges were built all at once, but they give a similar impression of a casual group rather than a studied composition.

Not many architects would have the self-confidence to adopt such a low-key approach, especially for a client with pockets as deep as Alice Walton's. But after a career that has spanned almost fifty years and scores of projects, Safdie no longer has to prove himself. Or at least that is the feeling I got during a recent public conversation with the architect before a packed audience at the University of Pennsylvania. At one point, we spoke about Frank Lloyd Wright, who has a popular reputation for arrogance. Safdie took a different view. "I think Wright is an architect with humility," he said. "When he comes to a site, when he's using materials, when he's creating a space for people, there is a *deep* humility, because he is—it sounds a bit corny to say—at the time at the service of what he's doing."

Safdie might have been talking of himself, for his designs tend to be at the service of their sites, materials, and programs. This has produced a rather diverse body of work; unlike Gehry, Piano, and Meier, Safdie does not have an identifiable personal style. Perhaps that is one reason that, unlike them, he has not been awarded a Pritzker Prize, sometimes called the Nobel Prize of architecture. Another reason is less obvious: despite his fame and the prominent projects, Safdie remains something of an outsider in the architectural world. Modernist architects, having dispensed with figural and decorative ornament, have favored abstract designs that have tended to create environments that are spare and austere, with space, light, materials, and details combining to create a subtle interplay. Such buildings often reveal themselves slowly; some require interpretation and are not immediately appreciated by the layman. Safdie, although a confirmed modernist, designs buildings whose literal meaning is easily grasped. His United States Institute of Peace in Washington, D.C., for example, has undulating glass roofs that resemble the wings of a dove. The Yad Vashem Holocaust museum in Jerusalem is a single long prismatic structure that peels open at one end, revealing a view of Jerusalem. Marina Bay Sands is made up of three hotel towers supporting a dramatic sky park, big as an aircraft carrier, fifty-six stories in the air. This is not subtle stuff: with Safdie, what you see is what you get. In that regard, he resembles Eero Saarinen, a mid-twentieth-century modernist, the range of whose work likewise made his contemporaries nervous—and jealous. For Saarinen, the projects came hard and fast, each different, each an opportunity to explore new materials, new structural techniques, new shapes. Like Safdie, Saarinen achieved wide popularity among clients and the public, even as critics and academics deplored his "stylish packaging forms," in the Yale historian Vincent Scully's words. Scully preferred more cerebral architects such as Louis Kahn and Robert Venturi, but in a recent essay he admitted, "At the time I did not like Saarinen's buildings very much but I respect and admire them now. They have rather surprisingly worn very well."

Time, not prize-giving juries, is the ultimate judge of a building's worth. Habitat, now almost fifty years old, has worn very well, indeed; it looks as visionary as ever, it has grown on Montrealers, and it is much appreciated by its occupants. I am not sure what people will think of Crystal Bridges in the year 2060. Buildings are not static; functions change, tastes change, people change. I hope that the blocked-up skylights will be reopened and that some happier solution is found to those boxy partitions in the galleries. Eventually, someone may add a new pavilion. But Safdie's design will accommodate these changes. If his concept is sound, and I think it is, Crystal Bridges will likely grow on people, too. Although the noisy and excited crowds I saw during my visit seemed to like it just fine.

I met Safdie in 1963 when he was an invited critic in my fourth-year studio at McGill, and my first job after graduating was in his Montreal office. Habitat was under construction, and one of my tasks was to compile punch lists of quality-control issues on the site. Climbing ladders from one concrete box to another was like being in a modern version of a southwestern pueblo.

The Zen Master

Bing Thom wears a discreet Order of Canada lapel pin. Otherwise, like so many architects, he is dressed entirely in black: black T-shirt, black trousers, black jacket, black shoes. But instead of looking severe or forbidding, he comes across as avuncular. A small man in his early seventies with a shock of white hair, he resembles a wise and benevolent Zen master—think Mr. Miyagi in *The Karate Kid*. Thom is presenting a project to neighborhood groups and local residents in Washington, D.C. About thirty people are gathered in a meeting room of the Capitol Skyline Hotel. They all know who Bing Thom is because, while based in Vancouver, he is a minor celebrity here, thanks to his involvement with Arena Stage, a local theatrical institution that he recently enlarged to great acclaim. "It took an outsider, a Canadian architect, to break with the usual habits of large civic architecture in the nation's capital," wrote the architecture critic of *The Washington Post*, who described the striking timber-and-glass building as "both structurally and symbolically brilliant."

The Arena Stage is in what Washingtonians call Southwest, the location of Thom's current project. Although it's only a short walk from the U.S. Capitol, the neighborhood is a part of the city that few tourists ever see. A focus of urban renewal in the 1950s, the area was essentially bulldozed and replanned as a collection of superblocks following the idealistic but misguided urban design formulas of that era. The result is a mixture of Brutalist-style federal office buildings, apartment blocks, public housing projects, parking, and lots and lots of wide open space. "A five-minute walk can seem awfully long if there's nothing there," Thom tells his listeners. He reminds them that he first came to Southwest in 1965, as an architecture student on a scholarship tour. He recalls being appalled by the devastating effects of urban renewal and saying to himself, "There must be a better way to build cities."

After describing the general context of Southwest, Thom asks people to gather around a small architectural model that he uses to explain his concept. This is an unusual project. Thom's clients are Mera and Donald Rubell, wealthy art collectors from Miami. The Rubells have decided to build a gallery in Washington to house their notable collection of contemporary art, but being business-minded (they own the Capitol Skyline Hotel, which is across the street from the proposed gallery), they have partnered with a developer specializing in urban housing to include five hundred apartment units on the large site. The site is unusual, too, for it contains an old abandoned high school, the Randall School, which, despite its shuttered condition, is a cherished local landmark.

Thom explains that the original portion of the school, a listed Colonial Revival structure of the early twentieth century, will be restored and will house the art gallery as well as a restaurant and a cooking school. Behind the old building will be a courtyard surrounded by new apartments. These mid-rise buildings have large openings, both at ground level and above. "We've tried to free up the space so that the building can breathe," he says. "It's very open, to allow the public to come through and wander in the courtyard."

Returning to his slide presentation, Thom takes people through the building plans, floor by floor. His is a conversational style, simple and unaffected, without the usual jargon that afflicts so many architects today. He doesn't make a formal presentation as much as tell stories. "When I first met Mera Rubell, I told her that

I was interviewing her as much as she was interviewing me," he says. "She was a little taken aback, and I explained that I didn't want to spend my life with people I didn't like." His point was that good architecture is the result of active collaboration. And not just with clients; Thom once told an interviewer, "My client is more than the person who pays me; my client is society and the public." He stresses the civic responsibility of the architect, and his message to the Southwest community is that making architecture, especially good architecture, is a long and arduous process that requires support from many sides. "We have to deliver this baby, and it will take a lot of effort."

Thom has been coming to Washington regularly for the last thirteen years, and the city has become, if not exactly a second home, a familiar place. He is designing two other projects here: a neighborhood branch library in Woodridge, in the northeastern corner of the city, and a large $625 million mixed-use development in Silver Spring, Maryland. He has been invited to join the mayor's commission on the nearby Anacostia River waterfront, and he is also collaborating in a study with the city's planning office. Thom likes this long-term involvement. "It is nice to know that you're not just a hired gun," he says.

It's time for questions from the audience. In Washington, neighborhood issues, such as traffic, zoning, and economic development, are overseen by locally elected commissioners, who are also here today. Local demands can hold up projects and require concessions, so this meeting is important to the future of Thom's project. Much of the discussion is focused on what is generally called gentrification, that is, the tendency of new development to raise real estate values, which can be a mixed blessing for existing residents. A local community organizer observes, "Every time low-income tenants see a dump truck going down the street, they feel that much closer to being pushed out of their homes." A black woman expresses concern about the fate of those who live in public housing. How will the proposed project help them? A retired architect sums up the general mood of the meeting. "You're going to be the five-hundred-pound gorilla in this neighborhood. We'd like you to be a friendly gorilla." Everybody laughs; the mood is upbeat. People have been won over by Thom's low-key approach. They like the fact that the boarded-up school, which has stood empty for decades, will be renovated and put to use. They also like the openness of Thom's design and the mixture of uses. "This will be a twenty-four-hour place," a resident says approvingly.

"I like buildings that create crossovers that normally wouldn't happen, combining an art gallery with a cooking school and housing," Thom observes after the meeting. This attitude to design is probably influenced by his early experience with Arthur Erickson, whom he worked for in the 1970s. At the time, Erickson, who died in 2009, was Canada's premier architect—the first Canadian architect ever to garner international recognition. Thom oversaw two of Erickson's highest-profile urban projects: Roy Thomson Hall in Toronto and Robson Square in Vancouver. The best Erickson buildings have a timeless quality. "Arthur always said that he was not interested in what changes, but in what doesn't change," Thom recalls.

After leaving Erickson in 1981, Thom opened his own office. His early work was in Vancouver, but the Canada pavilion at Seville's Expo '92, a striking box clad entirely in zinc, brought him national recognition. Five years later, he designed the Chan Centre, a performing arts complex at the University of British Columbia. The twelve-hundred-seat concert hall, housed in an ivy-covered concrete drum, received rave reviews. *The Globe and Mail* called it "one of the most architecturally innovative and musically rewarding performance spaces in Canada."

The Chan Centre led directly to Arena Stage—and Washington. He took on other projects as well, including Tarrant County College, a downtown campus in Fort Worth, Texas; a town center for Surrey, British Columbia, that includes a university campus improbably located on top of an existing shopping mall; and a striking public library, also in Surrey. The architectural style of these buildings defies easy categorization. Erickson was largely impervious to architectural fashions and did not have a signature style, and Thom has followed his lead. Sometimes Thom's buildings incorporate high-tech details that recall Renzo Piano, but warm and woodsy rather than cool and machinelike. The Surrey town center and Arena Stage are all swooping curves and glass walls supported by timber masts. The Surrey library goes even further, and its plastic forms reminded me of the early German expressionist Eric Mendelsohn. The Randall School project, on the other hand, will be a disciplined composition of rectangular volumes, piled up on one another like children's building blocks.

Thom learned another lesson while working for Erickson: what happens when an architect takes on too much work and spreads himself too thin—by 1980, Erickson's best work was behind him. "Some firms grow very large and end up chasing clients—and chasing fame," says Thom. "When I started the office, I was determined not to be that kind of architect." Bing Thom Architects, run by Thom and his longtime partner, Michael Heeney, currently has forty employees, which is unusually small at a time when star architects regularly employ a hundred people or more. "The size of my practice is limited, since I can only keep four or five projects in my head at a time," says Thom. "But we are a top-heavy firm. More than a third of the staff are senior, experienced people who have been with me a long time. That makes a big difference."

·

Following the Washington meeting, Thom leaves for Hong Kong, where he is starting a major new project. The Xiqu Centre is a performing arts center dedicated to the revitalization of *xiqu*, the traditional Chinese opera that is a stylized combination of singing, acting, music, dance, and martial arts. The $350 million building, one of the largest civic buildings ever undertaken by Bing Thom Architects, may well be the capstone of Thom's career. It has already resoundingly cemented his standing as an A-list architect, because the design competition for Xiqu Centre featured some of the best architects in the world: the international powerhouse Norman Foster; Moshe Safdie, who had just completed an acclaimed performing arts center in Kansas City; Jack Diamond, who had opera houses in Toronto and St. Petersburg under his belt; and the Dutch firm Mecanoo, which has built award-winning cultural buildings all over Europe.

Thom dislikes entering competitions, because he believes that they are too impersonal and make it impossible to work directly with the client. "In my whole career of thirty years, I haven't done more than ten competitions," he says. But this time, he had made an exception. The subject of *xiqu* interested him (his wife is a dancer), and the chance to build an important cultural landmark in the city of his birth—he came to Vancouver with his parents at age ten—was too good to pass up.

Xiqu Centre will be the gateway to the West Kowloon cultural district, an ambitious effort to position Hong Kong as an Asian cultural hub. Thom and his collaborator, the local architect Ronald Lu, raised the main auditorium up in the air to create a large weather-protected public space at ground level that is open to the street through the four corners of the curvaceous building, whose form is said to be based on a traditional Chinese lantern. The jury, which voted unanimously for Thom's entry, said it was won over by the way that his modern design embodied the essence of Chinese opera through its openness to street life, its sense of a gateway, and its evocation of a traditional courtyard. It also singled out the curvilinear form of the building as an imaginative expression of the ancient Chinese concept of qi, or life force. Score one for the Zen master.

I have known Bing Thom since 1965. We were both students on the scholarship tour that visited Washington's Southwest, as well as public housing projects in New York, Philadelphia, and Baltimore, where we witnessed the ravages wrought by urban renewal firsthand.

The Smart Man from Hollywood

In 1986, the Walker Art Center in Minneapolis organized an exhibition of the "major works" of the American architect Frank Gehry. Although Gehry was fifty-seven, only a few large projects were exhibited—a branch library, a law school, an aerospace museum— and my chief recollection is of models and drawings of many small buildings, unbuilt as well as built. Most of the buildings were in Los Angeles. At the time, Gehry had achieved a small notoriety for making lumpy furniture out of corrugated cardboard. He was also known for incorporating prosaic materials such as chain-link fencing and tar-paper shingles into his architecture. This roughness and studied cheapness set him apart from most of his contemporaries. He didn't fit easily into an architectural mold. Unlike the buildings of postmodernists, his work contained no historical allusions; he was obviously a modernist, though neither a refined stylist like Richard Meier nor a technological maven like Norman Foster. Rather, he came across as an inventive Southern California bohemian, something of an outsider. That didn't seem to bother Gehry. "Being accepted isn't everything" was the nose-thumbing epigram he provided for the Walker exhibition catalog.

That was then. Today, Frank Gehry is definitely accepted. More, he is acclaimed, feted, lionized. In 1989, he was awarded the Pritzker Prize, the Nobel of the architectural world. He has won almost every major architectural award available, including the

Japanese Praemium Imperiale and the Wolf Foundation Prize, and he was the first recipient of the Dorothy and Lillian Gish Prize, a $250,000 arts award. In 1994, *Progressive Architecture* rated Gehry the world's No. 1 architectural prizewinner with almost half a million dollars in awards, more than twice the runner-up, the Japanese minimalist Tadao Ando. Gehry subsequently added the Chrysler Award for Innovation in Design, the Frederick Kiesler Prize, and the National Medal of Arts to his trophy case. Last year, even the staid American Institute of Architects, which thus far had shunned him in lieu of more mainstream practitioners, awarded Gehry its top accolade, the AIA Gold Medal.

Prizes are one thing, but there is no doubt that Frank Gehry is the most important twentieth-century architect since Louis I. Kahn. Like Kahn, he was a late bloomer. Kahn was fifty years old when, after a conventional career, he built his first significant building: the Yale University Art Gallery. Gehry was forty-eight when he was noticed. It was for his own remodeled house in Santa Monica: a nondescript California bungalow encased in an unsettling Cubist composition of unpainted plywood, corrugated metal, and chain-link fencing. That design was only the beginning. "What does the building want to be?" was Kahn's fey demand. "What do I want it to be?" is the question Gehry asked—and answered—again and again, producing no fewer than eighty-five projects in the decade after 1986.

Gehry's extraordinary self-confidence, his highly developed spatial imagination, and his fearless disregard for convention bring to mind an earlier American maverick: Frank Lloyd Wright. Wright, an accomplished self-promoter, wrote more than half a dozen books over the course of his long career and coined such catchy if obscure terms as "Prairie style," "organic architecture," and "Usonian." Ever since, practitioners have felt that to be taken seriously, they must create a theoretical underpinning for their work—or have critics and academics do it for them. The problem

is that these explanations are often obscure, frequently obfusca-
tory, sometimes downright bogus. Gehry, unlike so many of his
contemporaries, has been reluctant to provide architectural theories. When he does talk about his work, he is refreshingly unaffected. Here is his explanation of his Santa Monica home: "I was
interested in making the old house appear intact inside the new
house, so that, from the outside, you would be aware always that
the old house was still there. You would feel like this old house was
still there, and some guy just wrapped it in new materials." While
Gehry is interested in modern art—more than most architects—
he seems to have taken to heart Edwin Lutyens's prescient warn-
ing: "All this talk about architecture and art is very dangerous: it
brings the ears so far forward that they act as blinkers to the eyes."

The Guggenheim Museum in Bilbao, Spain, opened to universal
acclaim at the end of 1997. Built on the site of a former shipyard on
the south bank of the Nervión River in this old industrial city, it is
an astonishing building. The walls curve, twist, and turn. Part
of the museum slides under an adjoining bridge; another section
emerges from a reflecting pool. The seeming disorder—a chaotic
collision of forms—has no architectural antecedent. This is not
sculptural architecture; it is sculpture, pure and simple. *Bilbaínos*
refer to the museum as the "artichoke," which comes close to describing it, if you can imagine a gleaming artichoke made out of
titanium and more than two hundred feet high.

Gehry's buildings usually start with scribbled sketches, a squig-
gle of lines that resembles nothing much at all. Just impressions,
you think. Then come the models: paper crudely taped together,
crumpled aluminum foil, still squiggles but now three-dimensional.
All right, you say, he's still playing around. He can't be serious.
But these very models are turned into construction drawings—
squiggles and all—and are translated into finished buildings.

"The plan is the generator," preached Le Corbusier, but with Gehry the plan is the *result*. He designs from the outside in. The building as a composition comes first; the interior spaces follow. This implies that he shoehorns functions into the building, which is not the case. The Guggenheim Foundation, for example, required three distinct types of gallery spaces: traditional, skylit rooms for displaying its permanent collection of early modern art; a large space for temporary installations; and eleven smaller galleries, each with its own character, each dedicated to the works of a selected living artist. The artichoke accommodates all of these. The permanent collection is housed in a rectangular box, the temporary gallery in a long boatlike space that extends under the bridge; and the specialized galleries are scattered in various parts of the building. Haphazard the building may appear, but there is nothing haphazard about the way it is organized. Gehry's talent is his formal imagination; his skill is reconciling the forms he imagines with the functional demands of his client.

This building is a sculpture, but the orchestration of spatial experiences is architectural. From the plaza, a long staircase leads to the entrance. After passing through a modest lobby, the visitor enters a 150-foot-high atrium, an expressionistic space that manages to be vertiginous, awesome, and cheerful all at once. From here one looks out over the reflecting pool to the river. The entrances to the galleries are conveniently clustered around the atrium.

The aim of the Guggenheim Foundation, which initiated this project and is responsible for the artistic direction of the museum (the $100 million building was built by the Basque Administration), was obviously to create a European counterpart to its famous building in New York. The Bilbao museum is at least as striking as Wright's spiraling building. But in New York, the splendid circular ramp tends to overwhelm the exhibits; the Bilbao museum, on the other hand, is generally considered a sympathetic setting for modern art.

The antecedent to the Bilbao Guggenheim in Gehry's work is the Walt Disney Concert Hall in downtown Los Angeles. Gehry won the architectural competition for the hall in 1989, but programmatic changes, higher-than-expected costs, and sluggish fund-raising delayed and almost halted the project. With the success of the Guggenheim, and the consequent rise of Gehry's reputation, it now appears likely that construction of the Disney hall will begin soon. If it is built, it will likely outshine even the Bilbao Guggenheim. It, too, is an *assemblage*, a three-dimensional collage of billowing forms, covered not in titanium but in limestone. Models of the interior of the twenty-four-hundred-seat hall promise a beautiful room: warm wood, sail shapes on the ceiling, and, a rarity in modern concert halls, natural light. It will probably sound good, too, for Gehry has been cannily conservative in adopting a traditional boxy shape for the room, designed in collaboration with the Japanese acoustician Minoru Nagata.

An architecture critic once described Gehry as "a smart man from Hollywood." This nicely captures the architect's blend of exuberant showmanship and behind-the-scenes savvy. Gehry is not a preindustrial romantic like Ando or Steven Holl, who are fascinated with craft; he is a *post*industrial romantic. His forms are as naturalistic as anything imagined by the Catalan architect Antoni Gaudí or the Finnish master Alvar Aalto, but both the design and the construction of Gehry's buildings are the result of extremely sophisticated technology. The Disney hall, for example, was one of the first large building designs produced by the Gehry office using the three-dimensional capabilities of the computer. CATIA is a program originally developed by Dassault Systèmes for the design of Mirage fighter jets. The computer program allows Gehry and his staff to digitize handmade models by tracing their shapes with a laser stylus. From these digitized images come three-dimensional views and architectural as well as construction and fabrication drawings. Without the computer, buildings like the

Disney hall and the Guggenheim Museum could be imaged; however, without CATIA, they could not be built.

An interest in new technology and unusual materials links Gehry to Wright. A less obvious architectural antecedent is Bruce Goff, the midwestern maverick who died in 1982. Goff is probably best remembered for a series of peculiar houses that defied conventional taste. He used corrugated aluminum (in the 1950s), outrageous colors, and, in one infamous case, a ceiling covered in white goose feathers. "He expressed an interest in the precarious, pushing ideas to their limits," Gehry has written of Goff. "He talked about awkwardness, irresolution, and the unfinished. These are all issues and ideas that move me also."

Gehry characterized Goff as "the model iconoclast, the paradigm of America . . . the antidote to Gropius's pontifical European presence." He could have been describing himself, for Gehry, too, challenges modernist orthodoxy. Not only are his buildings designed from the outside in; the interiors and the exteriors often appear quite different: different materials, different architectural vocabularies. This discontinuity is rare in modern work (although common in Baroque architecture). Gehry's chaotic compositions also undermine the modernist emphasis on structural rationalism and industrial standardization.

Like Norman Foster and Richard Rogers, Gehry enlists up-to-date technology in his designs, yet there is no evidence that he particularly admires technology. This is visible in Gehry's approach to details. "God is in the details," Mies van der Rohe is supposed to have said, and ever since architecture has been distinguished from run-of-the-mill building by unusual—and often unusually contrived—details. Taut cables instead of ordinary stair balustrades, impossibly thin window mullions supporting heavy plate glass, invisible joints instead of ordinary moldings. Most modern architects devote a lot of time to getting the details right: lining up the bolt heads just so, hiding unsightly intersections, picking the right door handle. In the case of high-tech buildings, pristine details are important to provide the requisite machinelike character; in minimalist architecture, details are crucial because often that is all there is.

Gehry's sculptural effects do not depend on fussy or precious details. He is inventive, but he resolves the details of construction simply and unaffectedly (which is harder to do than it sounds). There are details in Gehry's designs, but one is less aware of them than in most modern buildings. Space, light, the texture of materials, the shapes of walls and ceilings—these are the things that count.

Stephen A. Wynn is chairman of Mirage Resorts Inc., a billion-dollar corporation that owns gambling casinos in Las Vegas and other American cities. In 1997, when Wynn decided to expand into Atlantic City, he chose Gehry to be the architect of a $2 billion hotel-and-casino complex. Wynn definitely has an eye for dramatic buildings. After all, he is responsible for the erupting volcano on the Las Vegas strip and has just opened Bellagio, which he describes as "the most beautiful hotel in the world." But the choice of Gehry represented Wynn's first foray into high-art architecture. In any event, the partnership did not last, and Gehry withdrew from the project last year. Still, it was a tantalizing temporary merger: one of the most successful and flamboyant corporate titans in the country and the most celebrated architect of our times.

Wynn's was an unexpected but not an illogical choice. It's hard to imagine any other Pritzker winner (except perhaps Philip Johnson, who agreed to work with Gehry on the Atlantic City project) being asked to design a multibillion-dollar casino. The result would be either too elegant or too severe; in any case, it would not be fun. Gehry is that rare combination of a serious architect who is also a crowd-pleaser. Perhaps that is why, at a time when the chief clients of most serious architects are museums, public libraries, and universities, Gehry's client list includes real estate developers as well as institutions.

In fact, Gehry has a great deal of experience designing commercial buildings. When he sprang on the architectural scene with his remarkable house in Santa Monica, he was hardly a novice. He had been a practicing architect, running his own successful office in Los Angeles, for almost twenty years. He had built shopping centers, suburban offices, department stores, apartments, and housing developments. His largest single client was the Rouse Company, a major real estate developer for whom he built several buildings, including a large shopping mall in Santa Monica. The architecture of these early buildings does not anticipate Gehry's later oeuvre, but it obviously provided the architect with valuable experience. "Working with developers, seeing them always trying to make things cheaper, I was intrigued with the idea of making something inexpensive and getting more out of it," Gehry has written. He continues to do commercial work. One of his recent clients has been the Chiat/Day advertising agency, for whom he has designed a West Coast company headquarters, as well as offices in London and Toronto. Developers have commissioned Gehry to design large commercial projects in New York, Los Angeles, and Mexico City. In 1988, he proposed a building in the shape of a huge lighthouse as the centerpiece of Canary Wharf; had it been built, it would have livened up that lackluster project. One of his most original designs is a skewed office building in Prague, built by a Dutch developer. German businessmen in particular seem to have cottoned to Gehry. The DG Bank, a mixed-use building with an extraordinary conference room shaped like a horse's head, is going up in Berlin, and a three-building office complex is in the final stages of completion in Düsseldorf. Gehry has produced more than 250 buildings and projects over the last forty years. There is no doubt that he has, as Henry James once said of John Singer Sargent, "a knock-down insolence of talent."

•

This essay was written in 1999. Walt Disney Concert Hall was built after all—in stainless steel, not limestone—and it is perhaps the best work of architecture in the United States of the past fifty years. Gehry, now an octogenarian, has not slowed down. Major projects are under way in Canada, France, Australia, and Abu Dhabi. Nor has he stopped working with developers, as his remarkable seventy-six-story residential tower in New York demonstrates.

Afterword and Acknowledgments

My first essay collection, *Looking Around*, was published in 1992. Much has changed in the intervening two decades. For one, I moved from Canada to the United States. The move did not provide me with new publishing opportunities, because except for the Canadian monthly *Saturday Night* the places where my journalistic writing appeared were mostly American newspapers and magazines. But crossing the border involved a major change. When I wrote about American buildings and cities while living in Canada, I did so as an outsider. It was easy to write about American urbanism, for example, from the comfortable vantage point of rural Quebec and quite another thing to be surrounded by the problems of a declining Rust Belt city such as Philadelphia, where I now live.

Another change has been the spread of the Internet. In the 1990s, I was still consulting my dictionary and thesaurus, leafing through library card catalogs, squinting at microfiche readers, and prowling the stacks of the university library. By the end of that decade, however, my computer—increasingly at home—had become my chief research tool. The Internet did not just change the way I searched for information; it also provided many new places to read about architecture. When I started writing, the only architecture critic I read with any regularity was Paul Goldberger in the Sunday *New York Times*. I was aware of Allan Temko and Robert Campbell, but I had no access to either the *San Francisco*

Chronicle or *The Boston Globe*, nor to the handful of other newspapers that had architecture critics. As for the architecture magazines, they contained little reading matter; I only looked at the pictures.

The Internet changed all that. Newspapers—from here and abroad—are available online, and I can read about architecture in the *Los Angeles Times*, the Toronto *Globe and Mail*, and *The Guardian*. Online architecture columns, blogs, and websites have proliferated. Moreover, Internet blogs have spurred the architecture magazines—and their websites—to publish critical prose again. Is this a new golden age of architectural writing? Not quite. While there is more writing about architecture than ever before, the quality is not high. Posts on the Web do not receive close editing and fact-checking. Moreover, while there is more coverage of architecture than ever before, the range of opinions expressed is surprisingly narrow; on the Internet, the herd instinct prevails. In part this is due to the lack of time for reflection, and in part it is the nature of mass culture, which favors entertainment over reflection, leading to oversimplification and caricature rather than considered judgment. And when critical disagreement does occur, as it has over Gehry's proposed design for the Eisenhower Memorial, it tends to take the form of people shouting at each other, an architectural *Firing Line*.

If there was a golden age of architectural prose, it might have been the 1960s and 1970s, thanks to magazines such as *The Architectural Forum* in the United States and *AD* in Britain, the criticism of Lewis Mumford, Reyner Banham, and Martin Pawley, and the scholarship of John Summerson, James Ackerman, Nikolaus Pevsner, and Vincent Scully. These writers have remained, for me, models of how one ought to write about architecture.

I have had the luxury of picking my own topics rather than being assigned subjects, so if the choice sometimes seems eccentric, there is no one to blame but myself. I have been given the opportunity to write for a wide variety of publications: newspapers, monthly magazines, book reviews, quarterlies, and literary journals. I would like to acknowledge my editors, especially Bill Whitworth and Corby Kummer at *The Atlantic Monthly*, Henry Finder at *The New Yorker*, Robert Silvers at *The New York Review of Books*, Holly Eley at *The Times Literary Supplement*, Jay Tolson and Steven Lagerfeld at *The Wilson Quarterly*, John Fraser at *Saturday Night*, and Nathan Glazer at *The Public Interest*. For seven years, I was the architecture critic for *Slate*. I have not included any of my *Slate* posts in this collection, but I learned a lot from Jacob Weisberg, Meghan O'Rourke, and Julia Turner.

I agree with William Wurster's wise observation that architecture is "the picture frame and not the picture," and I have written about the broader setting of our metropolitan world and the even broader context of modern life. "Mysteries of the Mall," "The Fifth City," "The Master," "A Distinguished Failure," and "Call Arup" appeared in *The New York Review of Books*; "Downsizing Cities," "Show Dogs," "A Good Public Building," and "Sounds as Good as It Looks" in *The Atlantic*; "Downtown," "Why We Need Olmsted Again," and "Why Wright Endures" in *The Wilson Quarterly*; "Tomorrowland" and "Designs for Escape" in *The New Yorker*; "The Story King" and "The Biggest Small Buildings" in *Architecture*; "A Humble Architect" and "The Zen Master" in *The Walrus*.

"The Unreal America" appeared in *The New York Times Book Review*; "Big-City Amenities. Trees. High-Tech Jobs. Cappuccino. Retirement Paradise. Nose Rings" in *The New York Times Magazine*; "New York's Rumpus Room" in *The New York Times*; "When Buildings Try Too Hard" in *The Wall Street Journal*; "We're All Venetians Now" in the *Financial Times*; "The Smart Man from Hollywood" in *The Times Literary Supplement*; "Mr. Success" in *The Washington Post*'s *Book World*; "A Blight at the Opera" in *Saturday Night*; "Bauhaus Blunders" in *The Public Interest*; "Tocqueville, Urban Critic" in *City Journal*; "Palladio in the Rough" in *The*

American Scholar; "Thoughts on *Home*" in *Apartamento*; "Godfa-
thers of Sprawl" in the *Wharton Real Estate Review*; and "Bollard
Burg" in *Foreign Policy*. "Corbu" was written for Time/CBS News's
People of the Century (1999). "The Unfettered Eclectic" was written
as an introduction to *Robert A. M. Stern: Houses and Gardens* (2005).

I have written more than 350 essays and book reviews since
Looking Around. The task of culling a manageable and meaningful
collection from this motley output and editing the result for gram-
matical consistency and to eliminate redundancy fell to my supportive editor, Eric Chinski; thanks too to Peng Shepherd, Susan
Goldfarb, and all the rest at FSG.

Index

9 780374 538095